To my grandchildren,

Luke Kenneth Perkins
Emily Dawn Talley
London Mark Perkins
Anna Carter Talley

Port Economics

Wayne K. Talley

Routledge
Taylor & Francis Group

LONDON AND NEW YORK

First published 2009
by Routledge
2 Park Square, Milton Park, Abingdon, Oxon, OX14 4RN

Simultaneously published in the USA and Canada
by Routledge
270 Madison Avenue, New York, NY 10016

Routledge is an imprint of the Taylor & Francis Group,
an informa business

Typeset in Times New Roman by Keyword Group Ltd
Printed and bound in Great Britain by TJ International Ltd, Padstow,
Cornwall

British Library Cataloguing in Publication Data
A catalogue record for this book is available from the British Library

Library of Congress Cataloging in Publication Data
Talley, Wayne Kenneth.
    Port economics / Wayne K. Talley.
    p. cm.
    1. Harbors–Economic aspects. I. Title.
HE551.T35 2009
387.1–dc22
2008041761

ISBN13: 978-0-415-77721-6 (hbk)
ISBN13: 978-0-415-77722-3 (pbk)
ISBN13: 978-0-203-88006-7 (ebk)

ISBN10: 0-415-77721-6 (hbk)
ISBN10: 0-415-77722-4 (pbk)
ISBN10: 0-203-88006-4 (ebk)

Contents

Figures

Tables

Abbreviations

AEO	authorized economic operator
AFC	average fixed cost
AGV	automatic guided vehicle
APL	American President Line
ASC	automatic stacking crane
BLO	build-lease-operate
BOST	build-operate-share-transfer
BOT	build-operate-transfer
CARB	California Air Resources Board
CBP	Customs and Border Protection
CLIA	Cruise Line International Association
COLA	cost-of-living adjustments
CPA	Canadian Port Authority
CSI	Container Security Initiative
CSO	company security officer
C-TPAT	Customs–Trade Partnership Against Terrorism
DEA	data envelopment analysis
DHS	Department of Homeland Security
EBITDA	earnings before interest, tax, depreciation, and amortization
EDI	electronic data interchange
EPA	Environmental Protection Agency
EU	European Union
FBI	Federal Bureau of Investigation
FC	fixed cost
FEU	forty-foot equivalent
FMC	Federal Maritime Commission
FOC	flag of convenience
GAI	guaranteed annual income
HIT	Hong Kong International Terminals
HMT	harbor maintenance tax
HMTF	Harbor Maintenance Trust Fund
HSC	high-speed craft
ICC	Interstate Commerce Commission

IDC	International Dockworkers Council
ILA	International Longshoremen's Association
ILO	International Labour Organization
ILWU	International Longshore and Warehouse Union
IMO	International Maritime Organization
IOS	International Organization for Standardization
ISPS	International Ship and Port Facility Security
IT	information technology
ITF	International Transport Workers' Federation
LAITC	long-run average incremental total cost
LATC	long-run average total cost
LMC	long-run marginal cost
LNG	liquefied natural gas
LPG	liquefied petroleum gas
LTC	long-run total cost
LTL	less-than-truckload
MARAD	Maritime Administration
MARSEC	maritime security
MCA	Motor Carrier Act
MEPC	Marine Environment Protection Committee
MTSA	Maritime Transportation Security Act
NOAA	National Oceanic and Atmospheric Administration
NOL	Neptune Orient Line
NOx	nitrogen oxides
NPV	net present value
NVOCC	non-vessel operating common carrier
OD	origin-to-destination
OECD	Organization for Economic Cooperation and Development
OOCL	Orient Overseas Container Line
OSHA	Occupational Safety and Health Administration
PDA	product diversification analysis
P&O	Peninsular and Orient Line
PFSO	port facility security officer
PMA	Pacific Maritime Association
POMTOC	Port of Miami Terminal Operating Company
PPA	product portfolio analysis
PSA	Port of Singapore
PSC	port state control
RDC	regional distribution center
RFID	radio frequency identification
RO-RO	roll on-roll off
RPM	radiation portal monitor
RTGs	rubber-tired gantry cranes
SATC	short-run average total cost

SAVC	short-run average cost
SB	social benefits
SC	social costs
SMC	short-run marginal cost
SO	secure operator
SOx	sulfur oxides
SPA	strategic position analysis
SSA	shift-share analysis
SSAS	ship security assessment
SSC	ship security certificate
SSO	ship security officer
SSP	ship security plan
STC	short-run total cost
SVC	short-run variable cost
TBT	tributyltin
TEU	twenty-foot equivalent unit
TL	truckload
TR	total revenue
TSA	Transportation Security Administration
TWIC	transportation worker identification credential
UN	United Nations
UP	Union Pacific
USDOT	U.S. Department of Transportation
VTS	vessel traffic service

Preface

Port economics is the study of the economic decisions (and their consequences) of the users and providers of port services. Port users include shippers, passengers, and carriers. Port (or terminal) operators are the primary service providers; other service providers include, for example, ship agents, customs brokers, ship pilots and towage, stevedores and freight forwarders. Maritime economics consists of port and shipping economics. This book is an introduction to port economics. Although a textbook, it is expected to be useful in maritime research, to port user and service-provider decision makers, and to those of the general public who are interested in port issues.

In 1984, I and two other business professors established the center, Maritime, Trade and Transport (MTT), at Old Dominion University. Given that Norfolk, Virginia (where the university is located) has one of the largest container ports on the U.S. east coast, the center's mission was to perform high-quality maritime research to promote the Port of Virginia and international trade in the region. Prior to 1984, although a transportation economist, I was not a student of maritime economics. However, MTT provided me with the opportunity to become knowledgeable in the subject. In 1986, MTT was renamed the Virginia Center for World Trade and established as an economic development agency of the Commonwealth of Virginia. Given the success of MTT, the International Maritime, Ports, and Logistics Management Institute (Maritime Institute) was established in 1994 at Old Dominion University to provide graduate maritime management education – a maritime concentration in the Master in Business Administration and Master in Public Administration degrees and a maritime management certificate.

I have taught port economics in the Maritime Institute's educational program since 1994. Since a textbook in port economics did not exist, I have used a course pack, consisting of journal articles and book chapters, as the text for these classes. However, in 2006, I decided to write a port economics textbook based upon the syllabus of my port economics course. This book is a result of that decision.

This book has benefited from my numerous maritime-related activities over the years such as presentations before and discussions with my port economics students and presentations and discussions at the annual conferences of the International Association of Maritime Economists. It has also benefited from serving as a visiting professor at the Institute of Transport and Maritime Management, University of Antwerp (Belgium); the Centre for Shipping, Trade and Finance, Cass Business School, City University (UK); the Institute of Transport Studies, University of Sydney (Australia); the Department of Transport and Regional Economics, University of Antwerp (Belgium); the Centre for Transport Policy Analysis, University of Wollongong (Australia); and the Transport Studies Unit, University of Oxford (UK).

Further, it has benefited from serving as a Senior Research Fellow at the Marine Policy Center, Woods Hole Oceanographic Institution (U.S.A.); a Research Scientist at the Institute for Water Resources, U.S. Army Corps of Engineers (U.S.A.); and the Editor-in-Chief of *Transportation Research Part E: Logistics and Transportation Review*. Serving as Executive Director of the Maritime Institute at Old Dominion University since 1999 has, in particular, been beneficial – e.g., working with the Institute's Advisory Council, graduate assistants Eric Custar and Jeremy Sykes, and Sara Russell, Instructor in Maritime and Supply Chain Management. I would like to thank Dean Nancy Bagranoff of the College of Business and Public Administration of Old Dominion University for her support of the Maritime Institute. Finally, I would like to thank my wife Dolly for her support in the writing of this book.

Wayne K. Talley
Norfolk, Virginia
August 24, 2008

1 Introduction

What is a port?

A port (or seaport) is a place at which the transfer of cargo and passengers to and from waterways and shores occurs. The transfers are made to and from vessels. The port may be a cargo port (handling only the transfer of cargo), a passenger port (handling only the transfer of passengers), or a combination cargo/passenger port (handling the transfer of both cargo and passengers).

Ports are typically cargo ports. Cargoes include general and bulk cargoes. General (dry non-bulk) cargoes are either goods of various sizes and weights shipped as packaged cargo or goods of uniform sizes and weights shipped as loose (non-packaged) cargo. The former is either container or breakbulk cargo, while the latter is neobulk cargo. Container cargo is general cargo stored in standardized containers, generally 20 or 40 feet in length without wheels – i.e., as a TEU (20-foot equivalent unit) or as a FEU (40-foot equivalent unit). Breakbulk cargo is general cargo that is packaged on pallets or in wire or rope slings for lifting on and off a vessel. Examples of neobulk cargo include automobiles, steel, and lumber. Bulk (dry and liquid) cargoes are cargoes that are neither packaged nor of uniform sizes and weights. Examples of dry-bulk cargo include coal and grains; crude oil and refined petroleum products are examples of liquid-bulk cargo.

Cargo ports are described by the prominent type of cargo handled. If a port, for example, handles mostly container (breakbulk) cargo, it will be described as a container (breakbulk) port. Passenger ports are classified by the prominent type of passenger vessel (rather than by the type of passenger) that calls at the port. For example, a passenger port may be a cruise (ferry) port, where calls by cruise (ferry) vessels are prominent.

A marine terminal is a distinct infrastructure within a port for the transfer of cargo and passengers to and from vessels. A port may have several marine terminals – for handling the same type of cargo or different types of cargo. A port's marine terminals may be common-user or dedicated. If common-user, vessels of all shipping lines are allowed to call at the terminal subject to existing government regulations. If dedicated, the terminal is restricted to vessel calls by the shipping line (or party) that owns or leases the marine terminal.

A port is an economic unit. It provides a transfer service as opposed to producing a product as for a manufacturing firm. The amount of this transfer service is often referred to as the port's throughput, i.e., the number of containers (or tons of cargo) and passengers moved through the port. Ports utilize resources such as labor, mobile capital (e.g., cranes) and infrastructure (e.g., wharfs) in transferring cargo and passengers to and from vessels. If the port seeks to be technically efficient, it will seek to maximize its throughput in the employment of a given level of resources.

Ports may be commercial – privately owned, seeking to make a profit – or public – owned by government (local, state, or federal), generally not seeking to make a profit. A public port's objectives may include promoting regional employment, economic development, and the export of commodities for which the region has a comparative advantage. Public ports are typically managed by public port authorities. A public authority is an independent (or quasi-independent) agency that has been given the authority by the government owner of the port to manage the port.

In most places in the world, ports are located on the shore lands of cities. These lands are highly valued with many alternative uses. Not only may the land be used for marine terminals, but also for tourism and recreation industries, residential and office buildings, nature parks, and commercial fishing industries. Consequently, port land expansions are often entrusted to governments and regulatory authorities to reconcile the interests of all parties competing for the land.

A port is a place at which terminal services are provided to transportation carriers such as shipping lines, railroads, and trucking firms. These services include, for example, vessel and vehicle maintenance and the assembling and sorting of vehicles, cargo, and passengers. Carriers may also have administrative offices at ports.

A port is a node in a transportation network. A transportation network is a spatial system of nodes and links over which the movement of cargo and passengers occurs. A node is a center in a transportation network from which cargo and passenger movements emanate. A link between two transportation nodes is the transportation way (e.g., waterway, highway, railway, and airway) distance between the nodes. Important determinants in the location of transportation nodes are accessibility and capacity to hold cargo and passengers. For ports, however, it often will be physical geography that determines whether a particular location will be selected for a port node.

Port economics is the study of the economic decisions (and their consequences) of the users and providers of port services. Port users demand port services, while port service providers supply port services to port users. Port users use the port as part of the transportation process of moving cargo and passengers to and from origin and destination locations. Port users include shippers and individuals that provide cargo and themselves as passengers to be transported, and carriers (e.g., shipping lines, railroads, and truck carriers) that do the transporting. The port (or terminal) operator that operates a port or one (or more) of its marine terminals is the primary service provider of a port. Examples of other port service providers are ship agents, stevedores, freight forwarders, third-party logistics firms, custom brokers, ship pilots, and ship towage firms. Port economics and shipping economics comprise the branch of economics known as maritime economics.

Vessel port calls: networks

Both liner and tramp vessels may call at a port. Port calls by liner vessels are scheduled, i.e., each vessel that calls at a port follows a time schedule. Port calls by tramp vessels are non-scheduled (or chartered).

A vessel's transportation network may be an origin-to-destination (OD), a mainline-feeder (MAIN-FEED), or a mainline-mainline (MAIN-MAIN) transportation network (Chadwin *et al.* 1990). In an OD network, the same vessel transports cargo from its origin port through the network to its destination port. In the MAIN-FEED and MAIN-MAIN networks, the same vessel does not necessarily transport cargo from its origin port to its destination port. These networks consist of sub-networks that are connected by a common port. For the

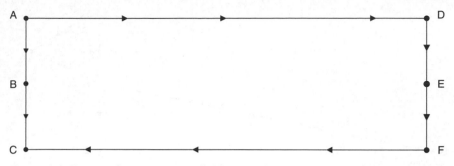

Figure 1.1 Constant frequency port-call OD network

MAIN-FEED network, the sub-networks consist of a mainline network over which cargo is transported in relatively large vessels and a feeder network over which relatively small vessels feeder cargo to and from the mainline network via the connecting (or feeder) port. When cargo is transferred from one vessel to another at a given port, the cargo is referred to as transshipment cargo. The MAIN-MAIN network consists of two mainline networks, where cargo is transferred from one mainline network to another at a port that is common to both mainline networks. By contrast, an OD network is one for which there is no transshipment of cargo among the network's ports.

An OD network may be a constant or a variable frequency port-call network. A constant frequency port-call network is one over which a vessel calls at all ports in the network the same number of times (generally once) on a given round trip. A variable frequency port-call network is one over which a vessel calls at some ports more than others on the same round trip.

A constant frequency port-call OD network is depicted in Figure 1.1. The figure has two separate ranges of ports separated by an ocean, with ports A, B, and C on one side and ports D, E, and F on the other side of the ocean. A vessel calls once at each port on each round trip, covering a broad range of ports. If the number of port calls on the network increases, vessel schedule adherence (and thus the reliability of service) is likely to be adversely affected.

A variable frequency port-call OD network is depicted in Figure 1.2. It depicts the network in Figure 1.1 except the vessel calls at port A twice while maintaining one call at each of the remaining ports on each round trip. A broad coverage of ports is maintained on a variable frequency port-call OD network, while providing more frequent vessel calls at ports where there are higher volumes of cargo.

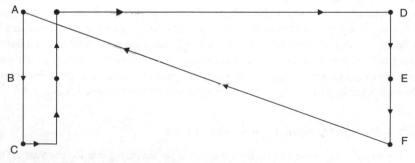

Figure 1.2 Variable frequency port-call OD network

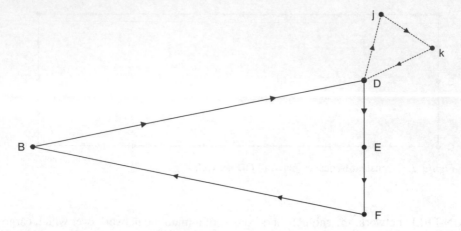

Figure 1.3 Mainline-feeder network

A mainline-feeder network is depicted in Figure 1.3. The mainline network DEFB has a connecting feeder network Djk, feedering cargo into and out of feeder port D, a port common to both networks. Relatively large vessels serve mainline network DEFB and relatively small vessels operate over feeder network Djk. The vessel service achieves broad coverage in the DEF port range, takes advantage of a vessel's cost economies of vessel size at sea by calling at only one port on the ABC port range, and takes advantage of a vessel's cost economies of vessel utilization (or load factor) in port from the increase in the concentration of cargo at port D.[1]

Cost savings to the shipping line in the network in Figure 1.3 are expected to arise from feedering cargo on a relatively small vessel from port j to port D and then combining this cargo with cargo already at port D for transport on a relatively large vessel to destination port B – as opposed to providing direct service between ports j and B and between ports D and B. However, with these cost savings, a loss in revenue to the shipping line is also expected. Feeder vessel service generally is a poorer quality of service than direct vessel service. For example, the sum of the transit times of cargo moving from port j to port D and then to port B will be greater than the transit time of direct service between ports j and B. If the shipping line seeks to maximize profits, it will have been rational in establishing a feeder port at port D if the cost savings related to the feeder port are greater than the revenue lost.

In Figure 1.4, a mainline-mainline network is depicted, consisting of mainline networks ABCE and GHIE, having the common port E. At port E, cargo is transferred to and from the two networks from one vessel to another. Since relatively large vessels are used on mainline networks, the vessel service is able to take advantage of cost economies of vessel size (i.e., utilizing a larger vessel) at sea. The shipping line will have been rational in establishing a transshipment port at port E if the cost savings related to the transshipment port are greater than the revenue lost. In Figure 1.5, a combination of mainline-feeder and mainline-mainline networks has been created by merging the networks depicted in Figures 1.3 and 1.4.[2]

Vessel port calls: world, country, and vessel type

In Table 1.1 the world's top-ranked ports for vessel calls for seven regions for the year 2006 are presented. In the regions of Africa, Asia, Australasia, Europe, North America, South America,

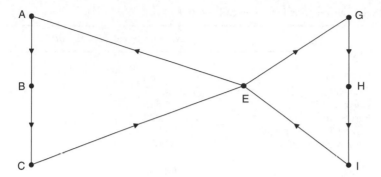

Figure 1.4 Mainline-mainline network

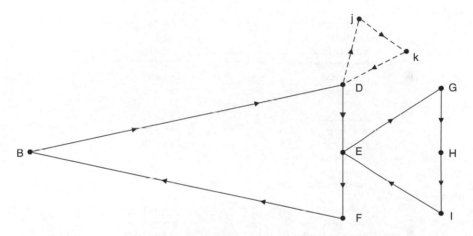

Figure 1.5 Mainline-feeder and mainline-mainline networks

and West Indies/Central America, the ports with the most vessel calls in 2006 were the ports of Las Palmas, Singapore, Melbourne, Rotterdam, Houston, Santos, and Freeport, respectively.

The region in the world with the most vessel port calls in 2006 was Europe with 700,239 port calls, followed by Asia with 562,375 port calls. Among all regions, the five top-ranked ports for vessel port calls in 2006 were the ports of Singapore, Hong Kong, Rotterdam, Busan, and Kaohsiung with 60,548, 31,493, 28,461, 22,480, and 15,565 vessel port calls, respectively.

In Table 1.2 vessel port calls by country and type of vessel for the year 2006 are presented. The countries are ranked by the number of vessel port calls. The five top-ranked countries for vessel port calls in 2006 were Japan, China, the United States, the United Kingdom, and Italy with 106,608, 105,827, 100,154, 97,766, and 72,050 calls, respectively. The countries with the greatest number of container, general cargo, tanker, dry bulk, and passenger vessel calls in 2006 were China (46,321 container vessel calls), Japan (32,637 general cargo vessel calls), the United States (23,632 tanker vessel calls), the United States (16,864 dry bulk vessel calls), and Italy (19,439 passenger vessel calls), respectively.

Table 1.1 The world's top-ranked ports for vessel calls (2006)

Region/rank	Port	Number of vessel port calls
Africa		
1	Las Palmas	5,060
2	Alexandria	4,711
3	Durban	4,325
4	Port Said	3,022
5	Santa Cruz de Tenerife	3,017
	Total regional calls	87,615
Asia		
1	Singapore	60,548
2	Hong Kong	31,493
3	Busan	22,480
4	Kaohsiung	15,565
5	Shanghai	15,371
	Total regional calls	562,375
Australasia		
1	Melbourne	3,441
2	Brisbane	2,593
3	Botany Bay	1,614
4	Freemantle	1,587
5	Gladstone	1,437
	Total regional calls	36,452
Europe		
1	Rotterdam	28,461
2	Antwerp	15,329
3	Hamburg	14,499
4	Barcelona	9,242
5	Zeebrugge	8,322
	Total regional calls	700,239
North America		
1	Houston	7,451
2	New York	5,598
3	Port Everglades	4,423
4	Long Beach	3,766
5	Port Arthur	3,228
	Total regional calls	114,090
South America		
1	Santos	5,556
2	Buenaventura	4,759
3	Cartagena	4,000
4	Turbo	2,836
5	Puerto Cabello	2,342
	Total regional calls	78,454
West Indies/ Central America		
1	Freeport	2,933
2	San Juan	2,852
3	St. Thomas	2,276
4	Puerto Limon	2,201
5	Philipsburg	1,990
	Total regional calls	59,224

Source: Staff (2007) *Lloyd's List Ports of the World 2008*, London: Informa.

Table 1.2 Vessel port calls by country and type of vessel (2006)

Country/type of vessel	Container	General cargo-breakbulk	Tanker	Dry bulk	Passenger	Other	Total
Japan	35,416	32,637	10,188	12,182	1,634	14,551	106,608
China	46,321	24,768	11,839	13,458	3,931	5,510	105,827
United States	20180	7,957	23,632	16,864	11,463	20,058	100,154
United Kingdom	8,142	28,359	17,556	3,223	8,214	32,272	97,766
Italy	9,613	14,324	12,002	3,916	19,439	12,756	72,050
South Korea	18,107	21,609	8,651	5,570	1,767	7,722	63,426
Singapore	16,490	7,975	15,523	8,187	780	13,336	62,291
Spain	8,450	15,553	6,682	4,941	11,506	10,865	57,997
The Netherlands	7,377	16,855	10,111	2,561	2,753	14,300	53,957
Norway	1,863	19,747	6,450	2,674	4,459	11,863	47,056
Indonesia	4,616	13,706	10,683	3,964	2,236	8,573	43,778
Germany	10,413	14,970	5,320	1,902	1,863	7,473	41,941
Russian Federation	2,256	20,229	7,853	3,091	957	4,359	38,745
France	4,637	8,578	8,870	1,857	6,932	5,773	36,647
Taiwan	14,752	9,148	4,786	5,341	153	2,000	36,180
Belgium	4,953	7,429	4,565	1,227	1,971	11,257	31,402
Turkey	4,429	15,547	4,564	1,911	979	3,201	30,631
Malaysia	11,984	7,041	6,228	1,635	425	2,657	29,970
Brazil	8,933	3,137	5,178	7,819	459	2,917	28,443
Sweden	1,605	12,593	6,094	827	1,343	5,481	27,943
Rest of world	94,048	150,758	89,073	66,186	38,272	87,300	525,637
World total	334,585	452,920	275,848	169,336	121,536	284,229	1,638,449

Source: Staff (2007) *Lloyd's List Ports of the World 2008*, London: Informa.

Ports and economic development

A port is an "engine" for regional economic development by increasing employment, labor incomes, business earnings, and taxes in the region. These benefits arise in the construction (or expansion) and operation of the port. During construction, regional construction contractors and workers are hired and regional construction materials are purchased. Jobs in the operation of a port include those of port operators, users (shippers and ocean and inland carriers), and other service providers (e.g., ship agent, ship repair, freight forwarding, marine insurance, pilotage, and towage service providers).

Port construction and operation jobs are the *direct regional jobs* created by the port. Jobs, labor incomes, business earnings, and tax revenues generated by port construction and operation activities represent the *direct regional benefits* of the port. It is implicitly assumed that these benefits would not exist in the region without the existence of the port.

Secondary benefits of a port arise when its initial generated labor incomes, business earnings, and tax revenues are subsequently spent or partially spent in the region. These expenditures (e.g., at restaurants and for entertainment and professional services) generate additional labor incomes, business earnings, and tax revenues within the region. This process continues to second, third, and further rounds of re-spending. When the re-spending is exhausted, the total labor earnings, business earnings, and tax revenues in the region will have increased by more than their initial amounts by a factor greater than one (i.e., by the multiplier coefficient). If the region's marginal propensity to spend of labor incomes and business earnings is 0.8 (i.e., $0.80 is spent out of each additional dollar of income and business earnings), the multiplier coefficient will be 5 for labor incomes and business earnings expenditures.[3] Thus, the increase in total spending in the region will be the initial spending plus the secondary spending. The secondary benefits of generated jobs, labor incomes, business earnings, and tax revenues from the spending and re-spending are the *indirect regional benefits* of the port.

The above benefits of the port, however, will be reduced if there are regional leakages. For example, in construction or expansion of a port, workers may be employed and materials purchased from outside the region. Consequently, the direct benefits that would have occurred in using regional labor and materials purchased are lost to other regions. Similarly, the direct benefits of the port will be less if the recipients of labor income and business earnings from operation of the port are not residents of the region.

When direct benefits are lost, indirect (or secondary) benefits will also be lost, since the latter arise from the former. In fact, if none of the port's direct benefit incomes and business earnings is spent in the region, the corresponding indirect benefits from these expenditures to the region will be zero. Also, if the resident recipients of the direct-benefit incomes and business earnings spend a part of these in other regions, the region's marginal propensity to spend will decline, thus resulting in a smaller multiplier effect. For example, suppose the marginal propensity to spend within the region drops from 0.8 to 0.5; hence, the corresponding multiplier coefficient will drop from 5 to 2 for the region.

Note that if the region of the port is increased in size, for example, to that of its state or province, there may be no leakages. If there are no leakages, the port's direct-benefit incomes and business earnings that are spent would now be entirely spent within the larger region. However, the assumption that the regional benefits attributed to the regional port would not occur without the existence of the port may not hold. That is to say, with a larger redefined region, it may be the case that some of the benefits could occur without the existence of the given port, e.g., there may be a nearby port for the larger region through which carriers and shippers could move their cargo.

Rather than positive benefits, the existence of a regional port may also generate negative benefits (or losses) for a region, e.g., from business earnings losses from foreign competition, higher regional taxes to subsidize the port, and losses in regional property tax revenue (from not being able to tax the government property of the port). If so, a port's positive benefits would have to be adjusted downward by its negative benefits in order to obtain a true measure of the port's net benefit (positive minus negative benefits) to the region. If not, "it is easy to exaggerate the existing and potential role of ports in regional economic development" (Gripaios and Gripaios 1995: 22).

In addition to the direct and indirect benefits of a port, the port may also generate tertiary and perpetuity benefits. Tertiary (or third-order) benefits stem from improvements (in infrastructure and quality of service) in the region's transportation system because of the existence of the port. For example, improvements may occur in the region's highway system and rail and trucking services – resulting in reductions in transit times for cargo movements within the region, increases in the frequency of pickups and deliveries, and increases in the accessibility of shippers to regional, national, and international markets. However, if cargo movements to and from the port rise to the extent that they result in highway congestion, negative tertiary benefits would be generated by the port.

Perpetuity benefits stem from the dynamic economic impact of a port, i.e., the port acts as a catalyst for greater economic growth within the region. For example, U.S. container ports have been a catalyst for the location of distribution warehouses by such retailers as Wal-Mart, Target, and Home Deport within the regions of the ports.[4]

A port in one region may also have spillover effects on another region. A study by Cohen and Monaco (2008) of U.S. ports and states indicates that a 1 percent increase in the infrastructure of ports in the neighboring states of a particular state leads to a 0.129 percent increase in the particular state's manufacturing costs, the rationale being that the neighboring states draw away productive resources from the particular state, leading to higher manufacturing costs in the particular state. The study also concludes that increasing the infrastructure of ports in a particular state by 1 percent will decrease manufacturing costs in that state by 0.043 percent.

Containerization

Over the centuries, various attempts have been made to simplify the ocean transportation of cargo. Limitations in the technology of cargo handling often defeated these efforts. However, advancements in the handling of bulk commodities occurred when barrels and casks were replaced by specially designed ships into which oil, coal, or grain could be poured, but the advancement in the transportation of general cargo has been limited.

Through the 1950s, general cargo continued to be handled as breakbulk. This meant the movement of cargo, generally one pallet at a time, onto a rail car or truck that carried it from the factory or warehouse to a port's docks. There each pallet was unloaded and hoisted, by cargo net and crane, off the dock and onto the vessel. Once the pallet was in the vessel's hold, it had to be positioned precisely and braced to protect it from damage during the ocean crossing. This process was performed in reverse at the other end of the voyage, making the ocean transportation of general cargo a slow, labor-intensive, and expensive process.

All of this began to change in 1955 when Malcom McLean, believing that individual pieces of general cargo needed to be handled only twice – at their origin when stored in a standardized container box and at their destination when unloaded – purchased a small tanker company, renamed it Sealand, and adapted its vessels to transport truck trailers. On April 26, 1956, the first voyage of a Sealand containership occurred when the vessel left Newark, New Jersey, for Puerto Rico. However, confrontations with railroads, shipping lines, and unions delayed Sealand's maiden international voyage to Rotterdam until 1966. The containerization of international trade had begun.

Prior to containerization, general cargo was loaded/unloaded from breakbulk vessels having on-board cranes and docked at finger piers – piers extending into the water, perpendicular to port berths – and was stored in warehouses. With the redesign of containerships to be non-self-sustaining, i.e., with no cranes aboard, breakbulk ports aspiring to become container ports had to become more capital intensive, not only investing in dockside cranes but also in various types of infrastructure and mobile capital. Finger piers were eliminated. Berths were redesigned so that containerships could be docked parallel to them for easier loading/unloading by dockside cranes. Warehouses were removed and land cleared for open-land storage of containers. If land was plentiful, containers were stored on truck chassis for easy movement to and from vessels; if not, they were stacked on land one upon another, several containers high.

The increased use of containers, coupled with new cargo-handling techniques, resulted in a significant decrease in the demand for port labor. Huge job losses resulted, ranging from 40 to 60 percent in many countries (Zarocostas 1996). In the United Kingdom, dockworker jobs fell from 80,000 in 1967 to 11,400 in 1986 and further declines of 44 percent occurred between 1989 and 1992 (Talley 2000).

A gang of 20 dockworkers could load 20 tons of cargo per hour on a breakbulk ship, whereas on a containership, one crane and perhaps half as many dockworkers could load 400 to 500 tons per hour. While a breakbulk ship often took a week to unload and reload, a containership might be in port for only 12 hours for the same amount of cargo. Less time in port meant not only lower time-in-port charges but also fewer ships were needed to transport cargo.

A significant trend in containerization is the increase in the size of vessels employed. Between 1992 and 2002, the size of the largest containership in service increased from 4,500 TEU to 8,400 TEU. New vessels, now on order, exceed 14,000 TEU.[5] The introduction of larger containerships in worldwide service places pressure on container ports to increase: (1) water depths in entrance channels and alongside berths; (2) channel widths to have sufficient vessel turning circles; (3) the size of shoreside container cranes to have longer outreach, loading capacity, and lift height; (4) terminal storage capacity; and (5) truck and railroad facilities (Baird 2002).

World container ports

The world's largest container ports, ranked by TEU throughput, appear in Table 1.3. These ports are often described as load center ports (analogous to hub airports), having one or both of the location attributes: (1) centrality, a strong traffic-generating local market, and (2) intermediacy, an attraction to distantly located traffic-generating regions, i.e., the ability to capture transshipment cargo (Hayuth and Fleming 1994).

Table 1.3 The world's 20 largest container ports (2007)

Rank	Port	TEU throughput (1,000,000s)	Percent change in TEU throughput from 2006	Country
1	Singapore	27.93	12.7	Singapore
2	Shanghai	26.15	20.5	China
3	Hong Kong	24.00	1.9	China
4	Shenzhen	21.10	14.2	China
5	Busan	13.26	10.1	South Korea
6	Rotterdam	10.79	11.8	The Netherlands
7	Dubai	10.65	19.4	U.A.E.
8	Kaohsiung	10.26	4.9	Taiwan
9	Hamburg	9.89	11.6	Germany
10	Qingdao	9.46	22.9	China
11	Ningbo-Zhoushan	9.43	32.1	China
12	Guangzhou Harbor	9.26	39.0	China
13	Los Angeles	8.36	(1.4)	United States
14	Antwerp	8.18	16.5	Belgium
15	Long Beach	7.31	0.3	United States
16	Port Kelang	7.12	12.5	Malaysia
17	Tianjin	7.10	19.4	China
18	Tanjung Pelepas	5.50	15.3	Malaysia
19	New York-New Jersey	5.30	4.2	United States
20	Laem Chabang	4.64	12.6	Thailand

Source: Staff (2008) "The JOC's Top 50 World Container Ports," *Journal of Commerce*, 9, July 28: 28, 30, 32, 34 and 36.

The three top-ranked container ports in the world in 2007 with respect to TEU throughput were Singapore, Shanghai, and Hong Kong. Hong Kong was ranked number two in 2006, but dropped to number three in 2007. Singapore is a major transshipment port, used by container shipping lines as an interchange point between mainline and feeder services. Among the world's twenty largest container ports, seven are located in China – Shanghai, Hong Kong, Shenzhen, Qingdao, Ningbo-Zhoushan, Guangzhou Harbor, and Tianjin. In 2007, China became the first country in the world to handle more than 100 million TEUs (i.e., 102 million TEUs) through its ports; this 2007 TEU level exceeded China's 2006 level by 21.7 percent. Excluding Hong Kong, the range of the percent increase (from 2006 to 2007) in the TEU throughput of the above Chinese ports is 14.2 to 39.0 percent.

The combined 2007 TEU volumes (15.67 million TEUs) for the Ports of Los Angeles and Long Beach would rank the Los Angeles-Long Beach port complex as the fifth largest container port in the world. In 2007, however, the Port of Los Angeles experienced a decrease of 1.4 percent in its TEU throughput, while the Port of Long Beach experienced the very small percent increase of 0.3. The above decline and slow growth in TEU throughput are attributable to increases in long-haul intermodal rail rates, additional throughput capacity at the Canadian ports of Vancouver and Prince Rupert, and shippers opting for Panama/Suez Canal alternatives to the U.S. East and Gulf Coasts (Higginbotham 2008).

Busan serves South Korea as well as being a transshipment port for Chinese and Japanese cargo. Kaohsiung and Dubai are major transshipment ports. Rotterdam, Hamburg, and Antwerp are centrality hubs. Among North American container ports, New York-New Jersey is a centrality hub, whereas Los Angeles and Long Beach are centrality and transshipment hubs (for distantly located regions).

Summary

A port is a place that provides for the transfer of cargo and passengers to and from vessels. Also, it is an economic unit, a place that provides terminal services to transportation carriers and a node in a transportation network. A vessel's transportation network may be an origin-to-destination, a mainline-feeder, or a mainline-mainline network.

The benefits of a port to its region include direct regional, indirect regional, tertiary, and perpetuity benefits. Containerization has resulted in the redesign of ports. Breakbulk ports aspiring to become container ports have become more capital intensive: finger piers have been eliminated, and berths have been redesigned so that containerships can be docked parallel to berths for easier loading/unloading by dockside cranes. As larger and larger containerships are employed in world trade, container ports are under pressure to increase channel and berth water depths, channel widths, the size of shoreside cranes, terminal storage capacity, and truck and railroad facilities.

Notes

1 For support for the case of cost economies of vessel size at sea, see Talley (1990) and Chadwin *et al.* (1990). For support for the case of cost economies of vessel utilization in port, see Gilman (1983). Also, see Talley *et al.* (1986).
2 For a discussion of vessel transportation networks, see Gilman (1981), Pearson and Fossey (1983), Chadwin *et al.* (1990), Gilman (1999), and Cullinane and Khanna (1999).
3 Suppose there is an additional $1,000 in regional spending and the region's marginal propensity to spend is 0.8. In the first round of spending, the $1,000 is spent in the region; the second round of spending is $0.8 \times \$1,000 = \$800$; the third round of spending is $(0.8)^2 \times \$1,000 = \$640$; the fourth

round of spending is $(0.8)^3 \times \$1,000 = \$512$; etc. When the re-spending is exhausted, it can be shown that the initial spending of $1,000 will have increased to an expenditure of $[1/(1 - 0.8)] * \$1,000 = \$5,000$ in the region. The multiplier coefficient is $[1/(1 - 0.8)] = 5$.

4 For a discussion of the tertiary and perpetuity effects of airports, see Button (2004).

5 A discussion of the economic viability of mega containerships is found in Imai *et al.* (2006).

Bibliography

Baird, A. J. (2002) "The Economics of Transhipment", in C. Grammenos (ed.) *The Handbook of Maritime Economics and Business*, London: Informa, 832–859.

Bichou, K. and Gray, R. (2005) "A Critical Review of Conventional Terminology for Classifying Seaports", *Transportation Research Part A*, 39: 75–92.

Button, K. J. (2004) "Economic Development and Transport Hubs", in D. Hensher, K. Button, K. Haynes, and P. Stopher (eds) *Handbook of Transport Geography and Spatial Systems*, Amsterdam: Elsevier, 77–95.

Chadwin, M. L., Pope, J. A. and Talley, W. K. (1990) *Ocean Container Transportation: An Operational Perspective*, New York: Taylor & Francis.

Cohen, J. P. and Monaco, K. (2008) "Ports and Highways Infrastructure: An Analysis of Intra- and Inter-State Spillovers", *International Regional Science Review*, 31: 257–274.

Cullinane, K. and Khanna, M. (1999) "Economies of Scale in Large Container Ships", *Journal of Transport Economics and Policy*, 33: 185–208.

Gilman, S. (1981) *Container Logistics and Terminal Design*, Washington, DC: International Bank for Reconstruction and Development.

—— (1983) *The Competitive Dynamics of Container Shipping*, Aldershot, UK: Gower.

—— (1999) "The Size Economies and Network Efficiency of Large Containerships", *International Journal of Maritime Economics*, 1: 39–59.

Gripaios, P. and Gripaios, R. (1995) "The Impact of a Port on its Local Economy: The Case of Plymouth", *Maritime Policy and Management*, 22: 13–23.

Hayuth, Y. and Fleming, D. K. (1994) "Concepts of Strategic Commercial Location: The Case of Container Ports", *Maritime Policy and Management*, 21: 187–193.

Higginbotham, K. (2008) "Study: Cargo Diversions Contributing to SoCal Ports Volume Decline", *Shippers NewsWire*. Available online at http://www.shipper.com (accessed 4 March 2009).

Imai, I., Nishimura, E., Papadimitriou, S. and Miaojia, L. (2006) "The Economic Viability of Container Mega-Ships", *Transportation Research Part E: Logistics and Transportation Review*, 42: 21–41.

Oliver, D. and Slack, B. (2006) "Rethinking the Port", *Environmental Planning A*, 38: 1409–1427.

Pearson, R. and Fossey, J. (1983) *World Deep-Sea Container Shipping*, Aldershot, UK: Gower.

Robinson, R. (2002) "Ports as Elements in Value-Driven Chain Systems: The New Paradigm", *Maritime Policy and Management*, 29: 241–255.

Staff (2003) *Lloyd's List Ports of the World 2004*, London: Informa.

—— (2005) "The JOC's Top 50 World Container Ports", *Journal of Commerce*, 6, August 15: 12A–16A.

—— (2007) *Lloyd's List Ports of the World 2008*, London: Informa.

—— (2008) "The JOC's Top 50 World Container Ports", *Journal of Commerce*, 9, July 28: 28, 30, 32, 34 and 36.

Talley, W. K. (1990) "Optimal Containership Size", *Maritime Policy and Management*, 17: 165–175.

—— (2000) "Ocean Container Shipping: Impacts of a Technological Improvement", *Journal of Economic Issues*, 34: 933–948.

Talley, W. K., Agarwal, V. and Breakfield, J. (1986) "Economies of Density of Ocean Tanker Ships", *Journal of Transport Economics and Policy*, 20: 91–99, reprinted in M. Brooks, K. Button, and P. Nijkamp (eds) *Maritime Transport* (2002), Cheltenham, UK: Edward Elgar, 478–486.

Zarocostas, J. (1996) "Port Industry Jobs Worldwide Continue to Decline, Study Says", *Journal of Commerce*, May 12: 8B.

2 Port users and service providers

Introduction

Port users are those that utilize the port as part of the process in moving cargo and passengers from a given origin location to a given destination location. These movements are referred to as freight and passenger transportation trips. In order for a transportation trip to occur, two parties must be in agreement: (1) transportation carriers, e.g., shipping lines, railroads, trucking firms, and ferry companies, must be willing to transport cargo and passengers and (2) shippers and passengers must be willing to provide their cargo and themselves to transportation carriers to be transported. If either party is not in agreement, a transportation trip will not occur. Thus, port users are transportation carriers, shippers, and passengers that utilize ports in the creation of freight and passenger transportation trips.

Port service providers are those that provide services to the users of a port. The primary port service provider is the port's terminal operator that operates the port or one (or more) of its marine terminals. Other service providers include, for example, ship agents, freight forwarders, and custom brokers.

In the following section, the various types of transportation carriers that use port facilities are presented – container shipping lines, short sea shipping carriers, ferry carriers, cruise lines, railroads, and truck carriers – followed by a discussion on pages 23–26 of shippers and passengers that also use port facilities. Port service providers are discussed on pages 26–31. A summary of the discussion is found on page 31.

Users: carriers

Container shipping lines

Ocean container transportation accelerated in the 1980s, in particular the growth of the Asian container shipping lines, e.g., Hanjin, Yang Ming, Orient Overseas Container Line (OOCL), and Evergreen. By 1986 Evergreen had become the world's largest ocean carrier of containers. The Asian lines operated 30 percent of the world's container fleet, while the world's share operated by North American and Western Europe lines declined to 50 percent. Sealand and American President Lines (APL) were the largest and second largest U.S. flag container shipping lines, respectively.

Containership tonnage in the Far East–North American trade more than doubled in the five years between 1983 and 1988. In 1988 alone, the tonnage in the North Atlantic trades increased by 25 percent when the Danish line, Maersk, entered the market and Sealand deployed the energy efficient, but slow, "Econships" on the same routes. The excess ship capacity and declining profits in the industry, however, forced a number of container shipping lines to diversify or leave the industry, while others were involved in mergers or acquisitions by larger transportation firms, e.g., the purchase of Sealand by the U.S. railroad, CSX.

The container shipping lines that remained in the industry adapted to the increasingly complex and dynamic container shipping environment by adopting different service strategies. Some adopted the load-center strategy of calling at only one or two ports on a range. Others adopted the multi-port strategy of calling at several ports along the same coast. Some maintained their service over the large-volume, highly competitive routes between North America, Europe, and Asia, while others focused on less competitive, north–south routes. Some shipping lines, such as Sealand, sought to provide door-to-door service, utilizing their own facilities and equipment, while others contracted for rail, truck, and other intermediary services. Evergreen, Nedlloyd, and Senator Lines adopted round-the-world services. For the latter, Evergreen used relatively large ships in continuous eastbound and westbound circuits.

By 1997 the world's twenty largest shipping lines (ranked by TEUs transported) accounted for 78.2 percent of the TEUs transported by the largest hundred lines (Talley 2000). Among these twenty lines, the top three – Sealand, Evergreen, and Maersk – accounted for 33.2 percent of the TEUs transported.

By the late 1990s the container shipping line industry was experiencing financial difficulties. The estimated collective losses of the container shipping lines operating in the transpacific, transatlantic, and Europe/Far Asia trades in 1996 were \$411 million (Porter 1996). The losses reflected the continuing imbalance between market supply and demand, exhibited by excess ship capacity and declining freight rates. Finding it difficult to raise freight rates, container shipping lines sought to reduce costs – by forming alliances, undertaking mergers and acquisitions, and investing in larger (more cost-efficient) ships – in order to improve their financial conditions.

A number of the largest container shipping lines formed alliances. By sharing vessels and terminals, the lines could reduce operating costs without sacrificing frequency of service, while retaining their independence. For example, a line's alliance partner may have a ship berthed at a given port. If this ship has space for the line's containers at this port, the line may choose to have its containers loaded on this ship rather than having one of its ships call at the port. By reducing its number of port calls, the line would save port-call ship capacity as well as reduce transit times on a given route. The saved ship capacity, in turn, could be diverted to new service routes or for increasing the frequency of port calls on existing routes. By August 1995 four major alliances were in existence: (1) the Global Alliance of APL, OOCL, Mitsui OSK Line, and Nedlloyd; (2) the Grand Alliance of Peninsular and Orient Line (P&O), Hapag Lloyd Line, Neptune Orient Line (NOL), and NYK Line; (3) the Sealand/Maersk Alliance of Sealand and Maersk Line; and (4) the Tricon Alliance of Cho Yang Shipping Company, DSR-Senator Lines, Hanjin Shipping Company, and the United Arab Shipping Company.

Realizing that the anticipated cost savings from alliances would not be quickly realized, a number of container shipping lines entered into mergers and acquisitions as another means of reducing costs. P&O (a British carrier) and Nedlloyd (a Dutch carrier) surprised the maritime community by announcing that they would merge on January 1, 1997, forming P&O Nedlloyd, creating the world's largest container shipping line. The annual cost savings of the merger were projected to be US\$200 million, 65 percent of which would be immediate from eliminating duplicated overhead, far in excess of the cost savings from an alliance (Wastler 1997; Tirschwell 1997). In April 1997 NOL of Singapore agreed to acquire APL, identifying US\$130 million in annual cost savings from consolidating information technology and vessel, container, and inland services and from reduced terminal expenses (Tirschwell 1997). In 1999 Maersk acquired Sealand for a price of US$800 million, creating the world's largest container shipping line, Maersk-Sealand. During the years 2000–2003 a number of major lines acquired smaller lines to bolster their commercial presence on specific trade routes, e.g., four-teen acquisitions were made by Maersk-Sealand, P&O Nedlloyd, CP Ships, CSAV, Hamburg Sud, CMA-CGM, and Wan Hai. In 2005 the largest acquisition in the history of liner shipping occurred when Maersk-Sealand acquired P&O Nedlloyd, creating the world's largest container shipping line, Maersk. This merger was followed by the acquisition of CP Ships by Hapag Lloyd.

Liner mergers and acquisitions have implications beyond that for the lines themselves. First, they raise doubts about the future of alliances. Second, they reflect increasing pressures on lines to become global companies. Third, they reflect the fading importance of national flag lines. Although doubts continue about the future of alliances, alliances are still in exis-tence. In 2003 the New World Alliance included APL, Mitsui OSK lines, and Hyundai and the Grand Alliance included Hapag-Lloyd, NYK Line, P&O Nedlloyd, OOCL, and MSC.

Container shipping lines have also sought to reduce their costs by investing in larger containerships, the rationale being that non-self-sustaining (or cellular) containerships exhibit cost economies of ship size at sea. For example, a 4,000 TEU ship has a 30 percent to 40 percent per TEU cost saving over a 2,500 TEU ship and a 6,000 TEU ship has an 18 percent to 24 percent per TEU cost saving over a 4,000 TEU ship (Talley 2000). A 12,000 TEU ship on the Europe–Far East route has an 11 percent per TEU cost saving over an 8,000 TEU ship (Notteboom 2004).

The Maersk 6,000 TEU ship that was launched in 1996 is 1,049 feet in length and wide enough to carry 17 containers across, having a cruising speed of more than 25 knots and a fifteen-person crew and powered by the world's largest diesel engine (at the time of con-struction). The largest containership employed in service in early 2005 was the Colombo Express – a 8,750 TEU ship employed by Hapag-Lloyd. In early 2007 the Emma Maersk, a 13,000 TEU containership, was employed.

In Table 2.1 the world's twenty largest container shipping lines as of August 2007 are found. The lines are ranked by the TEU carrying capacity of their fleet of ships; their number of ships is also presented. The largest container shipping line in the world, Maersk Line, held almost 19 percent (as of August 2007) of the fleet ship TEU carrying capacity and approximately 17 percent of the number of ships utilized by the twenty largest lines. Together, the five largest lines held 52.3 percent of the ship fleet TEU carrying capacity and 50.7 percent of the number of ships utilized by the twenty largest lines. The twenty largest lines in Table 2.1 held 73.4 percent of the world's ship TEU carrying capacity (12,211,101 TEUs) and utilized 33.5 percent of the world's number of ships (8,666 ships).[1] In 2007, the percentage of the ships utilized by the five largest container shipping lines found in Table 2.1, Maersk Line, Mediterranean Shipping, CMA CGM, Evergreen Line, and Hapag-Lloyd, that were chartered (as opposed to being owned by the lines) was 64.9, 42.7, 75.8, 38.9, and 56.8 percent, respectively (Leach 2007).

Short sea shipping carriers

Short sea shipping (or coastal shipping) is commercial waterborne freight transportation (by vessel and barge) that does not transit an ocean, but rather utilizes inland and coastal water-ways to move cargo to and from ports. In Europe and the United States, short sea shipping has been promoted as an alternative to truck transportation in order to reduce highway con-gestion. The extensive coastline, inland waterways, and numbers of ports in Europe have contributed to the success of the Europe short sea program. In 2000 approximately 2 billion

Table 2.1 The world's 20 largest container shipping lines (August 2007)

Rank	Shipping line	Fleet ship TEU carrying capacity (in 1000s of TEUs)/percent of total	Number of ships/ percent of total	World headquarters
1	Maersk Line	1,700/18.96%	507/17.48%	Copenhagen, Denmark
2	Mediterranean Shipping	1,140/12.71	346/11.93	Geneva, Switzerland
3	CMA CGM	765/8.53	301/10.38	Marseilles, France
4	Evergreen Line	609/6.79	178/6.14	Taipei, Taiwan
5	Hapag-Lloyd	479/5.34	138/4.76	Hamburg, Germany
6	China Ocean Shipping Company (COSCO)	440/4.91	151/5.21	Shanghai, China
7	China Shipping Container Lines	423/4.72	124/4.27	Shanghai, China
8	American President Line	364/4.06	109/3.76	Singapore
9	Nippon Yusen Kaisha (NYK Line)	343/3.83	114/3.93	Tokyo, Japan
10	Orient Overseas Container Line (OOCL)	340/3.79	84/2.90	Hong Kong
11	Hanjin Shipping Co.	322/3.59	76/2.62	Seoul, South Korea
12	Mitsui O.S.K. Lines	306/3.41	98/3.38	Tokyo, Japan
13	Kawasaki Kisen Kaisha (K Line)	284/3.17	88/3.03	Tokyo, Japan
14	Yang Ming Marine Transport	273/3.04	87/3.00	Keelung, Taiwan
15	Compania Sud Americana de Vapores	251/2.80	87/3.00	Valparaiso, Chile
16	Zim Integrated Shipping Services	243/2.71	98/3.38	Haifa, Israel
17	Hamburg Sud	235/2.62	100/3.45	Hamburg, Germany
18	Hyundai Merchant Marine	175/1.95	41/1.41	Seoul, South Korea
19	Pacific International Lines	154/1.72	101/3.48	Singapore
20	Wan Hai Lines	121/1.35	73/2.52	Asia
	Total	8,967	2,901	

Source: Staff (2007) *Top 20 Container Lines*. Available online at http://www.lloydslist.com (accessed 29 August 2007).

tons of short sea cargoes were transported throughout Europe, 700 million tons of which were transported in the United Kingdom and Italy (Europa 2004). The Europe short sea program accounts for 40 percent of Europe's transportation ton-kilometers and has resulted in a 50 percent reduction in heavy truck traffic in Europe. The significant growth in short sea shipping, however, has placed greater demand on Europe's port infrastructure – i.e., the increase in short sea cargo volumes and vessel calls has contributed to Europe's port congestion, e.g., from the interference between vessel calls by blue water and short sea fleets.

Short sea shipping in the United States is in its infancy stage. The Maritime Administration (MARAD) of the U.S. Department of Transportation has promoted short sea shipping via its Short Sea Shipping Initiative. The objective of the initiative is to use the U.S. domestic waterway system (coastal and inland) to ease congestion on the U.S. highway and rail systems by transporting containers on small coastal vessels and barges. The energy consumed and the cost and pollution per ton-mile by short sea shipping are less than that by truck.

A disadvantage of the U.S. Short Sea Shipping Initiative is that non-Jones-Act vessels cannot participate. Specifically, the U.S. Jones Act requires that all vessels that move cargo from one U.S. port to another must be U.S.-built, -crewed, and -flagged. Hence, foreign flag vessels cannot participate in the initiative. Will there be enough Jones-Act vessels to meet a significant growth in the demand for U.S. short sea shipping?

Must union dockworkers be used to load and unload short sea vessels? If so, the prices for U.S. short sea cargo movements may not be price competitive with those for truck movements. On the U.S. East Coast, the International Longshoremen's Association (ILA) has a master's contract (that covers ports from Maine to the Gulf Coast) that entitles the ILA union members to handle all port container movements for vessels involved in international voyages. However, the ILA may seek to extend this jurisdiction to Jones-Act vessels. Another concern is that short sea shipping may result in a significant increase in vessel calls and cargo volumes at U.S. ports, thereby contributing to greater congestion at these ports (Russell and Talley, forthcoming).

Ferry carriers

Ferry carriers provide ferry transportation services that are scheduled and provided by vessels over a fixed water route. Ferry vessels may carry passengers, passengers and their vehicles, and vehicles (truck and rail) transporting cargo. Ferry services are provided between origin and destination locations where a bridge (or tunnel) does not exist or where the width of the body of water between these locations would make the construction of a bridge (or tunnel) impractical. Ferry services are usually found in coastal urban regions, but also may be found in inter-island and inter-coastal regions. Ferry service is a less costly transportation service alternative per passenger and per ton of cargo moved to the bridge and tunnel for crossing a body of water when the demand for the crossing is relatively low. When the demand is relatively high, a bridge and tunnel may be less costly per passenger and per ton of cargo moved than ferry service, i.e., when the construction cost is amortized over the lifetime of the structure and then is divided by the number of transportation movements utilizing the structure.

Vehicle-carrying ferries are roll on-roll off (RO-RO) vessels that provide for the loading and unloading of vehicles through bow and stern doors. If these doors are breached while ferries are underway, allowing water to enter, ferries can list and sink. Conventional vehicle-carrying ferries generally operate at a speed of 22 knots. High-speed ferries (hovercrafts and catamarans) can operate at speeds exceeding 30 knots. Hovercrafts are supported by cushions of air, having boundaries defined by rubber skirts in which the crafts sit. Lift is provided by a fan system which blows air into the cushion; propulsion is provided by engines. Catamarans are twin-hull vessels with slender hulls and are most commonly used by passenger ferry operators.

Ferry carriers that operate large ferries around the world include Sealink (operating between the United Kingdom, Ireland, and Europe), Washington State Ferries (operating in the U.S. state of Washington), and British Columbia Ferry Corporation (operating in the Canadian province of British Columbia). The latter operates some of the busiest ferry marine terminals in the world. The world's largest ferries can carry more than 2,000 passengers and up to 700 vehicles on three vehicle decks. Marine terminals where such ferries berth are likely to be equipped with ramps that enable vehicles to be loaded and unloaded simultaneously from two decks of a ferry.

Cruise lines

Cruise lines are water carriers that provide passenger transportation (getting from origin A to destination B), tourism, and leisure services. Tourist trips on cruise vessels have been characterized "as one of the most augmented tourism products in the world as they offer a nearly all-inclusive vacation" (Lois *et al*. 2004). The trend in cruise vessel construction is to build larger vessels that can accommodate more than 1,500 passengers. Larger cruise vessels can exploit economies of vessel size at sea (lower cost per passenger) and increased on-board revenues from accommodating additional amenities. The larger cruise vessels are placing greater demands on cruise ports and marine terminals to: (1) enlarge their facilities to handle the loading and unloading of larger numbers of passengers, (2) increase the water depths of their channels, and (3) widen their channels so that two cruise vessels can pass each other at the same time. Cruise ports may also provide passengers with shore facilities such as shops, foreign exchange bureaus, and tourism information offices.

There are three types of passenger cruise vessels – ocean cruise, inland waterway cruise, and harbor/dinner cruise. As of January 1, 2004, 339 ocean cruise vessels with 296,000 passenger berths were in operation around the world. Among these vessels, 141 with 193,000 berths served the U.S. market at some time during 2003 (Ebersold 2004). Inland waterway and harbor/dinner cruise vessels are primarily found in North America and Europe.

There is considerable concentration in the worldwide cruise line industry. Carnival, Royal Caribbean, and Star/NCL lines together control 35 percent and 68 percent of the world's cruise vessels and berths, respectively. Carnival is the world's largest cruise line, controlling 22 percent and 39 percent of the worldwide cruise vessels and berths, respectively (Ebersold 2004).

The non-profit Cruise Lines International Association is North America's largest cruise industry organization, representing the interests of its twenty-four member cruise lines. These twenty-four lines are found in Table 2.2. The lines are ranked by the number of ship passenger berths found on their cruise ships. Note that the Royal Caribbean International is ranked number one with 60,586 berths, followed by Carnival Cruise Lines with 53,884 berths.[2]

Railroads

If ports have inadequate inland (rail, truck, and inland waterway/short sea shipping) transportation systems for moving cargo to and from inland locations, shipping lines (especially container shipping lines) may have to reroute their ships to neighboring ports. As larger and larger containerships call at fewer and fewer container ports, inland transportation carriers are relied upon more and more to distribute cargo over wider inland areas, placing an enormous strain on their infrastructure.

In 1984 the U.S. flag container shipping line, APL, began offering rail landbridge service[3] in the U.S. Rather than all-water service across the Pacific, through the Panama Canal, to the East Coast, its ships began calling at ports along the U.S. West Coast, where containers were unloaded and put on rail cars for the trip east. APL contracted with railroads to operate its double-stack trains over their rail lines. Double-stack trains consist of platform rail cars capable of moving containers stacked two high. Their appeal is their cost advantage over conventional COFC (container-on-flat car) trains: for slightly more locomotive power, the same labor and slightly more fuel, 200 containers can be transported on a double-stack train as opposed to 100 containers on a COFC train. By the late 1980s most of the containerized cargo from Asia bound for the U.S. East Coast did not arrive by ship, but rather was discharged on the U.S. West Coast, and hauled by rail across the continent, thereby placing

Table 2.2 Cruise Lines International Association's cruise lines, berths, and ships (2008)

Rank (by number of berths)	Cruise line	Number of ship passenger berths/ships
1	Royal Caribbean International	60,586/ 22
2	Carnival Cruise Lines	53,884/ 23
3	Princess Cruises	34,220/ 16
4	Norwegian Cruise Line	25,345/ 12
5	Costa Cruise Lines	23,330/ 12
6	Holland America Line	18,983/ 13
7	Celebrity Cruises	13,877/ 8
8	MSC Cruises	15,836/ 9
9	Hurtigruten (formerly Norwegian Coastal Voyages)	6,399/ 15
10	Cunard Line	6,397/ 3
11	Disney Cruise Line	5,400/ 2
12	Regent Seven Seas Cruises	2,418/ 5
13	Oceania Cruises	2,052/ 3
14	Crystal Cruises	2,020/ 2
15	Majestic American Line	1,537/ 6
16	Silversea Cruises	1,488/ 5
17	Azamara Cruises	1,388/ 2
18	Orient Lines	845/ 1
19	Seabourn Cruise Line	624/ 3
20	Windstar Cruises	608/ 3
21	Uniworld Grand River Gruises	592/ 9
22	American Cruise Lines	298/ 4
23	Seadream Yacht Club	220/ 2
24	Pearl Seas Cruises	214/ 1

Source: M. Silver Associates, Inc. (2008) *Cruise Industry Source Book*, Fort Lauderdale: Cruise Lines International Association.

West Coast ports in competition with East Coast ports. In comparison to all-water service via the Panama Canal to the East Coast, rail landbridge service (even by double-stack trains) is more costly, but it is five to six days faster. Today, shipping lines contract with railroads to transport containers by double-stack trains to and from ports on both the U.S. West and East Coasts.

Rail landbridging stimulated the growth of U.S. West Coast container ports (in particular the Ports of Los Angeles and Long Beach) to the detriment of East Coast container ports. In the mid-1980s, U.S. East Coast ports captured 22 percent of Asian ocean containerized cargo; by 1997 this share had declined to 15 percent (Mongelluzzo 1998). This decline would have been worse if not for the gains in container cargo by U.S. East Coast ports from all-water Asian trade via the Suez Canal – which grew from zero in 1991 to 6 percent of all ocean container service between Asia and the U.S. by mid-1996 (Talley 2000). The speed and the economies of larger containerships have made the Suez Canal trade somewhat competitive with that of the Pacific landbridging trade. All-water service via the Suez Canal from Singapore to the Port of New York-New Jersey, a 9,000 nautical mile route, takes 22 days, 1 to 2 days longer than passage across the Pacific to the Ports of Los Angeles and Long Beach and then rail landbridging to the U.S. East Coast. Although the freight rates of the all-water Suez service to the U.S. East Coast are 10 percent lower than those for water service to the West Coast and then rail landbridging to the East Coast, the freight revenue of the former goes to the shipping lines rather than being shared with railroads.

In January 1998 Panama's legislature privatized the state-owned Panama Railroad, awarding a 25-year lease to the U.S. companies, Kansas City Southern Railway and Mi-Jack Products. The rebuilt railroad is being used to provide landbridge service for containers that arrive (on either coast) in Panama on post-Panamax ships (i.e., ships too large to go through the Panama Canal). In addition, rail landbridging networks are found in Malaysia and Saudi Arabia. Also, Nicaragua is considering providing a landbridge network to compete with the Panama Canal and a Eurasia landbridge is being planned that would rail cargo to and from Rotterdam via China and Russia, linking Asia and Europe.

Besides stimulating the growth in the Ports of Los Angeles and Long Beach, rail land-bridging has also led to significant increases in highway congestion in these port cities. Congestion arises when highway traffic has to stop at rail crossings for trains entering and departing these ports. The problem of highway congestion was addressed by constructing the $2.4 billion Alameda Corridor – a high-capacity intermodal rail grade-separated (trench) corridor that consolidated more than 90 miles of rail operations into one 20-mile corridor, linking the Ports of Los Angeles and Long Beach and rail lines leading eastwardly. All rail-road crossings at street level (200 in number) along the corridor were eliminated. The cor-ridor was opened in 2002, charging $30 for each 40-foot equivalent unit (FEU) container that passed through the corridor. In 2002 the average number of trains (of the Union Pacific and Burlington Northern Santa Fe railroads) running per day on the Alameda Corridor was thirty-nine, increasing to fifty-five by 2006 and declining to forty-nine in 2007 (with a slight decrease in container volume due to more containers per train). The Alameda Corridor is the largest intermodal construction project in U.S. history.

Another negative of double-stack train landbridging may be the need to accommodate the height requirements of double-stack rail cars. That is to say, rail tunnels may not be high enough for double-stack trains to go through. If so, these tunnels must be heightened if they are needed for the provision of more direct double-stack train services (for lowering trans-portation times and costs) to certain destinations. On the U.S. East Coast, Norfolk Southern railroad is involved in the "Heartland Corridor" project for which mountain railway tunnels in the state of West Virginia are being heightened in order for double-stack trains from the Port of Virginia to be able to cut off significant distances in transporting containers to Chicago. A similar project, named the "Crescent Corridor," is also underway that involves the heightening of rail tunnels for more direct service by double-stack trains from the Port of New York-New Jersey to Memphis, Tennessee.

A shortage of rail equipment at ports can result in significant delays in the departure of port cargo to inland distances. In the summer of 1997, the Union Pacific (UP) railroad, which handles two-thirds of the Southern California container traffic, experienced a severe shortage of intermodal rail cars and locomotives in the region. This equipment shortage and the resulting backlog of containers for departure from the Ports of Los Angeles and Long Beach reached such a critical level that UP took the unprecedented step of chartering an APL ship – to transport containers from these ports, through the Panama Canal, destined for the Port of Savannah.

Furthermore, there was the related problem of a chassis shortage at the Ports of Los Angeles and Long Beach. With the delay in the departure of port containers that were stored on chas-sis, a shortage of truck chassis at the ports arose, thereby requiring the Ports of Los Angeles and Long Beach to store more containers by stacking (as opposed to by chassis), a more labor-intensive storage method. In recent years, the Ports of Los Angeles and Long Beach experi-enced a 20,000-chassis shortage, resulting in the ports using 30 percent to 35 percent more labor for storage-stacking of containers than if the containers were stored on chassis.[4]

Truck carriers

Truck carriers that transport cargo to and from ports (or intermodal truck carriers) include harbor drayage and over-the-road truck carriers. The former provides local truck service, e.g., moving containers from (to) the port to (from) local distribution warehouses and rail-yards. Over-the-road truck carriers provide intercity truck service, such as moving containers from (to) the port to (from) locations other than in the local area of the port. The form of payment for these two types of truck carriers differs markedly. Drayage trucker drivers are typically paid by the number of trips, while over-the-road truck drivers are typically paid by the mileage incurred. In the U.S. both types of truck drivers are usually owner-operators (also referred to as independent truck drivers) who own the trucks that they drive.[5] Brokerage firms typically keep 25 percent to 30 percent of the freight revenue of harbor drayage service with the remainder going to owner-operators (Mongelluzzo 2001).

The earnings of intermodal truck drivers are negatively affected not only by low truck rates but also by time-related costs and other costs imposed on them by ports and shipping lines. The higher costs when subtracted from trucking revenues result in lower earnings for harbor drayage (owner-operator) drivers. For example, truck drivers often incur port congestion from waiting in lines. Consequently, harbor drayage drivers, who are paid by the trip, have their earnings reduced when long waits result in fewer port trips per day. Solutions for reducing the waiting times of truckers at ports include: (1) providing additional truck lanes, (2) extending gate hours, (3) establishing port reservation systems, (4) encouraging local warehouses and distribution centers to remain open longer hours, and (5) charging truck idling and port congestion fees.

In 2002 the California legislature passed a truck idling (the Lowenthal) bill that stipulates a $250 fine on marine terminals for every truck that must wait (or idle) in line for more than 30 minutes. Fines, however, may be avoided by terminals keeping their gates open 60 to 70 hours per week.

In 2005 the Ports of Los Angeles and Long Beach adopted the Pier Pass program to relieve congestion at terminal gates and local highways by shifting port traffic to less-busy hours of the day. The Pier Pass program charges an $80-per-FEU (40-foot-equivalent-unit) fee on shippers when their cargo enters the ports by truck after 3 a.m. and before 6 p.m. during Monday through Thursday and during a day shift on Saturday. At other times of the day, the shipper can avoid the pier pass fee.

U.S. truck drivers moving container cargo to and from ports may also face additional costs attributable to container shipping lines. In the U.S. truck container chassis are owned by shipping lines. While chassis are in port, shipping lines are responsible for their repair, e.g., repair of defective brakes, lights, and tires. Once chassis have been turned over to a driver and have departed the port, the trucker is responsible for any highway fines that might occur. A trucker may not be aware of chassis defects – they may not have been reported or if reported, not repaired by the shipping line or its agent. Alternatively, a trucker may know of the defects but accepts the defective equipment and risks a fine to avoid losing the cargo or future cargoes to a competitor. If a trucker acknowledges defects of a chassis prior to its departure from a port, the trucker will be delayed in port while repairs are made.

In 2002 the California legislature passed a chassis roadability (the Romero) bill that makes marine terminals responsible for providing safe, roadworthy chassis to intermodal truckers. Specifically, terminal operators must certify that the chassis they tender to truckers are road-worthy and pay any fines that truckers receive for operating defective chassis. Similar chassis roadability legislation has been passed in the U.S. by South Carolina, Louisiana, and Illinois and has been proposed in New Jersey, Pennsylvania, Florida, Virginia, and Texas.

The Intermodal Association of North America has lobbied for a uniform national policy on equipment roadability. This policy was adopted when the U.S. Congress passed the Safe, Accountable, Flexible and Efficient Transportation Equity Act: A Legacy for Users in August 2005. The new law requires the owners of the estimated 750,000 chassis in the U.S. intermodal system to keep them in good condition. Specifically, a system of records on chassis is required; drivers will have to go through a safety checklist before taking a chassis on the highway; drivers are obligated to report any damage or defects to chassis while in transit; and the U.S. Department of Transportation will be able to levy fines for noncompliance.

As independent contractors, U.S. owner-operator truck drivers are prohibited under antitrust laws (in contrast to truck carrier employees) from forming collective-bargaining organizations (Peoples and Talley 2004). In an effort to increase the earnings of U.S. harbor drayage (owner-operator) truck drivers by allowing them to become members of a union, the Teamsters and the dockworker unions, the International Longshoremen's Association (ILA) and the International Longshore and Warehouse Union (ILWU), have agreed to form a national alliance to organize these drivers. The alliance seeks to persuade brokers of truck services to hire the estimated 50,000 nationwide harbor truck drivers as direct employees and lease the trucks from the drivers. As employees, the drivers would be eligible for membership in a union.[6]

Carrier demand for port service

The demand for port service at various prices by carriers that call at a port is represented by demand curve D_{CA} in Figure 2.1. At lower prices, more service is demanded and at higher prices, less service is demanded, other things remaining the same.

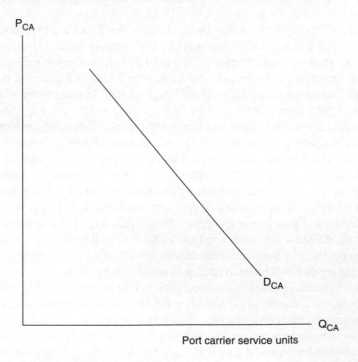

Figure 2.1 Carrier demand for port service

The responsiveness of the quantity demanded for a port service (Q_{CA}) by a carrier to changes in the price of this service (P_{CA}) may be measured by the carrier's price elasticity of demand (E_{CA}) for this service, i.e., the ratio of the percentage change in quantity demanded for the service to a percentage change in the price of the service, or

$$E_{CA} = \%\Delta Q_{CA}/\%\Delta P_{CA} \tag{2.1}$$

$E_{CA} < 0$, since a drop in the value of price P_{CA} will result in an increase in the value of quantity Q_{CA} and conversely. If $|E_{CA}| > 1$, the price elasticity of demand is price elastic; a given percentage change in price will result in a greater percentage change in quantity demanded. Thus, port carriers are very responsive to price changes in port carrier services. If $|E_{CA}| < 1$, the price elasticity of demand is price inelastic; a given percentage change in price will result in a lower percentage change in quantity demanded. Thus, port carriers are not very responsive to price changes in port carrier services. If $|E_{CA}| = 1$, the price elasticity of demand is unitary price elastic; a given percentage change in price will result in the same percentage change in quantity demanded.

Users: shippers and passengers

Shippers

For the shipper, the containerization of ocean transportation cargo meant less pilferage, since containers would be sealed at the origin and not opened until they arrive at the consignee. Less handling also meant less damage to the cargo. The delivery of cargo by containerships was faster and more reliable than the delivery by breakbulk ships, thereby resulting in substantial reductions in shipper inventories. A contributing factor to the faster deliver times of containerships is that they are in port less time than breakbulk ships.

Ocean container freight rates are increasingly based upon factors other than the value of cargo. As a result, ocean container rates for high-value cargo have declined relative to breakbulk rates, all else held constant. The general decline in container rates and the advantages of container over breakbulk ocean transportation service have contributed to the significant increase in the containerization of international trade. For the 1980–1996 time period, for example, containerized international seaborne trade increased 433 percent, from 36.4 million TEUs in 1980 to 157.6 million TEUs in 1996 (Talley 2000). By 2006 this number had increased to 442 million TEUs and is forecast to increase to 673 million TEUs by 2011 (Galhena 2008). Between 1996 and 2006 world container throughput increased by a compound annual growth rate of 10.8 percent. As of 2007, 50 percent of international cargo transported by water carriers was containerized. China accounted for 25 percent of the world's containerized exports.

In Table 2.3 the top-ten ranked U.S. exporters (or shippers) of ocean containerized cargo for 2007 are presented. The top-ranked U.S. exporter, American Chung Nam, exported 211,300 TEUs, followed by the second-ranked exporter, Weyerhaeuser, which exported 165,800 TEUs. The top-ten ranked U.S. exporters of ocean containerized cargo are often exporters of paper products and chemicals.

In Table 2.4 the top-ten ranked U.S. importers (or consignees) of ocean containerized cargo for 2007 are presented. Wal-Mart Stores imported 720,000 TEUs of retail (or generalized) cargo. Target was the second-ranked importer by importing 435,000 TEUs of retail cargo. TEU imports by Wal-Mart Stores were almost twice those of the third-ranked importer, Home Depot. The majority of the top-ten ranked U.S. importers of ocean containerized cargo are importers of retail cargoes.

Table 2.3 Top ten U.S. exporters of ocean containerized cargo (2007)

Rank	Exporter	TEUs (1000s)	Product	Headquarters
1	American Chung Nam	211.3	Paper	California
2	Weyerhaeuser	165.8	Forest/Paper Products	Washington
3	Cargill	123.8	Chemicals	Minnesota
4	Koch Industries	123.4	Conglomerate	Kansas
5	International Paper	100.9	Conglomerate	Tennessee
6	Dow Chemical	100.0	Chemical/Paper	Michigan
7	DuPont	93.1	Chemical/Plastics	Delaware
8	MeadWestvaco	77.9	Mfg/Consumer Products	Virginia
9	Procter and Gamble	73.8	Paper Products	Ohio
10	Archer Daniels Midland	73.3	Paper/Recyclables	Illinois

Source: Staff (2008b) "Top 100 Importers and Exporters", *Journal of Commerce*, 9, May 26: 13A and 34A.

Table 2.4 Top ten U.S. importers of ocean containerized cargo (2007)

Rank	Importer	TEUs (1000s)	Product	Headquarters
1	Wal-Mart Stores	720.0	Retail	Arkansas
2	Target	435.0	Retail	Minnesota
3	Home Depot	365.3	Retail	Georgia
4	Sears Holding	248.6	Retail	Illinois
5	Dole Food	223.2	Food	California
6	Costco Wholesale	183.8	Retail	Washington
7	Lowe's	182.1	Retail	North Carolina
8	LG Group	130.0	Conglomerate	New Jersey
9	Philips Electronics North America	127.2	Mfg/Electronics	New York
10	Chiquita Brands Int'l	116.3	Food	Ohio

Source: Staff (2008b) "Top 100 Importers and Exporters", *Journal of Commerce*, 9, May 26: 13A and 34A.

The demand for port service at various prices by shippers that provide cargo to a port is represented by demand curve D_{SH} in Figure 2.2. At lower prices, more service is demanded and at higher prices, less service is demanded, other things remaining the same. The responsiveness of the quantity demanded for a port service (Q_{SH}) by a shipper to changes in the price of this service (P_{SH}) may be measured by the shipper's price elasticity of demand (E_{SH}) for this service, i.e., the ratio of the percentage change in quantity demanded for the service to a percentage change in the price of the service, or

$$E_{SH} = \%\Delta Q_{SH}/\%\Delta P_{SH} \tag{2.2}$$

If $|E_{SH}| > 1, < 1$ and $= 1$, the shipper's price elasticity of demand for a port service is price elastic, inelastic, and unitary, respectively.

Passengers

By the late 1990s the number of ferry passengers in the U.S. had reached 134 million annually (Talley 2002). Washington State Ferries, the largest U.S. ferry carrier, operated 28 ferries

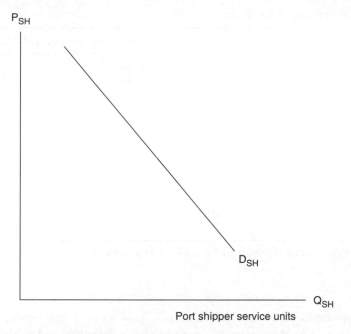

Figure 2.2 Shipper demand for port service

with a total capacity for 37,500 passengers. In 2003 the number of ferry passengers in Canada was 38.9 million, representing approximately 15 percent of the total worldwide ferry traffic (Transport Canada 2008).

In 2003 the number of ocean cruise passengers worldwide was approximately 11.5 million. The North American share of this total was 78 percent, followed by 18 percent and 4 percent for Europe and Asia/South Pacific, respectively (Ebersold 2004). The number of passengers carried worldwide in 2003 by the cruise lines of the Cruise Lines International Association (CLIA) was 9.5 million. The most popular destination for CLIA cruise ships is the Caribbean, accounting for 46 percent of the total bed-days on CLIA cruise ships in 2002. For the time period 1995–2002, the total CLIA ship bed-days in the Europe/Mediterranean and Alaskan markets grew at the annual rates of 15 percent and 21 percent, respectively. In 2007, 12.6 million passengers took ocean cruises worldwide, of whom, 10.3 million passengers took cruises in North America (Dunham-Potter 2008).

The number of North American passengers carried by CLIA lines for the years 1980–2004 is presented in Table 2.5. The average yearly growth rate in the number of CLIA North American passengers transported over the years 1980–2004 is 8.2 percent. The number of CLIA North American passengers transported in 2006 was 10.08 million, was estimated to be 10.33 million in 2007, and forecasted to be 10.5 million in 2008 (Cruise Passengers Predicted for 2008, 2008).

Major U.S. cruise departure ports include Miami, Port Canaveral, and Fort Lauderdale. In 2003 these three ports accounted for 49 percent of the total passengers departing on North American cruises. From 2001 to 2003, the ports of New York, Tampa, Galveston, and New Orleans experienced increases of 93 percent, 53 percent, 151 percent, and 140 percent, respectively, in cruise passengers departing from these ports (Ebersold 2004).

Table 2.5 Annual CLIA passengers in North America

Year	Number of passengers (1,000)	Year	Number of passengers (1,000)
1980	1,431	1993	4,480
1981	1,453	1994	4,448
1982	1,471	1995	4,378
1983	1,755	1996	4,656
1984	1,859	1997	5,051
1985	2,152	1998	5,428
1986	2,624	1999	5,894
1987	2,898	2000	6,882
1988	3,175	2001	6,906
1989	3,286	2002	7,640
1990	3,640	2003	8,195
1991	3,979	2004	9,107
1992	4,136		

Source: Cruise Lines International Association (2005). Available online at http://www.cruising.org/press/overview (accessed 7 November 2005).

The demand for port service at various prices by port passengers is represented by demand curve D_{PA} in Figure 2.3. At lower prices, more service is demanded and at higher prices, less service is demanded, other things remaining the same. The responsiveness of the quantity demanded for a port service (Q_{PA}) by a passenger to changes in the price of this service (P_{PA}) may be measured by the passenger's price elasticity of demand (E_{PA}), i.e., the ratio of the percentage change in quantity demanded for the service to a percentage change in the price of the service, or

$$E_{PA} = \%\Delta Q_{PA}/\%\Delta P_{PA} \qquad (2.3)$$

If $|E_{PA}| > 1, < 1$ and $= 1$, the passenger's price elasticity of demand for a port service is price elastic, inelastic, and unitary, respectively.

Service providers

Service providers of a port are those that provide services to the users of the port, i.e., to carriers, shippers, and passengers. The primary service provider of a port is the port (or terminal) operator.

Port operator

The port operator may be: (1) a port authority that operates its "common user" terminal (that is open to any vessel that makes arrangements to call there); (2) a private port terminal operator that contracts with a port authority or landlord port to operate its "common user" terminal or to operate a "common user" terminal that it owns; (3) a shipping line that acts as a port operator or its terminal operator division that contracts with a landlord port to operate its "common user" terminal or to operate a "common user" terminal that it owns; and (4) a shipping line that leases and operates a terminal of a landlord port as a "dedicated" terminal or operates a "dedicated terminal" that it owns (serving only its own vessels, alliance

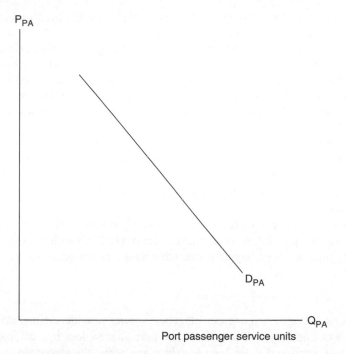

Figure 2.3 Passenger demand for port service

vessels, and customers). The port operator manages the interchange of cargo (the entry and exit of cargo to and from the port), yard operations, and use of the terminal's wharf space and equipment.

Port authorities operating their own container terminals are no longer the norm. Increasingly, port authorities are acting as landlord ports by hiring private port terminal operators to operate their terminals. There are a number of global (private) port terminal operators of container terminals. The largest is the Hong Kong-based Hutchison Port Holdings, which in 2006 handled 13.8 percent of the container liftings at container ports worldwide, followed by a 11.8 percent share for Denmark's APM Terminals and a 10.7 percent share for the Singapore-based PSA International (see Table 2.6). The world's seven largest global port terminal operators in 2006 handled 56.2 percent of the world's container throughput. In 2004 the seven largest operators handled 53 percent of the world's container throughput. Hence, concentration in the global port terminal operator industry is increasing. "The global terminal operators have increased their market share through better performance and the acquisition of additional concessions" (United Nations Conference on Trade and Development Secretariat 2007: 91).

DP World acquired CSX World Terminals, headquartered in the U.S., for US$1.2 billion in 2005 and P&O Ports, headquartered in the UK, for US$6.8 billion in 2006. In 2006 PSA International purchased a 20 percent share in its competitor, Hutchison Port Holdings, for HK$4.4 billion plus the right to purchase the remaining share should the parent company, Hutchison Whampoa, decide to sell. In 2007 PSA International's earnings before interest, tax, depreciation, and amortization (EBITDA) was US$1.462 billion (48.6 percent of annual revenue). For the same year, Hutchison Port Holdings' EBITDA was US$1.649 billion (33.9 percent of annual revenue) and DP World's EBITDA was US$1.1 billion (40.3 percent of annual revenue). In 2007 the TEUs handled by the world's largest global container port terminal operators increased at a faster rate than global trade and their EBITDAs as a percentage of annual revenue were generally higher than in 2006 (Staff 2008a).

Financial institutions have been particularly interested in investing in marine terminal operations. In 2007 Goldman Sachs Infrastructure, a unit of the New York investment bank, purchased 49 percent of SSA Marine; the Ontario Teachers' Pension Plan purchased U.S. and Canadian marine terminals from the shipping line Orient Overseas Container Line; and Macquarie Infrastructure Partners purchased marine terminals in Halifax and Vancouver, Canada (Mongelluzzo 2007).

Shipping lines that are active in expanding their terminal operations are CMA-CGM and Mediterranean Shipping Company. Some shipping lines are finding that the operation of ports provides higher profit margins than transporting containers between ports. By moving containers through terminals that they own, shipping lines are also able to avoid or reduce terminal congestion problems.

The amount of port service that a port operator is willing to supply at various prices is represented by the supply curve S_{PO} in Figure 2.4. At lower prices, the port operator is willing to supply less service, but will supply more service at higher prices, other things remaining the same.

Other service providers

In addition to the port operator, there are numerous other port service providers that provide services to carriers, shippers, and passengers that utilize a port. A stevedore is a company whose functions are to load, stow, and unload vessels. In many ports, the stevedore is an independent contractor that is hired by shipping lines to work their ships while in port, i.e., load and unload cargo. At unionized ports, the stevedore hires local union dockworkers to work ships. At a container port, the stevedore is responsible for removing containers from the staging area and loading them on a ship. Conversely, the stevedore also removes containers from the ship for placement in a staging area. In some container terminals, the stevedore also does stowage planning for ships, stages containers before the ship arrives, lashes above-deck containers on ships, and assists in line handling when a ship ties up and casts off.

A ship's agent is a company that looks after the interest of a ship and her master and crew while in port on behalf of the ship owner, e.g., making all necessary arrangements with the

Table 2.6 The world's largest global container port terminal operators (2006)

Rank	Operator	TEUs handled (millions)	Percent share of world TEU port throughput
1	Hutchison Port Holdings	60.9	13.8
2	APM Terminals	52.0	11.8
3	PSA International	47.4	10.7
4	DP World	41.6	9.4
5	Cosco Pacific	22.0	5.0
6	Eurogate	12.5	2.8
7	SSA Marine	11.9	2.7
Total		248.3	56.2
World TEU port throughput		441	100

Source: United Nations Conference on Trade and Development Secretariat (2007) *Review of Maritime Transport*, Geneva, Switzerland: United Nations.

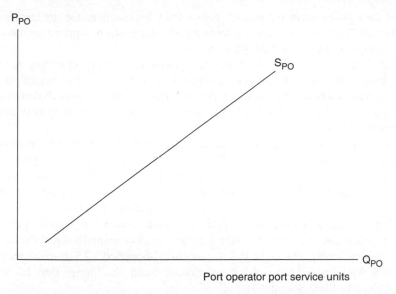

Figure 2.4 Port operator supply of port service

port and a stevedore while a ship is in port. The ship's agent may arrange for the pilotage, towage, and a berth for a ship, pay for charges incurred by the ship and handle relations with shippers, consignees, and government officials.[7] A company that supplies ships with stores and provisions is a ship chandler. Companies may also be available to provide ships with bunkers (ship fuel) while in port.

Pilotage is the assistance given by a pilot to a ship's master in navigating his ship when entering and leaving a port or in confined waters. The pilot is usually licensed and an experienced mariner familiar with the given port or place. Towage is the towing or pushing of ships in port, e.g., in the berthing and unberthing of ships, by a tug (a small power-driven vessel) and is provided by towage companies. Ships may also receive ship repair and maintenance services from ship repair and maintenance companies while in port. Surveyors of ship classification societies may also be at ports to undertake periodical surveys of ships to ensure that they meet the minimum standards for maintaining their classification society certificates, which are required by ships for obtaining of insurance.

A customs broker is a company that clears cargo through customs at a port on behalf of the consignee of imported cargo. The customs broker ensures that all customs fees are paid and releases are obtained, permitting the departure of cargo from the port. A freight forwarder is a company that arranges for the carriage of cargo on behalf of a shipper. The arrangements include booking space on a carrier's ship or vehicle (e.g., a railroad car or truck) and providing the necessary accompanying documentation. A third-party logistics (3PL) company integrates logistics activities, e.g., inventory management and warehousing, in the carriage of cargo and in some cases provides valued-added services such as assembly to cargo.

Government can also be a port service provider. At the U.S. federal level, the Army Corps of Engineers is responsible for constructing (deepening and widening) and maintaining harbor channels, disposal of dredged materials, and building harbor jetties and breakwaters.

Local ports and their government owners are responsible for maintenance dredging near their piers and berths. The U.S. Bureau of Customs and Border Protection grants permission for cargo to be brought into the U.S. through its ports.

The U.S. Coast Guard is responsible for constructing, maintaining, and operating navigational aids (e.g., buoys) in ports and neighboring waterways. A buoy is a small floating body, anchored to the waterway's bed, which marks a channel or alerts vessels to such dangers as wrecks or other waterway obstructions. The U.S. Coast Guard also has the authority to establish levels of security threats at ports.

In response to an alarming rate of vessel accidents at many U.S. ports and in coastal waters, the U.S. Congress in 1972 passed the Ports and Waterways Safety Act – giving the U.S. Department of Transportation (USDOT) the authority to establish and operate vessel traffic service (VTS) systems, subsequently establishing eight USDOT Coast Guard-operated VTS systems. A VTS system is a marine safety system that gathers, processes, and disseminates information between a land-based vessel traffic service center and vessels operating in the service area, but unlike an air traffic control center does not normally direct the movement of vessels (Talley 1998). The eight U.S. Coast Guard-operated VTS systems include the Houston, New York, San Francisco, Puget Sound, Sault St. Marie, Berwick Bay, Louisville, and Prince William Sound systems.

Local governments are usually responsible for providing accessible highways (and in some cases railways) to and from local ports, especially at container ports for the movement of containers to and from these ports by truck. If a port fire or security breakage occurs, the fire and police departments of the local government may be requested by the port to provide it with fire and police services.

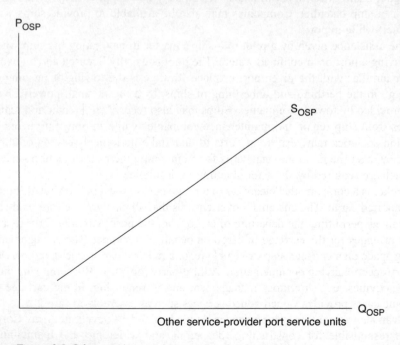

Figure 2.5 Other service-provider supply of port services

The amount of port service that other service providers (i.e., other than the port operator) are willing to supply at various prices is represented by the supply curve S_{OSP} in Figure 2.5. At lower prices, the other service providers are willing to supply less service, but they will supply more service at higher prices.

Summary

Port users are transportation carriers, shippers that provide their cargo to transportation carriers, and individuals who present themselves as passengers to transportation carriers and utilize ports as part of the process of creating freight and passenger transportation trips. Transportation carriers that utilize ports include, for example, shipping lines, short sea shipping carriers, ferry carriers, cruise lines, railroads, and truck carriers.

For the shipper, ocean container transportation service means less pilferage of cargo, less damage to cargo, faster delivery, and more reliable service than that of breakbulk service (resulting in substantial reductions in shipper inventories). The number of worldwide ocean cruise passengers in 2003 was approximately 11.5 million passengers. Major U.S. cruise ports include the ports of Miami, Port Canaveral, and Fort Lauderdale. In 2003 the number of ferry passengers in Canada was 38.9 million, representing approximately 15 percent of the total worldwide ferry traffic.

Service providers of a port are those that provide services to the users of the port, i.e., to carriers, shippers, and passengers. The primary service provider of a port is the port operator. Other service providers include, for example, stevedores, ship agents, customs brokers, pilot and towage companies, and various government agencies providing maintenance of harbor channels, customs, and vessel traffic service systems.

Notes

1 For a discussion of the world's fleet of commercial ships, see Hoffman *et al.* (2005).
2 A general discussion of various types of passenger vessels is found in Talley *et al.* (2006).
3 Some authors have distinguished between landbridging, minibridging, and microbridging: landbridging referring to cargo movement that crosses a body of land between two ocean legs, minibridging referring to cargo movement that crosses one ocean by ship and then crosses a body of land but ends at a port on another ocean, and microbridging referring to cargo movement that crosses one ocean by ship and then proceeds to an inland location (Chadwin *et al.* 1990). For this chapter, landbridging is an all encompassing term, capturing all three of these possibilities.
4 For a discussion of U.S. freight railroads, see Schwarz-Miller and Talley (1998, 2002) and Talley (2001).
5 U.S. owner-operator truck drivers are discussed in Peoples and Talley (2004).
6 For a discussion of U.S. truck carriers in general, see Talley (2001).
7 A ship's agent is a type of shipbroker. A shipbroker may also be a chartering agent that negotiates the terms for the charter of a ship on behalf of the charterer or ship owner. In addition, a shipbroker may be a loading broker whose business is to obtain cargoes for ships.

Bibliography

Chadwin, M. L., Pope, J. A., and Talley, W. K. (1990) *Ocean Container Transportation: An Operational Perspective*, New York: Taylor & Francis.
Cruise Lines International Association (2005) Available online at http://www.cruising.org/press/overview (accessed 7 November 2005).
Cruise Passengers Predicted for 2008 (2008) Available online at http://familyfriendly.wordpress.com/2008/01/21/cruise-passengers-predicted-for-2008-128 (accessed 3 June 2008).

Dennis, S. and Talley, W. K. (2007) *Railroad Economics: Research in Transportation Economics*, Amsterdam: Elsevier.

Dunham-Potter, A. (2008) "Tripso: Recession? Not for the Cruise Industry, Executives have Rosy Outlook Despite Record Oil Prices, Struggling Economy". Available online at http://www.msnbc.msn.com/id/23674324/ (accessed 10 April 2008).

Ebersold, W. B. (2004) "Cruise Industry in Figures", *Business Briefing: Global Cruise*, Burr Ridge, IL: Business Briefings, 15–16.

Europa (2004) *Press release*, Brussels, Belgium: European Commission.

Galhena, G. (2008) "Overcoming Obstacles", *Containerization International*, February: 55–56.

Hoffman, J., Sanchez, R., and Talley, W. K. (2005) "Determinants of Vessel Flag", in K. Cullinane (ed.) *Shipping Economics: Research in Transportation Economics*, Amsterdam: Elsevier, 173–219.

Leach, P. T. (2007) "That Sinking Feeling", *Journal of Commerce*, 8, December 10: 12–14, 16, 18, 20.

Lois, P., Wang, J., Wall A., and Ruxton, T. (2004) "Formal Safety Assessment of Cruise Ships", *Tourism Management*, 25: 93–109.

Mongelluzzo, B. (1998) "Work Stoppages Again Disrupt West Coast Ports", *Journal of Commerce*, July 15: 1A and 14A.

—— (2001) "Teamsters Target Port Drayage", *JOC WEEK*, 2, December 17–23: 31–32.

—— (2007) "SSA Marine Joins the List", *Journal of Commerce*, 8, July 16: 24.

M. Silver Associates, Inc. (2008) *Cruise Industry Source Book*, Fort Lauderdale, FL: Cruise Lines International Association.

Notteboom, T. E. (2004) "Container Shipping and Ports: An Overview", in W. K. Talley (ed.) *The Industrial Organization of Shipping and Ports*, a special issue of the journal *Review of Network Economics*, 3: 86–106.

Oliver, D. and Slack, B. (2006) "Rethinking the Port", *Environment and Planning A*, 38: 1409–1427.

Peoples, J. and Talley, W. K. (2004) "Owner-Operator Truck Driver Earnings and Employment: Port Cities and Deregulation", in J. Peoples and W. K. Talley (eds) *Transportation Labor Issues and Regulatory Reform: Research in Transportation Economics*, Amsterdam: Elsevier, 191–213.

Porter, J. (1996) "Continued Losses Swamp Container Lines in Sea of Red", *Journal of Commerce*, August 1: 2B.

Russell, S. and Talley, W. K. (forthcoming) "Coastal Shipping", in K. Button, P. Nijkamp, and H. Vega (eds) *Transportation Dictionary*, Cheltenham, UK: Edward Elgar.

Schwarz-Miller, A. and Talley, W. K. (1998) "Railroad Deregulation and Union Labor Earnings", in J. Peoples (ed.) *Regulatory Reform and Labor Markets*, Boston: Kluwer Academic Press, 125–153.

—— (2002) "Technology and Labor Relations: Railroads and Ports", in J. Bennett and D. Taras (eds) *Technological Change and Employment Conditions in Traditionally Heavily Unionized Industries*, a symposium issue of the *Journal of Labor Research*, 23: 513–533.

Slack, B. (1989) "The Port Service Industry in an Environment of Change", *Geoforum*, 20: 447–457.

Staff (2005) "BRA-Alphaliner's Top 50 Global Container Fleet Operators", *Journal of Commerce*, 6, December 5: 28.

—— (2007) *Top 20 Container Lines,* Available online at http://www.lloydslist.com (accessed 29 August 2007).

—— (2008a) "Container Terminals Post Strong Gains", *Containerization International*, May: 23.

—— (2008b) "Top 100 Importers and Exporters", *Journal of Commerce*, 9, May 26: 13A and 34A.

Talley, W. K. (1998) "Vessel Traffic Service Systems: Cost-Recovery Alternatives", *Maritime Policy and Management*, 25: 107–115.

—— (2000) "Ocean Container Shipping: Impacts of a Technological Improvement", *Journal of Economic Issues*, 34: 933–947.

—— (2001) "Wage Differentials of Transportation Industries: Deregulation Versus Regulation", *Economic Inquiry*, 39: 406–429.

—— (2002) "The Safety of Ferries: An Accident Injury Perspective", *Maritime Policy and Management*, 29: 331–338.

—— (forthcoming) "Ferry Services", in K. Button, P. Nijkamp, and H. Vega (eds) *Transportation Dictionary*, Cheltenham, UK: Edward Elgar.

—— (forthcoming) "Shipping", in G. Giuliano, L. Hoel, and M. Meyer (eds) *Intermodal Transportation: Moving Freight in a Global Economy*, Washington, DC: Eno Transportation Foundation.

——, Jin, D., and Kite-Powell, H. (2006) "Determinants of the Severity of Passenger Vessel Accidents", in P. Panayides (ed.) *IAME 2005 Conference Special Issue*, a special issue of the journal *Maritime Policy and Management*, 33: 173–186.

—— (2008) "Determinants of the Severity of Cruise Vessel Accidents", *Transportation Research Part D: Transport and Environment*, 13: 86–94.

Tirschwell, P. (1997) "NOL-APL: What Now?", *Journal of Commerce*, April 15: 1A, 4B.

Transport Canada (2008) "Transport Canada Media Room". Available online at http://www.tc.gc.ca/mediaroom/backgrounders/b05-M007e.htm (accessed 15 May 2008).

United Nations Conference on Trade and Development Secretariat (2007) *Review of Maritime Transport*, Geneva: Switzerland: United Nations.

Wastler, A. R. (1997) "Alliances: Not So Grand?", *Journal of Commerce*, April 16: 3B.

3 Ports in operation

Introduction

Container, breakbulk, neo-bulk, dry-bulk, and liquid-bulk cargo ports are ports where the prominent type of cargo handled is container, breakbulk, neo-bulk, dry-bulk, and liquid-bulk, respectively. If neo-bulk, dry-bulk, and liquid-bulk ports handle specific types of commodities such as auto, coal, and petroleum, respectively, they may be referred to as auto, coal, and petroleum ports. Further, if a cargo port has more than one marine terminal, each marine terminal may also be described by the prominent type of cargo handled. For example, a container port may have several container marine terminals, one auto marine terminal, and one petroleum marine terminal. If a cargo port (or marine terminal) has more than one berth for vessels, each berth may also be described by the prominent type of cargo handled.

Passenger ports are described by the prominent type of passenger vessel that calls at these ports, e.g., cruise and ferry ports are ports where cruise and ferry vessels call, respectively. If a passenger port has more than one marine terminal, each marine terminal may also be described by the prominent type of vessel that calls. For example, a passenger port may have cruise and ferry marine terminals.

Although differences exist among cargo ports due to the type of cargo handled, there are similarities in the design of all cargo ports. Furthermore, there are similarities in the design of cruise and ferry ports.

In this chapter the operations of container (cargo) and cruise (passenger) ports are presented. Specifically, the flow of containers in and the services of container ports are discussed. The port design and equipment of both container and cruise ports are discussed. It is assumed that a port has just one marine terminal. Thus, the discussion of a port in operation is also a discussion of a marine terminal in operation. Finally, specific ports in operation are discussed.

A container port

Container ports are often located on the shore lands of cities, e.g., at the cities of Rotterdam, the Netherlands; Antwerp, Belgium; Hamburg, Germany; and Los Angeles, United States. A container port is the place, where non-transshipment containers received from vessels are transferred to inland carriers such as railroads, truck carriers, and inland waterway and coastal (i.e., short sea) carriers, and vice versa, and transshipment containers are transferred from one vessel to another.

A container port resembles the operations of a manufacturing plant that receives "raw materials" that are transformed at the plant into "finished products" (Chadwin *et al.* 1990).

Containers arriving at the port resemble raw materials. Although containers do not undergo a physical transformation, operations on them by port labor and equipment give them added value. These operations include, for example, the loading and unloading of containers to and from ships, rail cars, and trucks, and sometimes the loading (stuffing) of cargo into and the unloading (stripping) of cargo from containers. Eventually, loaded containers leave the container port (via a ship or an inland carrier) as "finished products," referred to as the "container throughput" of the port.

A container port also performs many of the activities that are performed by a manufacturing plant. Similar to a plant's inventory control of raw materials and finished products, the container port must control the inventory of arriving and departing containers. A manufacturing plant achieves efficiency in production when it maximizes the amount of finished products in the utilization of given levels of resources. Similarly, a container port achieves efficiency in production when it maximizes its container throughput in the utilization of given levels of resources. By minimizing the time that containers are in port, a port is able to handle more containers and thus increase its container throughput. That is to say, by minimizing the number of times that containers are moved and time in storage while in port, port labor and equipment resources (that would be used otherwise) are freed up to receive more containers to the port and thus increase the port's container throughput.

The flow of port containers

Containers that move through a container port are involved in four basic port activities: (1) receiving, (2) loading/unloading, (3) staging, and (4) storage. Import containers enter the port via a ship and leave by an inland carrier; export containers enter the port via an inland carrier and leave by ship.

The receiving activity occurs when a container arrives at the port. Its arrival time and relevant information about the container, e.g., a description of its cargo, are recorded. The container will then be unloaded from the ship or vehicle and placed in the port's storage area, where it will be retrieved in the future to be loaded on another ship or vehicle for departure from the port.

For an export container, staging is the activity of preparing the container to leave the port by ship. Specifically, the container is moved from storage to a staging location within the port to be with other containers that are waiting for the arrival of a ship onto which they will be loaded. Containers in the staging location are organized according to an optimal ship loading process, i.e., the ship's stowage plan. The plan may be one that seeks to minimize the time in the loading/unloading of ship containers at the port and at future ports of call and to provide stability to the ship.

Suppose an export container arrives at the port's interchange gate by truck. Then, the truck moves to a location within the port, where the container is removed from the truck and placed in storage or at a staging location. If placed in a storage location, it will eventually be moved to a staging location to wait the arrival of the specific ship onto which it will be loaded.

The ship on which an import container is stowed docks at a berth of the port. The container is unloaded from the ship by a ship-to-shore crane and placed on the port's apron (the staging location). From the staging location, the container is moved to a storage location or loaded onto a truck for departure from the port. If placed in storage, it will eventually be removed by loading it onto a truck or rail car for departure from the port. The import container will leave the port through its interchange gate.

Containers may be stored on chassis or stacked in a storage location. A chassis is a trailer on which a container is carried when transported by a truck. Chassis storage is also referred to as an all-wheeled storage operation. Port chassis storage has a time advantage over stack storage for inland carriers and the port. Specifically, over-the-road truckers while in port do not have to wait for a container to be placed on a chassis as opposed to stack storage for departure from the port, since the container is already on a chassis. The time savings for inland carriers are also time savings for the port, since containers are in storage less time. A disadvantage of an all-wheeled storage operation is that it is land intensive. If port land is scarce and/or expensive, a port will likely utilize stack storage.

Stack storage occurs at a given location in the port, where containers are stacked on top of each other. An advantage of stack storage is that containers require less space and thus less land for storage. The disadvantage of stack storage is the difficulty of retrieving and moving containers from and to the storage location, making stack storage more time intensive than having containers stored on chassis. Stack storage is also capital intensive, since it requires specialized yard equipment for stacking and unstacking containers.

In addition to import and export containers, a port's containers may also be transshipment containers. A transshipment container is one that arrives at a port on one ship and is then transferred to another ship at the same port for departure, thereby not utilizing inland carriers. A port that handles transshipment containers is often referred to as a hub, main, or transshipment port. Such ports often have depth harbors that allow them to handle relatively large containerships (carrying large numbers of containers) that seek to call at a few ports so that they can spend more time at sea in order to take advantage of economies of ship size at sea. Examples of transshipment ports include Singapore, Hong Kong, and Shanghai. For the years 2000–2004, transshipment containers in Europe and the Mediterranean increased 58 percent (Penfold 2006).

Ports from which containers are transported on relatively small or feeder ships to and from main or transshipment ports are referred to as feeder ports. Containers destined to transshipment ports from feeder ports are export containers of the feeder ports but become transshipment containers of transshipment ports. Containers destined to feeder ports from transshipment ports are transshipment containers of transshipment ports but become import containers at feeder ports. Unlike non-transshipment ports, transshipment ports that handle only transshipment containers do not require inland interchange gates.

In Figure 3.1 containers at the smaller ports A, B, and D are being feedered to and from the main (or larger) port C in the region. The ports in the region where ports A, B, C, and D are located are linked to ports in another region where ports 1, 2, 3, and 4 are located by a mainline containership service route between the main ports C and 2 of the two regions. Containers at the smaller ports 1, 3, and 4 are being feedered to and from the main (or larger) port 2 in the region.

Port design

The common design features of container ports are: (1) harbor, (2) berth, (3) wharf, (4) apron, (5) container yard, and (6) inland interchange gate. A harbor is a natural or artificial body of water adjacent to the land area of the port, where ships may drop anchor (away from shipping lanes). In anchorage, a ship may wait for the availability of a port berth. A berth is the water area alongside a wharf (or quay), where a ship sits for its cargo to be unloaded or loaded; a berth frequently accommodates only one ship at a time. When a ship arrives, the port must decide where the ship is to be positioned at the berth and what

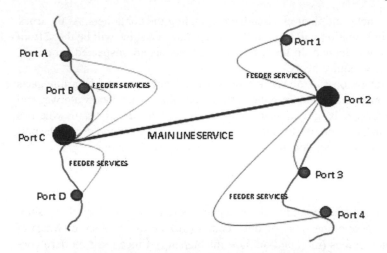

Figure 3.1 Feedering and main container ports in two trading regions

Source: Henesey, L.E. (2006) *Multi-Agent Systems for Container Terminal Management*, Karlskrona, Sweden: Blekinge Institute of Technology, p. 9.

resources are to be assigned to it, e.g., the number of cranes. A wharf (or quay) is a structure alongside a harbor (or waterway) to which ships are moored for the unloading and loading of cargo. The apron is an area of the wharf (or quay), where containers are staged, i.e., assembled before loading on a ship or after their unloading from a ship.

Inland from the apron is the container yard. The container yard consists of (1) various buildings for administrative activities and the stuffing and stripping of containers, (2) road-ways and pathways for the movement of containers within the port by trucks and various types of yard equipment, and (3) land area for the storage of containers, chassis, and equipment. The specific design of a port's container yard will depend upon the amount of land that is available. If land is scarce, the container storage area will be a stacking storage area; otherwise, it will be a chassis storage area. Alternatively, there may be a mixture of both, depending upon the requirements or desires of container shipping lines and shippers. Some container ports may use chassis storage as a buffer to stack storage. If the port has on-site rail service, the container yard will also have a rail yard that consists of railroad tracks and pathways for the loading and unloading of containers to and from trains.

Container ports have inland interchange gates for the entry and departure of containers by land (or inland waterways) to and from the port. An exception is the transshipment container port that handles only transshipment containers, i.e., no import and export containers. Containers that enter and leave the port (i.e., import and export containers) are subject to inspection for proper documentation and security requirements. Interchange truck gates are gates where over-the-road and drayage trucks are received into and dispatched from the container port. These gates consist of entry and departure gates. In some cases, a truck may arrive at the entry gate (from outside the port) with a chassis on which a container is mounted, only a chassis, or no chassis (to be obtained inside the port), and arrive at the departure gate (from inside the port) with a chassis on which a container is mounted, only a chassis (after dropping off a container or obtaining a chassis within the port), or no chassis (after dropping off a container and a chassis or dropping off just a chassis).

At the truck entry gate, relevant information regarding truck movements is recorded, i.e., information on containers being hauled (e.g., their cargoes), the ships on which the containers will be loaded, and the trucks and their chassis that are hauling the containers. At the truck departure gate, similar information will be recorded except now the ships will be those from which the containers were unloaded. In the U.S. departing chassis are inspected for adherence to safety and security requirements.

At container ports that have on-site rail service, there are also rail entry and departure gates for trains transporting containers to and from the port. At ports that have inland waterway and coastal container barge service, barges are usually unloaded and loaded at the same wharf as containerships. As for truck containers, rail and barge containers that enter and depart the port are checked for adherence to proper documentation and security requirements.

Port equipment

Containers are loaded to and from containerships (while moored at a port's wharf) by ship-to-shore gantry cranes. These cranes may be dock cranes (located on the dock or wharf of the port) or ship-mounted cranes (mounted on the containership). Since most modern containerships are non-self-sustaining (i.e., without ship-mounted cranes), they require the use of dock cranes while in port. The majority of ship-to-shore gantry dock cranes are rail cranes (although some are rubber-tired). Typically, they run along rail tracks on the port's wharf, thereby allowing several to be "ganged together" for working (i.e., unloading and loading containers from and to) large containerships simultaneously.

The crane's spreaders straddle rows of containers on a ship, picking containers from and placing containers onto the ship. They fit on the corner castings of containers and lock to these castings (fittings) via twist-locks. Dock cranes are sometimes referred to as bridge or quay cranes. In loading and unloading containers onto and from ships, their booms when lowered over the ships appear as bridges over these ships (see Figure 3.2). The largest dock cranes in operation (Suez dock cranes) can span across twenty-six rows of containers on a containership.

Figure 3.2 Ship-to-shore gantry crane

Dock cranes may place unloaded (import) containers from a ship onto port truck chassis, over-the-road truck chassis, or on the apron itself. If placed on port chassis, containers are hauled by port trucks, driven by port truck drivers (yard hustlers), to the port's stack storage area or rail yard. At the stack storage area, the containers are lifted from the chassis by yard gantry cranes and placed in stack storage. If placed on over-the-road truck chassis, containers are hauled by over-the-road trucks, driven by over-the-road truck drivers, to the port's truck departure gate. Containers that are placed on the port's apron may be transported by port straddle carriers to the port's stack storage area or rail yard.

For export containers, this process will be reversed. Dock cranes retrieve containers from port truck chassis, over-the-road truck chassis, or the apron itself for loading on a containership. In being mounted on rails, dock rail cranes thus move laterally along moored containerships (at the wharf) so they can load and unload containers to and from each bay of the ship.

A straddle carrier (or strad) is a wheeled rubber-tired vehicle that can lift containers within its own framework and transport them to and from various locations within the port (see Figure 3.3). At stack storage areas, it is used to place and pick containers to and from the stacks as well as to reposition containers in the stacks. In order to straddle stacked containers, straddle carriers require space among rows of stacked containers in order to be able to move among these rows. Another type of port equipment that can be used to both transport and stack containers is the top loader, a fork-lift truck equipped with a spreader bar (see Figure 3.4).

At the port's stack storage area and rail yard, containers can be stacked/unstacked and loaded/unloaded to and from rail cars by the port's straddle carriers, top loaders, and yard gantry cranes. Import containers arriving from ships and placed on port chassis are removed

Figure 3.3 Straddle carrier

Figure 3.4 Top loader

from the chassis at stack storage areas and stacked in storage. Export containers in stack storage are removed, placed on port chassis, and hauled to the port's apron, then removed from port chassis by ship-to-shore gantry dock cranes for loading on moored ships. Containers that arrived at the port on over-the-road chassis may remain on their chassis in chassis storage or removed from these chassis and placed in stack storage. Containers leaving the port are unstacked and placed on over-the-road or drayage chassis for departure from the port.

Yard gantry cranes (or transtainers) are similar to ship-to-shore cranes in that they attach their spreaders to containers for their lifting and lowering (see Figure 3.5). Transtainers may lift and lower containers from and to rail cars, truck chassis, and container stacks and may be rail or rubber tired. If rubber tired, they are referred to as rubber-tired gantry cranes (RTGs). RTGs are more mobile than rail-tired gantry cranes in moving from one container storage bay to another. However, the greater stability of the rail-tired gantry crane (in being mounted on rails) allows ports to use them to stack containers higher, thereby increasing the density of container stacks in storage areas.

Like straddle carriers, transtainers lift and lower containers from overhead. Unlike straddle carriers, transtainers have the disadvantage of not being able to transport containers from one designated area of the port to another in a timely fashion; the transportation of transtainer containers is usually performed by chassis hauled by trucks, thereby requiring additional equipment for their transportation.

Transtainers, however, have a selectivity-capability advantage over straddle carriers with respect to container stacks, i.e., they can generally pick and remove or relocate containers in the stacks faster than straddle carriers. This advantage increases with the height and the width of container stacks, which tends to increase with the value of port land. For example, at the Port of Hong Kong, where land is expensive, loaded containers are stacked six high. Also, transtainers have an advantage over straddle carriers with respect to how high containers can be stacked. Usually, straddle carriers only stack containers three high (Bielli *et al.* 2006). Furthermore, transtainers require less space for stacked-container bays than straddle carriers

Figure 3.5 Yard gantry crane

and top loaders, i.e., transtainers allow for greater density in stacked-container storage than straddle carriers and top loaders (Bielli *et al.* 2006).

Import containers from ships, mounted on port chassis, arriving at rail yards within the port are removed from the chassis and loaded on rail cars. Import containers in stack storage are unstacked from storage, placed on port chassis, hauled to rail yards, removed from the chassis, and loaded on rail cars. Export containers arriving at the port by rail are unloaded and placed on port chassis for movement to stack storage, where they are removed from the chassis and stacked. Also, they may be hauled to the port's apron and removed from the chassis by the port's dock cranes and loaded on ships.

Several container ports around the world utilize automated guided vehicles (AGVs) – transport vehicles that are automated and driven by automatic control systems. At the Delta port terminal at the Port of Rotterdam, the Netherlands, AGVs transport containers from the stack storage area to the terminal's apron and vice versa. A port's AGV control/management system consists of the vehicle (the AGV), the vehicle's onboard controller, a centralized management system with a data link to the vehicle, and the vehicle's navigation system. The vehicle may be electrical or fuel powered, having its propulsion, braking, steering, and other functions controlled by an onboard controller (see Figure 3.6). The centralized management system is responsible for the dispatching, routing, and traffic control of AGVs within the port. The vehicle's navigation system guides the vehicle to its destination and promotes safety by being able to detect obstacles along the vehicle's travel route. In the ports of Rotterdam and Hamburg (Germany), AGVs have improved operational efficiency, decreased vehicle accidents, and reduced labor costs.

AGVs are transitioning from wire-guided to free-ranging (Ioannou *et al.* 2000: 79). New guidance technologies for AGVs include laser scanners, microwave transponders, embedded magnets, camera vision systems, inertia gyros, and ultrasonic sensors.

There are two types of AGV – the traditional AGV and the cassette AGV. Containers are loaded on traditional AGVs for transport by these AGVs. Alternatively, containers are not loaded on cassette AGVs but rather on detachable cassettes for transport by these AGVs (see Figure 3.7). The term "cassette" comes from the Finish word *cassettie*, referring to the hauling

Figure 3.6 Automated guided vehicle (AGV)

Figure 3.7 Cassette AGV that is double-stacked loaded onto a cassette and transported by an AGV

Source: Henesey, L.E. (2006) *Multi-Agent Systems for Container Terminal Management*, Karlskrona, Sweden: Blekinge Institute of Technology, p. 32 (per permission of author).

of material in a wagon. Although the equipment was redesigned for container terminals, the equipment is still referred to as a cassette. The advantage of the cassette AGV over the traditional AGV is that the former can hold more than one container on its detachable cassette, thereby allowing for the transportation of more than one container at a time. Alternatively, the traditional AGV can transport only one container at a time. Another advantage of the cassette AGV is its storage advantage, i.e., containers can be stacked on cassettes without AGVs being attached.

The ports of Thamesport (southeast England) and Antwerp (Belgium) and the APM terminal in Portsmouth, Virginia (U.S.A.) are utilizing fully automated yard stacking equipment, automatic stacking cranes (ASCs). These cranes automatically reposition export containers in the stacks in order to allow for their efficient removal from the stacks for loading on ships according to the ship's stowage plans. Also, ASCs may reposition import containers in the stacks for subsequent efficient placement on over-the-road chassis and rail cars for their departure from the port (see Figure 3.8).

Port services

Services provided at a container port by its service providers consist of core (traditional port) and value-added (non-traditional port) services (World Bank 2001). Core services consist of marine, terminal, and repair services. Marine services include, for example, pilotage, towage, and vessel traffic management services. Examples of terminal services include vessel tie-up, container handling and transfers, container storage, and container stuffing and stripping. Examples of repair services include dredging and maintenance of channels, dry dock ship repairs, lift equipment repairs, container repairs, and chassis repairs.

Service providers at container ports are increasingly delivering nontraditional port services that expand their role in the supply chains of shippers. "These services create value for

Figure 3.8 Automatic stacking crane (ASC)

shippers by expanding the scope of markets that they can economically access, by reducing the delivered cost of products they sell, or by reducing the cost to complete buy/sell trans-actions" (World Bank 2001: 10). Nontraditional port services (e.g., information, office and equipment rental, and equipment maintenance services) typically add value to the logistics activities, e.g., inventory management and warehousing, of shippers.

A prominent value-added service provided by many container ports in the world is the freeport zone (or free trade zone) service. A freeport zone is a designated area by a port (within or outside a port), where imported goods are stored and/or processed and exported – free of all customs duties (Firoz 2003). A variety of activities can be undertaken in a freeport zone, e.g., packaging, assembling, cleaning, repackaging, sorting, testing, labelling, and combining imported goods with domestic goods or other foreign goods. Freeport zones boost the local port economy by employing labor and other resources and attracting foreign investment for the provision of freeport zone services. The goal of freeport zones is to max-imize the value of transshipment cargoes (Feng and Hsieh 2008).

A cruise port

The cruise product purchased by cruise passengers has several components: transportation (to and from cruise ports); on-board accommodation, dining, entertainment and recreational activities; cruise ports of call; and shore excursions. Ocean cruise itineraries vary according to vessel operating speed, embarkation port, voyage duration, and the spatial pattern of des-tination ports (Marti 2004). Voyage duration may be two days in length, longer journeys within large areas, and round-the-world cruises.

Critical to the overall quality of the cruise product is the service quality of each component (Teye and Leclerc 1998). Poor performance by one component may negate a high performance by another component. If competition among cruise lines and/or cruise ports intensifies, cruise ports will be under greater pressure to improve the quality of their services.

Port design

Cruise ports are similar to cargo ports in that they have harbors, berths, wharfs, and aprons. As for container ports, cruise vessels usually dock parallel to berths at cruise ports. Aprons are areas where passengers and their luggage assemble (stage) for embarkation to and after debarkation from moored cruise vessels. Also, vessel supplies assemble at aprons for vessel embarkation; vessel waste assembles at aprons after debarkation from moored vessels.

Cruise ports do not have yards and interchange gates as found at container ports. Unlike container ports, cruise ports have passenger ashore support facilities that include shops (food and retail), tourism information offices, and luggage interchange (between ship and shore) offices. For vessel itineraries that include international stops, foreign exchange bureaus may be available.

Cruise ports also have vessel ashore support facilities. These facilities are used in supply-ing cruise vessels with basic supplies such as water, food, and fuel. Also, cruise ports may provide waste handling and repair services for cruise vessels.

The increasing number of ocean cruise passengers and number and size of ocean cruise vessels will place greater demands on ocean cruise ports into the foreseeable future. In order to satisfy these demands, more cruise marine terminals at existing cruise ports or an increase in the number of new cruise ports may be needed. Port Canaveral, a U.S. cruise port, has six cruise terminals in operation, but two more are in the planning stages. Greater water depths at cruise vessel berths may be needed for the berthing of the larger cruise vessels. Also, the width of harbor channels may be problematic. At the Port of Tampa (in the U.S.), the cruise ship, the *Carnival Sensation*, is so large that no other ship can utilize the channel while it is moving through it.

Port equipment

Another difference between cruise and container ports is in their equipment requirements. Cruise ports do not require the heavy lifting equipment (e.g., ship-to-shore gantry cranes, straddle carriers, and transtainers) as found at container ports. Rather, they utilize smaller-sized equipment in loading luggage and supplies on cruise vessels and unloading luggage and waste from vessels. Also, cruise ports utilize passenger loading bridges, placed between the apron and the moored vessel, for the loading and unloading of passengers to and from cruise vessels. These bridges vary in design according to vessel portal heights and longitudinal positions, tide and vessel load line variation, vessel movements, and ramp slopes (Ledford *et al.* 1995). The types of passenger loading bridges include: gangways, ramps, rolling stairs, airport-type telescoping jetways, escalators, and gantry-mounted ramp systems.

In order to reduce air pollution from cruise vessels while in port, more cruise ports in the future are expected to provide shore-based electricity for cruise vessels – i.e., to allow for "cold ironing" of cruise vessels while in port, where engines are turned off and vessels are hooked to shore-based electricity sources. In San Francisco, a new electric substation is being built next to its cruise terminal for the purpose of providing electricity to cruise vessels moored at the terminal. The cruise terminal will be responsible for providing the equipment for transmission of electricity to moored cruise vessels. Cold ironing reduces carbon dioxide emissions from cruise vessels, i.e., emissions that occur when cruise vessels run their diesel engines in port for provision of onboard electricity.

Specific ports in operation

Port of Hong Kong

The Port of Hong Kong is the world's third largest container port based upon TEU throughput (see Chapter 1). It has nine container terminals with 24 berths and 2,009 kilometers of paved roadways. By 2020 six additional berths are expected to be in operation. Its container terminals are operated by five terminal operating companies: Modern Terminals, Hong Kong International Terminals (HIT), COSCO-HIT Terminals (a joint venture between China Ocean Shipping Company and HIT), DP World, and Asia Container Terminals. In addition to containers, liquid bulk (petroleum) and solid bulk (coal) cargoes, as well as cruise vessel passengers, are handled by the port. Hong Kong is a deep water port with water depths of 15.5 meters in its approach channel and at its berths. The port is located on a relatively small amount of land, thereby necessitating the stacking of stored containers. Transtainers are used in the stacking and unstacking of containers to and from its six-container-high stacks.

The Port of Hong Kong is a major transshipment container port, i.e., 21.2 percent of its total TEU throughput in 2006 was transshipment throughput (Wallis 2008). Hong Kong's throughput growth slowed in 2007 due in part to the growth in container throughput in the ports of southern China, especially at the Port of Shenzhen (Hong Kong 2008). The high cost of trucking cargo from China to Hong Kong has resulted in a number of southern China shippers choosing southern China ports over Hong Kong, e.g., truckers are required to have a license (at a cost of $HK800 or more) to transport containers from southern China to Hong Kong. As a result, the cost of transporting a 40-foot container from the east side of China's Pearl River delta to the U.S. West Coast is $HK277 higher through Hong Kong than through the Port of Shenzhen (Wallis 2008).

The Port of Hong Kong is at a competitive price disadvantage with southern China ports (for cargo originating in southern China) given its relatively high trucking and terminal handling prices. However, it has a competitive service advantage over southern China ports in terms of its (1) fast vessel turnaround times (averaging 13 hours per container vessel in 2006) and (2) accessibility to other major ports in the world, given that a large number of shipping lines call at the port, including the world's top-ten largest container shipping lines.

In 2003, China's government endorsed the concept of constructing a 22-mile bridge-tunnel complex linking Hong Kong with seaports in the Pearl River Delta region of southern China. However, it was not until 2008 that a financial plan emerged to pay for its construction (estimated between $HK4 to $HK6 billion dollars). Hong Kong, the administrative region Macau, and the province of Guangdong agreed to pay 50.2, 14.7, and 35.1 percent of the bridge-tunnel construction cost, respectively (Dibenedetto 2008). The estimated completion date is 2015. The Zhuhai-Macau-Hong Kong bridge-tunnel is based on the Chesapeake Bay bridge-tunnel in the U.S. state of Virginia. The two bridges for the former bridge-tunnel will be 18.2 miles in total length and six lanes in width. The tunnel will be more than 4 miles long and laid 70 feet below the water surface. Two artificial (man-made) islands, each more than a half-mile long, will be built to join the two ends of the tunnel to bridge segments.

A significant growth in container barge traffic (in response to the high trucking costs) has occurred in recent years. Hong Kong has a vessel traffic service (VTS) system that monitors the movement of vessels in its waters for the prevention of vessel accidents. The Harbor Patrol Section patrols the Hong Kong harbor to prevent and investigate pollution activities.

Port of Hamburg

The Port of Hamburg in Germany is the world's ninth largest container port based upon TEU throughput (see Chapter 1) and Europe's second largest container port (after the Port of Rotterdam). It has four container terminals and eight multipurpose terminals (that handle, for example, general, roll on-roll off, liquid, agriculture, chemical, food, and stimulant cargoes). In 2007 there were 74 calls by cruise vessels. Its four container terminals include 25 berths with alongside water depths that range between 15.2 to 16.7 meters in maximum depths. The port has 41 kilometers of quay walls and can accommodate 320 ocean-going vessels at its berths at the same time (Hamburg Port Authority 2008). The port lies 110 kilometers up the Elbe River. Transtainers are utilized by its container terminals with straddle carriers utilized by one terminal.

The Port of Hamburg is in competition with other ports along Europe's North Range – Rotterdam, Antwerp, Bremen, and Le Havre. It has a well-established relationship with China; more of its containers come from China than from any other nation, thereby attracting numerous vessel calls by shipping lines that also call at China ports. The Port of Hamburg's transshipment containerized traffic between the Far East/Asian and the Baltic Sea regions was 2.7 million transshipment TEUs in 2007, an increase of 280,000 TEUs from that of 2006 (Hamburg Port Authority 2008). The port is connected to inland (roadway and railroad) transportation systems that provide access to regions throughout central Europe. The Port of Hamburg is Europe's largest rail hub for the transport of containerized cargo.

The Port of Hamburg also has a free port for which there are few customs restrictions. Its port safety is enhanced by having a VTS system that allows it to communicate directly with vessels calling at the port.

Port of Le Havre

In 2006 the Port of Le Havre in France was the world's forty-third largest container port based upon TEU throughput, handling 2.13 million TEUs (Port of Le Havre Authority 2008). It is located on the northwest coast of France on the English Channel. It is the first port of entry into northern Europe (from the south), thereby giving it a 24–48 hour regional advantage in the berthing of vessels over its competing ports of Rotterdam and Antwerp. The Port of Le Havre has seven container terminals, two terminals for car ferries, a site dedicated for cruise vessels, one combi-terminal for general cargo and container vessels, and one roll on-roll off center for vessels carrying new vehicles (Port of Le Havre Authority 2008). It has 28 kilometers of quay walls. The Terminal de France, which opened in 2006, has a 700-meter quay length, two berths, a water depth of 14.5 to 16 meters, and six post-Panamax ship-to-shore cranes that can extend across 22 container rows of a containership. The Terminal Port Oceane that opened in 2007 has a 700-meter quay length, three berths, and four post-Panamax ship-to-shore cranes that can extend across 22 container rows of a containership.

Forty-five percent of the Port of Le Havre's imported cargo is destined for Paris (which is two hours transit by road) and 60 percent of French exports move through the port. Its short sea transportation of containers to Great Britain and Baltic destinations have increased; 160,000 containers were transported in 2007, a 400 percent increase in five years (Port of Le Havre Authority 2008). The major cruise lines call at the Port of Le Havre and its car ferries transport passengers and vehicles to and from England.

Port of Savannah

In 2006 the Port of Savannah was the world's forty-first largest container port based upon TEU throughput, handling 2.16 million TEUs (Port of Savannah 2008). It is also the second largest container port on the U.S. East Coast (second to the Port of New York-New Jersey) and is located on the Savannah River in the state of Georgia, 13 nautical miles from the Atlantic Ocean. The Port of Savannah is the fastest growing container port in the U.S. exhibiting a 12 percent growth in container throughput from 2005 to 2006 (Talley forthcoming). It has two terminals – the Garden City Terminal with eight berths for container, breakbulk, and project cargoes and one berth for liquid bulk and the Ocean Terminal with 11 berths for breakbulk, roll on-roll off, forest and solid wood, steel, project, and heavy-lift cargoes. It has a channel depth of 42 feet, to be deepened to 48 feet by 2012 (Port of Savannah 2008). The Garden City Terminal utilizes post-Panamax ship-to-shore cranes and transtainers (RTGs).

The compounded annual growth rate in TEU throughput of the Port of Savannah between 2001 and 2007 was 16.7 percent in comparison to the rate of 8.2 percent for all U.S. ports (Port of Savannah 2008). A number of factors have contributed to the Port of Savannah's high growth rate. A primary factor has been the marketing campaign undertaken by the Georgia Port Authority (the state authority) and Georgia (the state) to attract the construction of regional distribution centers (RDCs) in the Savannah area by such major retailers as Wal-Mart, Target, Dollar Tree, Home Depot, Kmart-Sears, Lowe's, Best Buy, Advanced Auto Parts, and Pier 1 Imports. With the establishment of RDCs, container shipping lines were effectively forced by the retailers (given the relatively large volume of cargoes being shipped to the RDCs) to call at the Port of Savannah. There are 17 import RDCs in the Savannah area, with over 14 million square feet of space, generating in excess of 500,000 import TEUs annually.

Major retailers have been willing to construct RDCs in the Savannah area due to (1) state and port tax incentives for construction of RDCs, (2) the relatively low cost for land, (3) two on-dock Class I railroads, (4) low port congestion, 5) convenient access to interstate highways, and (6) the relatively low cost for labor (by the port using a mixture of union and non-union labor). The latter is explained by the fact that the Georgia Port Authority (a public entity) operates the Port of Savannah. By law, state employees such as those of the Georgia Port Authority cannot belong to a union. Hence, Georgia Port Authority employees (who are paid less than union port workers) can perform jobs at the port that are not directly related to ships, e.g., working as inland gate operators and port truck drivers. Alternatively, an ILA (International Longshoremen Association) East Coast contract requires that containerships be worked by only ILA union members (who are paid higher wages than Georgia Port Authority employees).

Port of Miami

The Port of Miami is located in Miami in the U.S. state of Florida and is two and a half miles from the Atlantic Ocean. The channel from the ocean to the port has a depth of 44 feet and varies in width from 500 to 1,000 feet. The Port of Miami has three cargo terminals (Port of Miami Terminal Operating Company – POMTOC, APM Terminal, and Seaboard Marine) and six cruise passenger terminals. POMTOC is a common user container terminal that is owned by Miami-Dade County and operates on 117 acres. The APM Terminal is a dedicated container terminal for A. P. Moller vessels and those of alliance vessels and operates on 75 acres. The Seaboard Marine terminal occupies 70 acres and handles containerized refrigerated, heavy equipment, and roll on-roll off cargoes. The Port of Miami handles fewer than 1 million TEUs of cargo per year (Port of Miami 2008).

The Port of Miami markets itself as the "Cruise Capital of the World." Eight cruise lines call at the port (Azamara Cruises, Carnival Cruise Lines, Celebrity Cruises, Crystal Cruises, Fred Olsen Cruise Lines, Norwegian Cruise Line, Royal Caribbean International, and Oceania Cruises) and it is the home port to 18 cruise vessels. In 2007 the port had a passenger throughput of 3.75 million cruise passengers. Passenger facilities at cruise terminals D and E are among the most modern in the world, having, for example, a VIP lounge, a high-tech security screening facility for embarkation of passengers, an airport-style conveyor baggage system, and a one-stop multi-agency facility for passenger processing. Since Miami is in close proximity to the Caribbean, it has the advantage of short-time sea cruises to tropical island destinations.

Ports of Panama

The ports of the country of Panama are 18 in number, found on both the Atlantic and Pacific coasts of Panama. Eleven (mainly small ports) are managed by the Panama Maritime Authority; the remaining seven are managed and operated by private businesses. Container ports on the Atlantic Coast include Manzanillo (operated by the Stevedoring Services of America), Cristobal (operated by the Panama Ports Company, a division of Hutchinson Port Holdings), and Colon (operated by Evergreen Marine Corporation). The Port of Colon is a container transshipment hub between Latin American feeder and mainline east–west container line routes. The Port of Balboa is located on the Pacific Ocean and is operated by the

Panama Ports Company. The TEU throughputs of Manzanillo, Cristobal, Colon, and Balboa in 2006 (2005) were 1.2 (1.4), 0.07 (0.03), 0.5 (0.4), and 0.8 (0.6) million TEUs, respectively (Business Panama 2008). In 2006 all container ports of Panama had a throughput of 3.2 million TEUs. Seventy percent of this throughput was transshipment.

Cruise terminals include the Cristobal Cruise Terminal and the Colon 2000 Terminal on the Atlantic Coast and terminals at the ports of Fuerte Amador and Balboa on the Pacific Ocean. These terminals had a cruise passenger throughput of 305,000 passengers from January to November of 2006 (Business Panama 2008). Also, numerous cruise lines utilize the Panama Canal, i.e., in having their vessels transit to and from the Atlantic and Pacific oceans.

Panama's Colon Free Trade Zone is the largest free trade zone in the Americas and the second largest in the world (Business Panama 2008). A number of large container shipping lines (e.g., Maersk, CMA-CGM, Evergreen, and Hapag-Lloyd) call at the zone. The top importing countries to the zone are China, Taiwan, the U.S., Japan, and Korea. The top exporting countries from the zone are Colombia, Venezuela, Guatemala, and Ecuador.

Panama also offers rail landbridge service to and from the Atlantic and Pacific Coast ports. The Panama Canal Railway Company provides inter-oceanic rail landbridge freight and passenger service from coast to coast along the 47-mile route in under an hour.

Summary

Containers that move through a container port are involved in four basic port activities: (1) receiving, (2) loading/unloading, (3) staging, and (4) storage. The common design features of container ports are: (1) harbor, (2) berth, (3) wharf, (4) apron, (5) container yard, and (6) interchange gate. The container yard consists of various buildings, roadways, and pathways for the movement of containers within the port by trucks and various types of yard equipment, and land area for the storage of containers, chassis, and equipment. If land is scarce, containers will likely be stored in stacks, otherwise, they will be stored on chassis. If the port has on-site rail service, the container yard will have a rail yard that consists of railroad tracks and pathways for the loading and unloading of containers to and from trains.

The equipment at container ports for the lifting and lowering of containers includes (1) ship-to-shore gantry cranes, (2) straddle carriers, (3) yard gantry cranes (transtainers), (4) top loaders, and (5) automated guided vehicles (AGVs). Trucks with chassis and AGVs are used to move containers to and from different locations within the port.

Services provided at container ports consist of core and valued-added services. Core services consist of marine, terminal, and repair services. Value-added services are those that add value to the supply chains of shippers.

The design features of cruise ports are similar to those of container ports except for the container yards and interchange gates. Cruise ports have passenger and vessel ashore support facilities. Cruise ports do not require the heavy lifting equipment found at container ports; smaller-sized equipment is used for loading luggage and supplies onto cruise vessels and unloading luggage and waste from cruise vessels.

Bibliography

Bielli, M., Boulmakoul A., and Rida, M. (2006) "Object Oriented Model for Container Terminal Distributed Simulation", *European Journal of Operational Research*, 175: 1731–1751.

Business Panama (2008) Available online at http://www.businesspanama.com/investing/opportunities/ ports_maritime.php (accessed 3 June 2008).

Chadwin, M.L., Pope, J. A., and Talley, W. K. (1990) *Ocean Container Transportation: An Operational Perspective*, New York: Taylor & Francis.

Dibenedetto, B. (2008) "A 22-Mile Bridge-Tunnel will Span China's Pearl River Delta at Hong Kong", *Journal of Commerce*, 9, July 28: 18–20, 22.

Ebersold, W. B. (2004) "Cruise Industry in Figures", *Global Cruise 2004*, Burr Ridge, IL: Business Briefings.

Feng, C.-M. and Hsieh, H.-C. (2008) "Creating Value-Driven Port Logistics in Free Trade Zones", a paper presented at the 2008 International Forum on Shipping, Ports and Airports, Hong Kong Polytechnic University, Hong Kong.

Firoz, N. M. (2003) "Investing in China's Economic Development Zone: A Managerial Guide", *International Journal of Management*, 20: 223–232.

Hamburg Port Authority (2008) Available online at http://www.hamburg-port-authority.de (accessed 10 March 2008).

Henesey, L.E. (2006) *Multi-Agent Systems for Container Terminal Management*, Karlskrona, Sweden: Blekinge Institute of Technology.

Hong Kong (2008) *Hong Kong: The Facts*, Hong Kong: Information Services Department.

Ioannou, P. A., Kosmatopoulos, E. B., Jula, H., Collinge, A., Liu, C.-I, Asef-Vaziri, A., and Dougherty, Jr., E. (2000) *Cargo Handling Technologies: Final Report*, Los Angeles, California: Center for Advanced Transportation Technologies, University of Southern California.

Ledford, G., Schneider, G., and Mock, D. (1995) "Cruise Passenger Loading Bridges at Florida Ports", *Ports – Proceedings*, 1: 173–184.

Marti, B. E. (2004) "Trends in World and Extended-Length Cruising (1985–2002)", *Marine Policy*, 28: 199–211.

Penfold, A. (2006) *European and Mediterranean Container Port Markets to 2015*, Surrey, UK: Ocean Shipping Consultants.

Port of Le Havre Authority (2008) Available online at http://www.havre-port.net/pahweb.html (accessed 1 June 2008).

Port of Miami (2008) Available online at http://www.miamidade.gov/portofmiami (accessed 3 June 2008).

Port of Savannah (2008) Available online at http://www.seda.org/contents/display/105/transportation/port.html (accessed 1 June 2008).

Speares, S. (2005) "Cruise Lines Urged to Build New Vessels to Meet Demand", *Lloyd's List*. Available online at http://www.lloydslist.com, November 3.

Staff (2005) "Cruise Industry Worth More Than $30bn to US Economy", *Lloyd's List*. Available online at http://www.lloydslist.com, September 9.

_____ (2006a) "Cruise Conventions Ride Tide of Passenger Growth", *Lloyd's List*. Available online at http://www.lloydslist.com, January 17.

_____ (2006b) "Positive Outlook for Passenger Shipping as Capacity Comes Online", *Lloyd's List*. Available online at http://www.lloydslist.com, January 17.

Talley, W. K. (2000) "Ocean Container Shipping: Impacts of a Technological Improvement", *Journal of Economic Issues*, 34: 933–948.

—— (forthcoming) "Shipping", in G. Giuliano, L. Hoel, and M. Meyer (eds) *Intermodal Transportation: Moving Freight in a Global Economy*, Washington, DC: Eno Transportation Foundation.

Teye, V. B. and Leclerc, D. (1998) "Product and Service Delivery Satisfaction Among North American Cruise Passengers", *Tourism Management*, 19: 153–160.

Wallis, K. (2008) "Hong Kong Told to Slash Charges: Port Throughput Held Back by Inefficiencies", *Lloyd's List*. Available online at http://www.lloydslist.com, May 30.

World Bank (2001) *World Bank Port Reform Tool Kit: Module 1*. Available online at http://rru.worldbank.org/Documents/Toolkits/ports_fulltoolkit.pdf (accessed 4 March 2009).

4   Carriers

Introduction

A carrier is a firm that provides a transportation service – moving cargo and/or passengers from one location to another. These movements may occur by land, water, or air. At cargo ports, water carriers (shipping lines and barge carriers) and land carriers (truck carriers and railroads) move cargo to and from these ports. At passenger ports, water carriers (ferry and cruise lines) and land carriers (buses and taxis) move individuals to and from these ports. Also, carriers are used to move cargo and individuals to and from various locations within the port.

The carrier differs from a manufacturing firm. First, the output of a manufacturing firm involves the transformation of resources into a physical product (a tangible output), whereas the carrier utilizes resources to provide a service (an intangible output). Second, a manufacturing firm produces a physical product at a given location, whereas the carrier provides a service that involves changes in locations. Third, a manufacturing firm seeks to produce a homogenous product, whereas the carrier may seek to provide a differentiated (varying in quality) service.

This chapter presents the theory of a carrier in the provision of transportation service. Specifically, the resources utilized by carriers, the means by which carriers can vary the quality of their service, the measurement of the service output of carriers, and carrier cost characteristics, pricing, and objectives are discussed. The theory is applicable to any type of carrier that moves cargo and/or passengers to and from ports. The latter carrier is a port user that demands port services and makes port choices. The efficiency of a port affects the size of ships that call at the port.

Resources

The resources used by a carrier in the provision of a transportation service may generally be classified as (1) vehicles, (2) energy, (3) way, (4) labor, and (5) terminals. Vehicles of various sizes and shapes are used by carriers in the physical movement of cargo and/or passengers. Vehicles may be carrying units (e.g., ships, barges, rail cars, and truck trailers) that carry cargo and passengers or power units (e.g., tugboats, railroad locomotives, and truck tractors) that do not carry cargo and passengers but push and pull the carrying units. Towboats and railroad locomotives both push and pull carrying units.

Energy resources are used to power vehicles. Petroleum fuels are used to power ships, tugboats, railroad locomotives, and truck carriers; electricity is used to power railroad locomotives; and natural energy such as wind and water currents are used to power ships.

The way is the path over which the carrier operates and includes the right-of-way plus any additions provided by humans to the right-of-way. The right-of-way is that part of the way provided by nature, e.g., water, land, and air area, over which a carrier's vehicle travels. Additions to the right-of-way are provided to enhance the flow and safety of vehicles in the use of the right-of-way. For truck carriers, the way is the highway (motorway) and the right-of-way is the land area provided by nature; the additions are the pavement and traffic lights and signs. For railroads, the way is the railway and the right-of-way is the land area provided by nature; the tracks and signals are the additions. For water carriers, the way is the waterway that consists of natural bodies of water such as oceans and rivers and navigational aids such as channel markers.

Labor includes workers directly involved in the physical movement of cargo and passengers such as vehicle drivers and cargo loaders. Also, these workers may be involved in the maintenance of vehicles and the way. Further, they may be management who supervise, coordinate, and plan the movement of cargo and passengers.

Terminals are activity centers of carriers. They are places where freight and/or passengers are loaded to and from vehicles, vehicles are dispatched, cargo is stored, passengers purchase tickets and wait for departure, and administrative activities and vehicle maintenance are performed. Railroads and water carriers have rail and marine terminals, respectively.

As discussed in Chapter 1, a port (seaport) may have one or more marine terminals. A shipping line may use a marine terminal that it owns, i.e., a private marine terminal, and does not share with other shipping lines (i.e., a dedicated terminal). Alternatively, it may use a marine terminal owned by government, managed by a port authority, and shared with other shipping lines (i.e., a common-user terminal). The advantage of a private marine terminal is that the shipping line can coordinate its use with its other resources in minimizing the cost in providing transportation service. In utilizing a common-user terminal, it would be more difficult to do so.

Operating options

A carrier has a number of operating options with which to differentiate the quality of its service. These operating options include (1) speed of movement, (2) frequency of service, (3) reliability of service, (4) spatial accessibility of service, and (5) susceptibility of cargo to loss and damage and passengers to fatal and nonfatal injuries (Talley 1988). Depending upon the operating option, an increase or decrease in its level will improve the quality of the carrier's service.

The greater the speed in moving cargo and passengers to their final destinations, the higher the quality of transportation service by the carrier – since cargo and passengers arrive at their destinations within a shorter period of time. Frequency of service is how often the carrier provides transportation service between two locations within a stated time period. If the carrier is a container shipping line that provides liner service (i.e., scheduled service) between two ports and now provides service twice a month rather than once a month between these two ports, its frequency of service between the two ports has increased. The greater the frequency of service, the more likely the service will be available when a shipper or passenger desires it, thus, the higher the quality of service. Frequency of service is sometimes referred to as the time accessibility of service.

The reliability of service is the degree to which cargo and passengers arrive at their destinations at the time so specified by the carrier. Reliability may be measured by the variability between the expected time of arrival (as stated by the carrier) and the actual time of arrival. The greater the variability between the two times, the more unreliable the service and thus the poorer the quality of service.

Spatial accessibility of service is the degree to which a carrier's transportation service is spatially convenient to a shipper or passenger. A carrier's transportation service becomes more convenient when the carrier expands its network by serving more nodes in its network, i.e., providing service to more locations. The carrier's quality of service will have improved, since shippers and passengers have a greater number of origin-destination locations from which to choose.

The susceptibility of cargo to loss and damage is the probability that cargo transported by a given carrier will be lost or damaged. The susceptibility of passengers to fatal or nonfatal injuries is the probability that passengers transported by a given carrier will be fatally or nonfatally injured. The quality of the given carrier's service will have improved if there is a decrease in these probabilities.

Another operating option sometimes mentioned in the literature is the environment of the carrying-unit vehicle, e.g., its cleanliness and adherence to desired vehicle temperature. However, this operating option and susceptibility of cargo to loss or damage may be positively related. For example, a container used in ocean container shipping may have a residue remaining inside the container from its previous cargo that damages the cargo currently being shipped in the container. If the container is a refrigerated container (reefer), a container's non-adherence to a desired temperature can damage its cargo. Similarly, the vehicle-environment operating option and susceptibility of passengers to fatal or non-fatal injuries may be positively related. For example, an unclean carrying-unit vehicle may have trash on which passengers slip and become injured.

Changes in the levels of the operating options of a carrier will affect the resources that it employs. If there is no excess capacity for a given resource, i.e., the resource is being fully utilized, then a change in a given operating option that improves the carrier's quality of service will require that the carrier employ an additional amount of the resource. For example, a carrier will employ more vehicles in order to increase its frequency of service on all routes. Similarly, if the carrier is requested to transport more cargo and passengers and its resources are currently fully utilized, it will need to employ more resources to handle the requested increase in cargo and passengers to be transported.[1]

Output

A carrier is technically efficient when it maximizes its transportation service in the employment of given amounts of resources.[2] The investigation of technical efficiency in practice requires measuring the service output of carriers. The most commonly used service output measure for cargo carriers is the ton-mile (one ton of cargo moved one mile) or ton-kilometer (one ton of cargo moved one kilometer). For passenger carriers, the output measure is the passenger-mile (one passenger moved one mile) or passenger-kilometer (one passenger moved one kilometer). However, these units of measurement are not necessarily homogenous, which can be problematic in costing the transportation service provided by carriers.

The ton-mile and passenger-mile treat all cargo and passengers as if they were the same. For example, the transportation of 100 tons of iron ore is treated the same as the transportation of 100 tons of plastic foam for the same distance; the transportation of the same number of elderly passengers is treated the same as the transportation of the same number of non-elderly passengers for the same distance. Even though the same tonnage of cargo and number of passengers are being transported the same distance, incurring the same ton-miles and passenger-miles, the costs incurred by the carrier in doing so may differ. The transportation of plastic foam, for example, requires greater vehicle capacity than the transportation of iron ore (given that plastic foam takes up greater cubic space) for the same tonnage of cargo being transported, thereby incurring greater vehicle-related cost. The transportation of elderly passengers may require special vehicles for getting on and off, and thus will be more costly than vehicles used for transporting the same number of non-elderly passengers.

Ton-miles and passenger-miles of service can also be the same for the same type of cargo and the same type of passenger but for different distances, tonnage, and numbers of passengers. For example, one ton of iron ore (passenger) being transported 1,000 miles is treated the same as 10 tons of iron ore (passengers) being transported 100 miles, i.e., 1,000 ton-miles (passenger-miles). While the ton-miles and passenger-miles are the same, the resources required to provide the service will differ, e.g., different vehicle capacity will be required – thus the costs incurred by the carrier will differ.

The rationale for using the ton-mile and passenger-mile as measures of service outputs for cargo and passenger carriers is as follows. In order for cargo transportation service to occur, two parties must be in agreement – i.e., the shipper must be willing to provide the cargo (tons) to be transported and the cargo carrier must be willing to transport the cargo (incurring vehicle miles). If either party is not willing to participate, a cargo transportation service will not occur, i.e., without cargo, the carrier will be incurring empty vehicle miles. In order for passenger transportation service to occur, the passenger must be willing to provide himself/herself to be transported and the passenger carrier must be willing to transport the passenger (thereby incurring vehicle miles).

Cost

A carrier is cost efficient if its costs incurred in the provision of various amounts of a transportation service are minimum costs, given the prices to be paid for resources in provision of the transportation service.[3] These costs can vary with respect to time. For the short-run time period, the carrier has at least one resource that is fixed, i.e., the length of the period is sufficiently short so that the carrier is unable to vary the amount of every resource. For example, a carrier's terminal may be a fixed resource in the short run. For the long-run time period, the carrier has sufficient time to vary the amounts of all resources utilized.

Short-run cost

A carrier's short-run total cost consists of fixed and variable costs. Fixed costs are those incurred by fixed resources and thus do not vary with changes in the amount of carrier service. Fixed costs include, for example, depreciation and insurance premiums on terminal buildings. Variable costs are those incurred by variable resources and vary with changes in the amount of carrier service. They include, for example, payments for fuel and labor that vary with the provision of carrier service.

Figure 4.1 shows graphically the short-run total cost (STC), fixed cost (FC), and variable cost (SVC) for various amounts of ton-miles of service provided by a carrier. Observe that short-run variable cost is measured vertically from the horizontal axis at each level of output (Q). The amount of fixed cost is added vertically to the SVC curve to obtain the points on the total cost (STC) curve.

The above costs can be converted into unit costs by simply dividing them by their corresponding amounts of carrier output Q (e.g., ton-miles). Thus, average fixed cost (AFC) is FC divided by Q; short-run average variable cost (SAVC) is SVC divided by Q; and short-run average total cost (SATC) is STC divided by Q. It follows that SATC = AFC + SAVC. If fixed costs are a large percentage of total costs, SATC will decline from increases in ton-miles over a relatively large range of output.

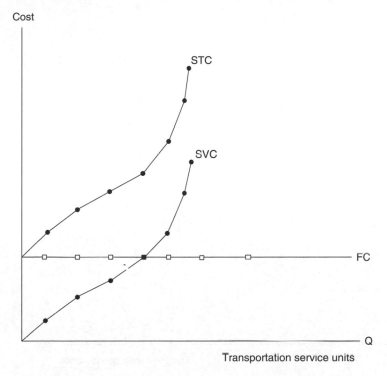

Figure 4.1 Carrier short-run total, fixed, and variable costs

The above unit costs are graphed in Figure 4.2. A carrier's short-run average total cost (SATC) is the vertical sum of average variable cost (SAVC) and average fixed cost (AFC) for a given amount of carrier output. AFC declines continuously as output increases, since a fixed or constant cost is divided by larger and larger amounts of output. As output increases from the increased utilization in variable resources, SAVC declines initially, reaches a minimum, and then increases. The addition to the carrier's short-run variable cost in providing an additional unit of service is the short-run marginal cost (SMC) for that unit of service, i.e., SMC = ΔSVC/ΔQ. As shown in Figure 4.2, the SMC curve intersects the SAVC and SATC curves from below at their minimum unit costs.

Long-run cost

In the long run, all carrier costs are variable. Figure 4.3a shows graphically the long-run total cost (LTC) for various amounts of service Q provided by a carrier. A carrier's long-run average total cost (LATC) is LTC divided by Q. The addition to the carrier's long-run cost in providing an additional unit of service is the long-run marginal cost (LMC) for that unit of service, i.e., LMC = ΔLTC/ΔQ (see Figure 4.3b).

In Figure 4.4a, the carrier's long-run average total cost is declining continuously as service expands. A carrier exhibits "economies of scale" for a given range of service provision if its LATC curve is negatively sloped over this range. Scale refers to the amount of service or output provided. If output increases by a certain percentage, the carrier's long-run costs will increase by a smaller percentage if economies of scale exist. If so, the carrier's LMC

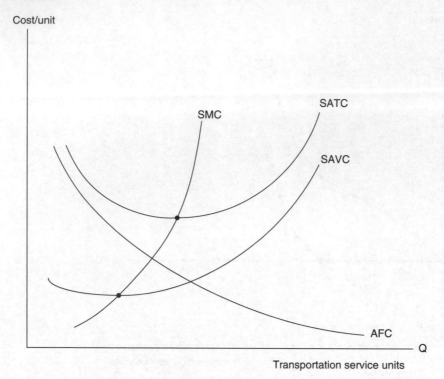

Figure 4.2 Carrier short-run unit and marginal costs

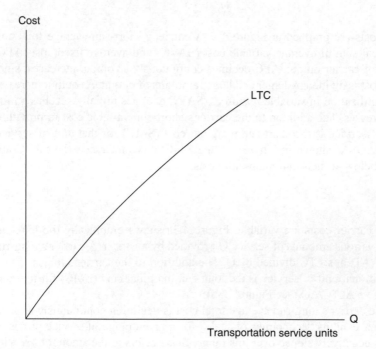

Figure 4.3a Carrier long-run costs

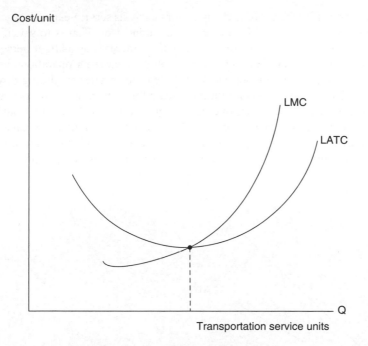

Figure 4.3b Carrier long-run unit and marginal costs

curve will lie below its LATC curve for a given output. Economies of scale may arise from labor and vehicle specialization. As output increases, the carrier is able to hire more specialized labor; rather than workers performing several tasks, workers can be hired to perform one task for which they have been trained. These workers will be more productive in performing individual tasks as opposed to workers performing several tasks, thereby contributing to declining unit costs. A similar analogy applies to utilizing specialized vehicles.

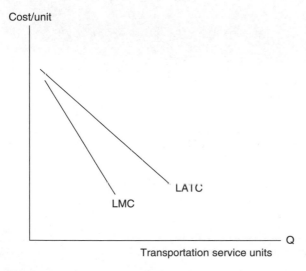

Figure 4.4a Carrier economies of scale

In Figure 4.4b, the carrier's LATC curve is rising continuously as service expands. A carrier exhibits diseconomies of scale if LATC increases as output rises. That is to say, if its output increases by a certain percentage, its long-run costs will increase by a larger percentage. The difficulty of efficiently coordinating and controlling a carrier's operations as it becomes a larger and larger service provider can contribute to the carrier exhibiting diseconomies of scale. A carrier exhibits constant returns to scale for a given range of service if long-run average total cost remains constant over this range (see Figure 4.4c). If its output increases by a certain percentage, its long-run costs will increase by the same percentage. In reality, a carrier may exhibit all three types of returns to scale – economies and diseconomies of and constant returns to scale – over a range of service levels (see Figure 4.5).

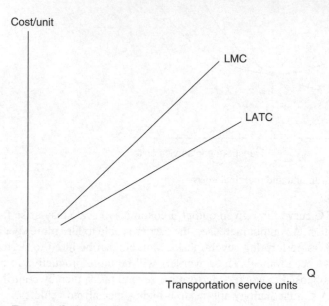

Figure 4.4b Carrier diseconomies of scale

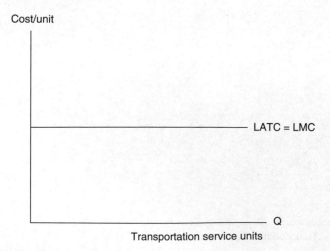

Figure 4.4c Carrier constant returns to scale

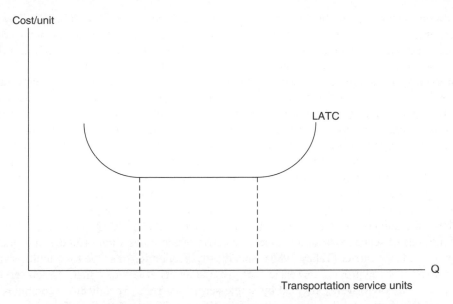

Figure 4.5 Carrier economies and diseconomies of and constant returns to scale

The type of returns to scale may also be described by the ratio of LATC to LMC for a given amount of output. Notice that for a carrier exhibiting economies of scale (see Figure 4.4a), LATC is greater than LMC at a given output, i.e., $S = LATC/LMC > 1$. In Figure 4.4b, LATC is less than LMC for the carrier exhibiting diseconomies of scale, or $S < 1$. In Figure 4.4c, LATC is equal to LMC for the carrier exhibiting constant returns to scale, or $S = 1$.

Long-run cost: multiple outputs

Heretofore, it has been implicitly assumed that the carrier provides one type of service, e.g., ton-miles. Suppose the carrier provides a freight service as well as a passenger service, measured in ton-miles and passenger-miles, respectively. Also, suppose that all costs incurred are variable, i.e., the carrier is in the long run. How would the carrier determine whether it exhibits economies or diseconomies of scale or constant returns to scale? How would it determine the unit costs of each of the two services? Would costs be less in providing these two services (at the same levels of provision) if provided by separate single-service carriers rather than by a two-service carrier?

Note that for a single-service carrier, $S = LATC/LMC$, may be rewritten as $S = (LTC/Q)/LMC = LTC/Q*LMC$. By analogy, S for the two-service carrier may be expressed as $S = LTC/[Q_1*LMC_1 + Q_2*LMC_2]$, where Q_1 may represent ton-miles and Q_2 may represent passenger-miles (Talley 1988). If $S > 1$, the two-service carrier exhibits economies of scale, i.e., if the amounts of the two services are increased by the same percentage, the long-run costs incurred by the carrier will increase by a smaller percentage. If $S < 1$, the two-service carrier exhibits diseconomies of scale, i.e., if the amounts of the two services are increased by the same percentage, the long-run costs incurred by the carrier will increase by a larger percentage. If $S = 1$, the two-service carrier exhibits constant returns to scale; the percentage increase in the amounts of the services will result in the same percentage increase in costs.

For a one-service carrier, its long-run unit costs (LATC) are found by dividing LTC by its corresponding quantity (Q). However, for a two-service carrier, its long-run total costs include costs that are incurred by both services, i.e., LTC/Q_1 is not the unit cost of ton-miles of service, since the cost of passenger-miles of service is also included in LTC.

Unit costs for multiple output carriers can be found by computing the long-run average incremental total costs for the outputs. For example, the long-run average incremental total cost ($LAITC_1$ or unit cost) for ton-miles of service Q_1 is the two-service carrier's long-run cost attributable to ton-miles of service divided by the ton-miles of service, i.e., the incremental (or addition to) cost incurred by the carrier in providing ton-miles of service divided by these ton-miles (Talley 1988). Specifically, the incremental cost of ton-miles of service is the cost in providing both services minus the cost of only providing the other type of service, i.e., passenger-miles of service Q_2. If LTC = $f(Q_1, Q_2)$, then the incremental cost of ton-miles of service Q_1 is $f(Q_1, Q_2) - f(0, Q_2)$. Thus, $LAITC_1 = [f(Q_1, Q_2) - f(0, Q_2)]/Q_1$. Similarly, the unit cost for passenger-miles of service is $LAITC_2 = [f(Q_1, Q_2) - f(Q_1, 0)]/Q_2$.

Economies of scope exist for a two-service carrier when it has a long-run cost advantage over a one-service carrier (Talley 1988). Specifically, economies of scope for a multiservice carrier exist if it can provide its services of given amounts at less cost than if each service (at the same amount) were provided by single-service carriers. Specifically, economies of scope exist for a two-service carrier when $f(Q_1, Q_2) < f(Q_1, 0) + f(0, Q_2)$. If the inequality sign is reversed to ">," then diseconomies of scope exist.

In a study by Kim (1987), diseconomies of scope were found for U.S. Class I railroads (the largest U.S. railroads). Fifty-six Class I railroads for the year 1963 were used in the analysis. The railroads provided both freight and passenger services, measured in ton-miles and passenger-miles. The presence of diseconomies of scope suggests that the same amounts of ton-miles and passenger-miles could be provided at lower cost by separate freight and passenger railroads. Specifically, the study concludes that the cost of providing freight and passenger services separately would be 41 percent less than the cost of providing them jointly. It is interesting to note that since 1970 U.S. intercity freight and passenger railroad services are no longer provided jointly. In 1970 the U.S. Congress established Amtrak (a passenger railroad), placing intercity passenger railroad services (75 miles or longer) that were previously provided by freight/passenger railroads under the provision of Amtrak.

Pricing

The pricing strategies of carriers will depend upon the degree of competition in the market and the carrier's operating objectives. The greater the degree of competition for carrier services, the less the control that carriers and the greater the control that the market will have in setting prices for these services. The market sets prices by the interaction of market demand and supply for carrier services. The less the market competition, the greater the control that the carriers will have in setting prices for their services.

If a carrier is privately owned, say by individual stockholders, it may have the objectives of maximizing profits or maximizing service output (e.g., ton-miles) subject to achieving a minimum level of profit (in order to increase market share) in the provision of a transportation service (Talley 1983). Profit for a carrier is the total revenue (TR) that it receives from users of its service minus the total cost that the carrier incurs in the provision of the service, i.e., short-run profit = TR − STC. Total revenue is the product of the price (P) per unit of transportation service charged by the carrier (and paid by users) and the amount of the transportation service utilized by users (Q), i.e., TR = PQ.

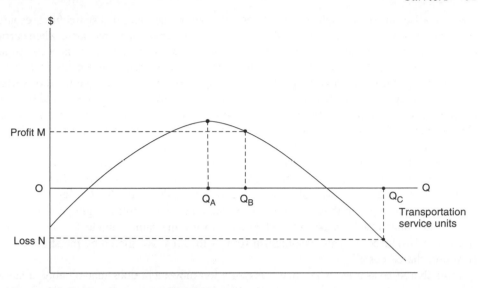

Figure 4.6 Carrier short-run profits and losses

In Figure 4.6, carrier short-run profit is measured on the vertical axis and the amount of carrier service is measured along the horizontal axis. The carrier maximizes profits in providing Q_A amount of service output. Service output is maximized subject to the minimum profit of OM at Q_B amount of service. If the carrier is owned and subsidized (in operation) by government and has the objective of maximizing service output subject to not exceeding a maximum operating deficit of ON (to be subsidized by government), this maximum service output will be Q_C. Note also that ON is the loss incurred by the carrier in providing Q_C amount of service, i.e., STC exceeds TR by the amount ON.

Depending on the extent to which a carrier has control over its prices, the carrier may seek to discriminate among groups of users of its service in order to increase total revenue and thus profits. Price discrimination occurs when a carrier sells a service at different prices to users and the prices do not reflect cost differences. For example, shippers of higher-valued cargo may be charged a higher price (or rate) than shippers of lower-valued cargo for transportation between the same origin and destination. The shipper of the higher-valued cargo is perceived to be willing to pay a higher price than the shipper of the lower-valued cargo, since the price elasticity of freight transportation demand for the higher-valued cargo tends to be price inelastic but price elastic for the lower-valued cargo.[4] Charging a shipper of higher-valued cargo a higher price than a shipper of lower-valued cargo for a service has been referred to as value-of-service pricing.

In passenger transportation, a higher-income individual (say a business traveler) may be charged a higher price (or fare) than a lower-income individual (say a nonbusiness traveler) for a transportation service. The higher-income individual is perceived to be willing to pay a higher fare than the lower-income individual, since the price elasticity of passenger transportation demand tends to be price inelastic for higher-income individuals but elastic for lower-income individuals.[5]

If a carrier seeks to set prices for its services (e.g., by route) that just cover the unit cost of these services, i.e., to set fully allocated cost prices where prices are equal to unit costs, a problem arises in how to allocate costs of resources among services that share these resources in the provision of services (Talley 1982). Fully allocated cost prices may arise when carriers are economically regulated by government and the government regulatory agency requires that the carriers establish fully allocated cost prices. Carrier shared costs are costs that cannot be traced to a particular cargo shipment or passenger. Shared costs may be fixed or variable and common or joint. The depreciation cost of a carrier's terminal is a fixed cost to be shared among cargo shipments (or passengers) that utilize the terminal. The variable costs of a vehicle trip such as the cost of fuel utilized by the vehicle and the driver's wage are variable costs that are shared by the cargo shipments (or passengers) of the vehicle trip.

Carrier shared costs are common shared costs if transported cargo and passengers that share these costs are not jointly determined, i.e., the transportation of a given cargo shipment (or passenger) does not unavoidably create the transportation of another (Talley 1988, 2001). For example, a shipment that is being transported on a vehicle from origin A to destination B does not unavoidably cause other shipments to use the same vehicle for transportation from A to B. The costs of the vehicle trip from A to B that are shared by the shipments are common shared costs.

Joint shared costs arise when one transportation movement does unavoidably create the transportation of another (Talley 1988, 1989). Joint costs, for example, arise when backhaul trips occur. If a vehicle that goes from origin A to destination B must return to A, the trip from A to B is a fronthaul vehicle trip and the trip from B to A is the backhaul vehicle trip of the round vehicle trip. The depreciation cost of the vehicle utilized in the round trip is a joint cost to be shared by the fronthaul and backhaul vehicle trips, since the fronthaul vehicle trip has unavoidably created the backhaul vehicle trip.

Carrier demand in port

In order for a port carrier service (i.e., a service to a carrier in port) to occur, the carrier must be willing to have one of its vessels (e.g., a ship or barge) or vehicles (e.g., a rail car or truck) to call at the port and the port must be willing to service this vessel or vehicle. If so, there will be two prices for the port carrier service, a money price and a time price to be paid and incurred, respectively, by the carrier (Talley 2006). The money price for the service is the money price (per unit of service) charged by the port for the service. The time price for the service is the time price (per unit of service) incurred by the carrier's vessel or vehicle that was involved in the provision of the port carrier service. Specifically, the carrier's time price in port is the product of the vessel's (vehicle's) value or cost of time per unit of time in port and the time that the vessel (vehicle) was involved in the provision of a unit of port carrier service. Examples of vessel and vehicle time costs include vessel and vehicle depreciation and insurance costs. Examples of port carrier services include vessel berthing and unberthing and loading and unloading cargo to and from vessels and vehicles.

In Chapter 2 the carrier demand for a port service was considered only from the perspective of the money price for the port service (see Figure 2.1). The carrier demand for a port service from the perspective of the full price appears in Figure 4.7, where the full price is the sum of the money price and the time price for the port carrier service. Specifically, the carrier demand for a port service with respect to the full price in Figure 4.7 is represented by the demand curve D_{FCA}. At lower full prices, more port service is demanded by carriers and less service at higher prices, other things remaining the same. The full price is $P_{FCA} = P_{CA} + P_{TCA}$, where P_{CA} is the money price charged by the port for the port carrier service per unit of service and P_{TCA} is the time price incurred by the carrier's vessel or vehicle in the provision of the port carrier service per unit of service.

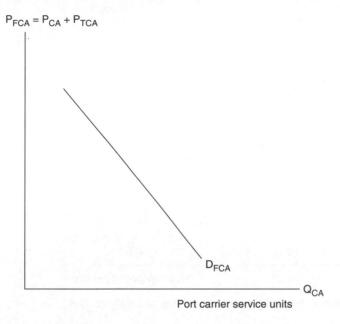

$P_{FCA} = P_{CA} + P_{TCA}$

D_{FCA}

Q_{CA}

Port carrier service units

Figure 4.7 Carrier demand for port service at full prices

Ports and ship size

Containerships and ships in general incur economies of ship size at sea. For a containership, economies of ship size at sea occur when ship cost per TEU moved (or transported) at sea decreases as ship size increases (Talley 1990). In Figure 4.8, ship economies of ship size at sea are exhibited. Ship size is measured by the transport capacity of the ship, i.e., by the number of TEUs that it can transport. The daily ship cost per TEU transported at sea decreases as the number of TEUs transported increase. Economies of ship size at sea arise due to the fact that ship costs in transporting containers at sea do not increase in proportion to the increase in ship size.

In port, however, containerships exhibit diseconomies of ship size, i.e., ship cost per TEU moved (loaded on and unloaded from a ship) in port increases as ship size increases (Talley 1990; Haralambides *et al.* 2002). In Figure 4.9, diseconomies of ship size in port for a containership are exhibited. The daily ship cost per TEU loaded on to and unloaded from a containership increases as the number of TEU movements increase. The diseconomies of ship size in port arise from the port having to assign a greater number of cranes (shore side and otherwise) to work larger ships, increasing the difficulty of moving containers to and from these ships. For example, two or more ship-to-shore trades may be used to simultaneously work a larger ship. Also, larger containerships have more TEU slot locations from which and to which containers may be moved.

Terminal operators at the Ports of Los Angeles and Long Beach discovered with the arrival of the first 8,000 TEU ship in 2004 that the working of this ship is more difficult than the working of two 4,000 TEU ships (Mongelluzzo 2006). Also, water depths of 50 feet, terminals that can devote at least 100 acres to unloading one 8,000 TEU ship, and on-dock or near-dock railroads that can carry the ship's unloaded containers away from the port are needed (Leach 2006).

Daily ship cost per TEU transported

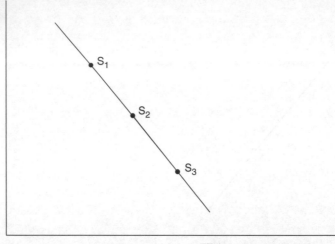

TEUs transported per day

Note: "S" represents the TEU carrying capacity of a ship, where $S_3 > S_2 > S_1$.

Figure 4.8 Economies of ship size at sea

A port's ship cargo handling capacity – the amount of cargo that can be loaded on and unloaded from a ship per hour – will affect the size of ships that call at the port. There is a positive correlation between a port's ship cargo handling capacity and the size of containerships that call at a container port (Talley 1990). That is to say, as a container port becomes more efficient in moving cargo to and from ships (i.e., more cargo moved per hour), the containerships

Daily ship cost per TEU loaded/unloaded

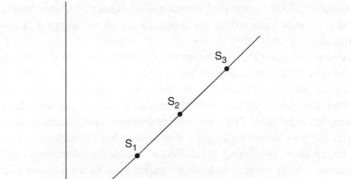

TEUs loaded/unloaded per day

Note: "S" represents the TEU carrying capacity of a ship, where $S_3 > S_2 > S_1$.

Figure 4.9 Diseconomies of ship size in port

that call at the port are expected to increase in size. There are two reasons for this occurrence. First, with an increase in a container port's ship cargo handling capacity, a larger containership will incur less time in port, thereby being able to spend more time at sea in order to take advantage of its economies of ship size at sea. Second, with an increase in cargo handling efficiency, a larger containership will incur less cost per container moved in port, since crane rental charges to the shipping line are usually by the hour and not by the number of containers moved. The lower cost per container moved in port from an increase in cargo handling efficiency can be shown graphically in Figure 4.9 by a shift in the unit cost curve to the right.[6]

Port choice and shipping lines

If a shipping line seeks to maximize profits, it will have been rational in including a port in its vessel transportation network if the revenue from this decision exceeds the cost. What are the factors that affect the revenue received and cost incurred by a shipping line's ship in the provision of service over a network? These factors may be described as determinants of a shipping line's port choice. One such factor is port consignment size, i.e., the amount of cargo to be loaded on ships. The larger the port consignment size, the greater the likelihood that a shipping line will have its ships call at a given port.

A shipping line's liner (scheduled service) pricing policy will also affect whether a port is included in a ship's transportation network. Equalization liner pricing is a port-to-port liner pricing scheme whereby the freight rate (or price) for cargo is the same from any main port in a port range (on one end of a ship's round-trip route) to any main port in a port range on the other end. If the shipper is responsible for inland transportation costs to and from ports, the shipper would minimize total transportation costs (ocean and inland) by having the cargo shipped to the port that is nearest to the shipper's location. Thus, equalization liner pricing results in natural hinterlands for ports, contributing to ships having multiport itineraries and the duplication of port calls on a round trip over a given network.

Absorption liner pricing is a door-to-door liner pricing scheme whereby shippers are charged a door-to-door rate independent of port choice. The rate is payment for ocean and inland transportation services. Absorption pricing dissipates the natural hinterlands of ports. Also, it shifts the port choice decision from the shipper to the shipping line. Under absorption pricing, the shipping line is responsible for obtaining land transportation carriers (e.g., truck and rail) for transportation of cargo to and from ports. In particular, the shipping line may use these carriers to transport cargo to and from one port in a range of ports. The port where cargo is concentrated is often referred to as a load-center port. A load-center port allows the shipping line to use relatively large ships to call at the port and thus to take advantage of ship cost economies of ship size at sea by calling at fewer ports.

The convexity ratio for ocean transportation is the ratio between maritime distance saved (or incurred) and inland distances thereby incurred (or saved) from a ship calling at a particular port. A ship call at a neighboring port may add little to the maritime distance of transported cargo, while perhaps achieving significant savings in inland distances, thereby increasing the likelihood that the ship will call at the neighboring port.

Shipping lines will seek to minimize the amount of time that larger ships are in port in order to take advantage of their ship cost economies of ship size at sea. Ports that can accommodate larger ships while maintaining fast ship turnaround times (i.e., time differences between ships entering and leaving a port) will likely see an increase in the number of calls by larger ships. Ports with relatively shallow water depths will likely experience a decline in ship calls over time as ships increase in size, conversely for ports with deep water depths.

If a port in a port range charges significantly lower port prices to shipping lines than another port in this port range, the greater is the likelihood that the former port will be chosen by shipping lines over the latter port in this port range. Also, if one port has superior inland transportation connections, existing port relationships (or a service history) with a given shipping line, and closer access to trade lanes, the given shipping line is more likely to choose this port over another port in a port range. If one port in a range of ports is subject to less port government regulation (e.g., economic, safety, and environmental regulation) than another port, the former will more likely be chosen as the port of call in this range than the latter, all else held constant.

Port calls may also be affected by mergers, acquisitions, and alliances in the shipping line industry. If a merger between two shipping lines occurs, a new shipping line is created consisting of the merged lines. If one shipping line acquires another through acquisition, the two shipping lines and their names will remain intact. The former line obtains ownership of the latter. Two or more shipping lines may also form an alliance to share ships. All three transactions – mergers, acquisitions, and alliances – may be undertaken to achieve lower unit costs through deployment of larger ships. If a shipping line that is involved in any one of these three transactions has dedicated marine terminals, the other lines involved in these transactions would be expected to shift their calls to these terminals and away from the common-user terminals (that were formerly used prior to the transactions) in a given port.

If the ownership of a port and/or its marine terminals changes, port calls by shipping lines may be affected. For example, a government-owned port may be privatized (i.e., sold to a private global terminal operator), resulting in an improvement in the quality of service provided and, in turn, an increase in port calls. Also, a former common-user marine terminal may be leased to a shipping line to become the line's dedicated terminal, therefore eliminating calls of ships at this terminal except for those of its own ships and those of the affiliated (via an alliance) shipping lines.[7]

Summary

A carrier is a firm that provides a transportation service, i.e., moving cargo and/or passengers from one location to another. The resources used by a carrier in the provision of a transportation service may generally be classified as (1) vehicles, (2) energy, (3) way, (4) labor, and (5) terminals. A carrier has a number of operating options with which to differentiate the quality of its service: (1) speed of movement, (2) frequency of service, (3) reliability of service, (4) spatial accessibility of service, and (5) susceptibility of cargo to loss or damage and passengers to fatal or nonfatal injuries. The most commonly used output measure for cargo carriers is the ton-mile (one ton of cargo moved one mile); for passenger carriers, it is the passenger-mile (one passenger moved one mile). However, these output units are not necessarily homogenous and thus their use can be problematic in costing transportation service.

A carrier's short-run total cost consists of fixed and variable costs. In the long run, all carrier costs are variable. A carrier exhibits economies (diseconomies) of scale when its long-run unit costs decline (rise) continuously as service expands. Economies of scope for a multiservice carrier exist in the long run if the carrier can provide its services of given amounts at less cost than if each service (at the same amount) were provided by single-service carriers.

The greater the degree of competition for carrier services, the less the control that carriers and the greater the control that the market will have in setting prices for these services.

Price discrimination occurs when a carrier sells the same service at different prices to users and the prices do not reflect cost differences, e.g., shippers of higher-valued cargo may be charged a higher price (or rate) than shippers of lower-valued cargo for transportation service between the same origin and destination locations. Regulated carriers in setting fully allocated cost prices (where prices are equal to unit costs) incur the problem of how to allocate shared costs to individual services.

In order for a port carrier service to occur, the carrier must be willing to have its vessels or vehicles to call at the port and the port must be willing to service these vessels and vehicles. If so, there will be two prices for the port carrier service, a money price and a time price to be paid and incurred, respectively, by the carrier.

Factors that affect a shipping line's port choice include, for example: consignment size; liner pricing policies; convexity ratios; ship time in port; port regulation; and mergers, acquisitions, and alliances in the shipping line industry. The efficiency of a port's ship cargo handling capacity can affect the size of ships that call at the port.

Notes

1 The relationship between the minimum amount of a given resource employed by a carrier and the levels of its operating options is the carrier's resource function for that resource. Also, the amounts and types of cargo and passengers to be transported by the carrier will also appear as independent variables in the resource function (Talley 1988).
2 The relationship between the maximum amount of service provided by a carrier and its levels of resources employed is the carrier's production function.
3 The relationship between the minimum costs incurred by a carrier in the provision of given levels of service is the carrier's cost function.
4 The responsiveness of the quantity demanded for transportation service by a shipper to changes in the price of this service may be measured by the shipper's price elasticity of freight transportation demand for this service, i.e., the ratio of the percentage change in quantity demanded for the service to a percentage change in the price of the service.
5 The responsiveness of the quantity demanded for transportation service by a passenger to changes in the price of this service may be measured by the passenger's price elasticity of passenger transportation demand for this service, i.e., the ratio of the percentage change in quantity demanded for the service to a percentage change in the price of the service.
6 A study by Sanchez *et al.* (2003) found that the maritime transportation costs between two ports decrease as the ports become more efficient in ship cargo handling. A study by Wilmsmeier *et al.* (2006) found an elasticity coefficient of -0.38, indicating that a 10 percent improvement in port efficiency in the handling of cargo for the ports is expected to reduce maritime transportation costs between the two ports by 3.8 percent.
7 See Lirn *et al.* (2004) and Guy and Urli (2006) for further discussion of port selection criteria by shipping lines.

Bibliography

Chadwin, M. L., Pope, J. A., and Talley, W. K. (1990) *Ocean Container Transportation: An Operational Perspective*, New York: Taylor & Francis.

Guy, E. and Urli, B. (2006) "Port Selection and Multi-Criteria Analysis: An Application to the Montreal-New York Alternative", *Maritime Economics and Logistics*, 8: 169–186.

Haralambides, H. E., Cariou, P., and Benacchio, M. (2002) "Costs, Benefits and Pricing of Dedicated Container Terminals", *International Journal of Maritime Economics*, 4: 21–34.

Kim, H. Y. (1987) "Economies of Scale and Scope in Multi-Product Firms: Evidence from U.S. Railroads", *Applied Economics*, 19: 733–741.

Leach, P. T. (2006) "Panama Canal Expansion Could Help New York-New Jersey, Virginia and Others Boost Share of Trans-Pacific Trade", *Journal of Commerce*, 7:12–15.

Lirn, T. C., Thanopoulou, H. A., and Beynon, M. J. (2004) "An Application of AHP on Transhipment Port Selection: A Global Perspective", *Maritime Economics and Logistics*, 6: 70–91.

Mongelluzzo, B. (2006) "East and Gulf Coast Ports Race the Clock as All-Water Services Escalate", *Journal of Commerce*, 7: 20, 22, 24–25.

Sanchez, R. J., Hoffmann, J., Micco, A., Pizzolitto, G. V., Sgut, M., and Wilmsmeier, G. (2003) "Port Efficiency and International Trade: Port Efficiency as a Determinant of Maritime Transport Costs", *Maritime Economics and Logistics*, 5: 199–218.

Talley, W. K. (1982) "Determining Fully Allocated Cost Prices for Regulated Transportation Industries", *International Journal of Transport Economics*, 9: 25–43.

—— (1983) *Introduction to Transportation*, Cincinnati, OH: South-Western Publishing Company.

—— (1988) *Transport Carrier Costing*, New York: Gordon and Breach Science Publishers.

—— (1989) "Joint Cost and Competitive Value-of-Service Pricing", *International Journal of Transport Economics*, 16: 119–130.

—— (1990) "Optimal Containership Size", *Maritime Policy and Management*, 17: 165–175.

—— (2001) "Costing Theory and Processes", in A. M. Brewer, K. J. Button, and D. A. Hensher (eds) *Handbook of Logistics and Supply-Chain Management*, Amsterdam: Elsevier, 313–323.

—— (2006) "An Economic Theory of the Port", in K. Cullinane and W. K. Talley (eds) *Port Economics: Research in Transportation Economics*, 16, Amsterdam: Elsevier, 43–65.

Wilmsmeier, G., Hoffmann, J., and Sanchez, R. J. (2006) "The Impact of Port Characteristics on International Maritime Transport Costs", in K. Cullinane and W. K. Talley (eds) *Port Economics: Research in Transportation Economics*, 16, Amsterdam: Elsevier, 117–140.

5 Shippers

Introduction

Shippers are business firms or persons that utilize carriers for the transportation of goods from origin to destination locations. The business firms or persons at the destination locations to whom the goods are delivered are the receivers (consignees) of these goods. Business shippers not only incur transportation costs in the carriage of their goods but also other costs that are related to this carriage – e.g., inventory, warehousing, order processing, production scheduling, materials handling, and packaging costs. The sum of these costs represents the business logistics costs incurred by the business firm in the carriage of its goods from origin to destination locations.

Business logistics management is the management of the integration of the business logistics activities of a firm, e.g., balancing production capacity against holding the finished product in inventory. Business logistics management generally does not consider the operating decisions of other firms, but rather is concerned with what happens within the firm's boundaries. Firms are assumed to make decisions that are independent of the decisions made by other firms, even though these decisions may affect the operations of other firms in a supply chain.

Supply chain management extends the focus of business logistics management by considering the decisions of other firms on a given firm's operations. The supply chain is both a system and a network. Supply chain management is the management of the complete process in the movement of raw materials to a firm's production sites and the movement of the firm's products from these sites to final users.

A shipper incurs two prices for a freight trip – the price paid to the carrier for transporting a shipment and a logistics price related to the shipment itself. A shipper also incurs two prices for a port service – the price paid to the port for providing the service and a logistics price related to the shipment itself while in port. The choice of ports by shippers is influenced by port money prices, port characteristics, and ship-schedule characteristics of ships that call at a port.

This chapter discusses shippers from the perspective of business logistics and supply chains. Transportation demand by shippers, shipper demand in port, port choice and shippers, and ports and supply chains are also discussed.

Business logistics management

In the 1970s there was interest in integrating a firm's supply and physical distribution activities. Physical supply activities are those associated with the movement of raw materials or products from suppliers' sites to a firm's production sites (plants). Physical distribution activities are those associated with the movement of the firm's finished products from its plants to its customers. Business logistics management is the management of the integration of these activities. It may also be defined as the coordination of a firm's physical supply and distribution activities so that the firm minimizes its costs while satisfying desired service levels for its customers. Business logistics managers manage the transportation, inventory, order processing, warehousing, production scheduling, materials handling, packaging, and location activities of the firm.

Transportation

The most important logistics activity for many business firms, not only in terms of cost but also in terms of service requirements, is transportation. No firm that produces a product can remain in operation without the availability of transportation – for the movement of products or raw materials to its plants and/or the movement of finished products from its plants to its customers. An efficiently managed business logistics system for a firm requires that the transportation activities of the firm be efficiently managed. However, the minimization of the firm's transportation costs in the movement of raw materials and products does not necessarily result in the minimization of the firm's total business logistics costs that are related to these movements.

Inventory

Firms whose inventory is too large may incur high carrying costs and potential obsolescence; too low an inventory may result in high restocking and production costs and the risk of lost sales. Inventory costs consist of stock-out and inventory carrying costs.

Stock-out costs occur when the supply of a firm's finished product is exhausted and the customer wishes to purchase the out-of-stock product. The amount of the firm's stock-out costs will depend upon whether the (1) sale is delayed, (2) the sale is lost, or (3) the customer is lost. Safety (or buffer) stocks of products are designed to prevent an excessive number of out-of-stock shortages of products.

A firm's inventory carrying costs consist of (1) storage costs for the space, e.g., in warehouses and storerooms, where the firm's inventory is stored; (2) obsolescence costs that arise when inventory gradually becomes out of date; (3) depreciation costs that are due to the deterioration of inventory related to time but not to usage; (4) insurance costs to protect inventory against theft, fire, flood, etc.; and (5) opportunity costs of the firm's money that is tied-up in inventory.[1]

A firm's inventory costs and the quality of its transportation service are negatively related (see Figure 5.1). As stated in Chapter 4, a transportation carrier has a number of operating options (e.g., speed of movement, frequency of service, and reliability of service) with which to differentiate the quality of its service. With faster deliveries and greater reliability in these deliveries, a firm will hold less inventory and thus incur less inventory carrying costs.

Order processing

From a shipper's perspective, order processing is the process of filling orders for its customers. This process affects the delivery time of the shipments to customers (or receivers). Delivery time, in turn, affects the inventory levels of both shippers and receivers. Order-processing costs include, for example, those related to document processing, credit checks, and managing information systems.

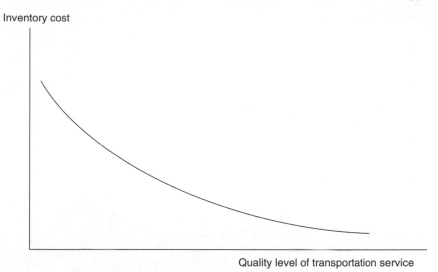

Figure 5.1 Inventory cost and the quality level of transportation service

If a shipper incurred no order processing costs, it would not maintain an inventory (aside from safety stocks); it simply would fill orders continually. Order processing costs tend to be minor in comparison to transportation and inventory costs. However, adherence to scheduled delivery times is often a critical factor for receivers of shipments.

Warehousing

A firm's warehousing logistics activity is the management of the space that holds its inventories. Warehouses consist of distribution and storage warehouses. Distribution warehouses assemble, mix, and segment products for shipment. Storage warehouses are used by firms with seasonal demand or supply patterns, thereby enabling these firms to avoid major peaks and lows in their production activities. Also, storage warehouses are used for the maturing or aging of products.

A major logistics decision that a shipper may face is to determine the number and the location of warehouses for minimizing its logistics costs. A firm's transportation costs will decrease as warehouses are added to its transportation network. Reductions in transportation costs result from consolidating volume shipments for long-haul trips from production sites to warehouses and then providing less-than-volume shipments for short-haul trips from warehouses to receivers. It is assumed (which is usually the case) that truckload and rail carload (or volume) shipments are charged lower transportation rates per ton of cargo shipped than less-than-truckload and less-than-carload (or less-than-volume) shipments per ton of cargo shipped.

In Figure 5.2 the transportation costs incurred by a shipper relative to its number of warehouses are presented. Transportation costs are those incurred by the shipper in transporting its product from production sites to customers. Initially, transportation costs decrease as the shipper's number of warehouses increase. The transportation cost savings from lower transportation rates in shipping volume shipments from production sites to warehouses exceed the transportation cost increases from higher transportation rates in shipping less-than-volume shipments from warehouses to customers.

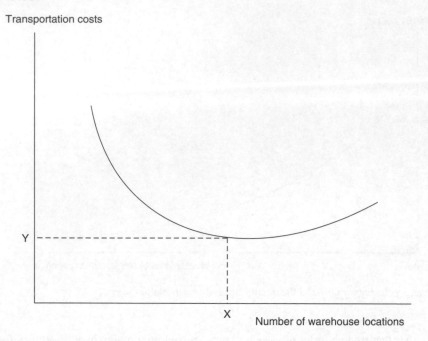

Figure 5.2 Transportation costs and the number of warehouse locations

At X number of warehouses in Figure 5.2, the shipper's transportation costs are minimized. Beyond this number of warehouses, transportation costs begin to increase with the addition of warehouses, since the number of volume shipments decreases and the number of less-than-volume shipments increases from production sites to warehouses. Specifically, the increase in transportation costs from the higher number of less-than-volume shipments exceeds the transportation cost savings from the lower number of volume shipments.

Production scheduling

Production scheduling for a shipper generates the following questions: What to produce? How much to produce? When to produce? It is not concerned with daily, detailed scheduling but rather with the overall level of production scheduling. The production scheduler coordinates production with other logistics activities of the firm – e.g., managing inventory, warehousing, and transportation – so that inventory shortages do not occur and warehouse space and transportation are available when needed.

Materials handling

Materials handling is the movement of raw materials and products to and from production sites and storage areas. Materials handling systems are either mechanized or automated. Mechanized systems utilize a combination of handling equipment and labor in the movement of raw materials and products. Examples of handling equipment include powered forklifts, conveyors, towlines, and trucks (for short- and long-distance movements). Automated systems require little or no labor (or physical handling) in the movement of the firm's raw materials and products.

Packaging

Shippers seek to transport undamaged products. Proper packaging of products helps to ensure that transported products remain damage-free. Government regulators of transportation modes may require that the cargo that they transport adhere to certain packaging requirements. One mode may have more restrictive packaging requirements than another mode. With the variance in packing requirements, expenses incurred by shippers in meeting these requirements will also vary. Hence, in selecting a transportation mode, a shipper must not only consider the cost of the mode's transportation service but also the cost in adhering to the mode's packaging requirements.

Location

The location of a firm's plants and warehouses has a direct effect on the shipper's transportation and inventory costs. The greater the distance between plants and warehouses and between warehouses and customers, the greater will be the distance for products to travel and thus greater the transportation costs to be incurred by the shipper. Assume that a customer does not take ownership of a shipped product until it is received. Hence, the product will remain in the shipper's inventory until it reaches the customer. Given the greater distance for transport and thus the greater length of time that the product will be in the shipper's inventory, the greater will be the shipper's inventory costs.

Plants and warehouses located in congested-transportation urban areas incur greater time in moving product from plants to warehouses and from warehouses to customers, thereby increasing the shipper's transportation and inventory costs. In the U.S., distribution warehouses are often found located near interstate highways in urban areas, thereby reducing the time of highway movement of products to and from these warehouses.

Supply chain management

Supply chain management is the integration of the activities of raw material suppliers, intermediate component product manufacturers, end-product manufacturers, warehouses, transportation carriers, ports (or terminals of transport carriers), end-product customers, and other stakeholders of the supply chain so that products and resources are distributed along the supply chain in order to minimize the chain's system-wide costs while satisfying customer service requirements. Supply chain management is an extension of business logistics management. While the latter is oriented toward the activities of a single firm (or shipper) in supplying products to customers, supply chain management is oriented toward the activities of the many firms that supply products to customers along a given supply chain.

The supply chain is not only a system of firms' activities but also a network. The raw materials of raw-material suppliers are transported directly to the plants of end-product manufacturers and/or to intermediate-component product manufacturers that use the raw materials to produce intermediate-component products that are, in turn, used by end-product manufacturers. The end-products are then shipped directly to customers or to warehouses of the end-product manufacturers from which they will eventually be shipped to customers.

A supply chain network

A simple supply chain network is presented in Figure 5.3, where end-products from an end-product manufacturer in country A are eventually shipped to a customer (e.g., a retail store)

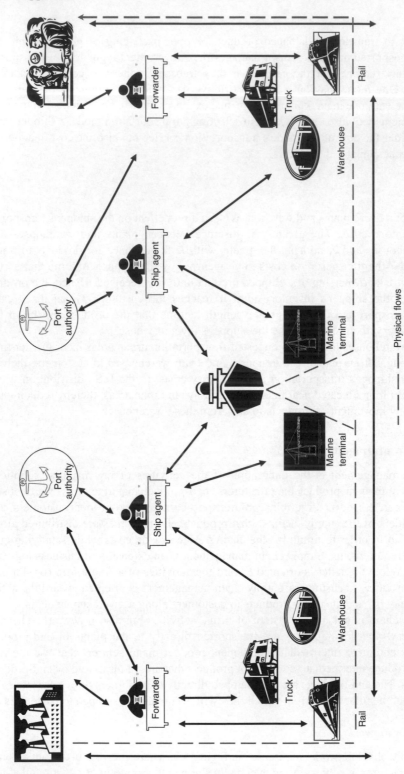

Figure 5.3 A supply chain network

in country B. Truck and rail carriers in country A transport end-products from the manufacturer directly to the port's marine terminal or to a warehouse, where they are transported at a later date by these carriers to the port's marine terminal. A freight forwarder and ship agent in country A represent the interests of the end-product manufacturer (or shipper) and the shipping line (whose ship will transport the end-products to country B), respectively, in the transportation of the end-products. The freight forwarder provides and receives information from the manufacturer, the truck and rail carriers, and the marine terminal's port authority. The ship agent provides and receives information from the warehouse, the port authority, the marine terminal, and the ship that is to transport the end-products to country B.

At the marine terminal of country B (the foreign country), the end-products arc unloaded from the ship and either transported directly to the customer or to a warehouse, where they will be transported at a later date to the customer by truck and rail carriers. A freight forwarder and ship agent in country B represent the interests of the customer (or consignee) and the shipping line (whose ship transported the end-products to country B), respectively. The freight forwarder provides and receives information from the customer, the truck and rail carriers, and the marine terminal's port authority. The ship agent provides and receives information from the warehouse, the port authority, the marine terminal, and the ship that transported the end-products to country B.

Supply chain activities

Supply chain management deals with a wide range of supply activities: (1) production, (2) purchasing, and (3) distribution (Schary and Skjott-Larsen 2001). Production is the transformation of raw materials and intermediate-component products into end-products. Supply chain production may have a push or a pull orientation. A push-orientation supply chain anticipates the demand by customers, i.e., production is based upon customer-demand forecasts that precede customer orders. Orders are filled from inventory; safety stock is used to manage demand variability. The lead time for push-orientation production is relatively long.

In a pull-orientation supply chain, production is initiated by customer orders. Products are customized – assemble-to-order, build-to-order, and make-to-order. Demand uncertainty is higher but lead time in production is significantly lower than in push-orientation supply chains. Furthermore, flexible capacity is used to manage demand variability.

Pull-orientation production is also referred to as just-in-time production, where a firm delays the final assembly of its products until customer orders are received. Pull-orientation (or just-in-time) production usually results in faster delivery times for products to customers and lower inventory levels for producers. Dell Inc. utilizes such a production system. Once Dell receives a computer order, it assembles the customer's computer from in-stock components and delivers the computer to the customer in just a few days. Thus, Dell can mass produce and deliver customized computers to its customers within a relatively short period of time.

Just-in-time production depends upon the quality of purchased components and production assembly processes. Hence, firms and supply chains that utilize such production systems often employ total quality management techniques to ensure quality compliance within their production facilities and from suppliers.

Purchasing is the act of a wholesaler or retailer firm purchasing product for resale or a manufacturing firm purchasing raw materials and intermediate-component products for conversion into an end-product. Purchasing is an important supply activity in supply chain management, since problems with suppliers of raw materials and intermediate-component products can have a negative effect on the quantity, quality, and price of end-products that are available to customers.

Supplier management is the means by which the purchasing firm is able to get its suppliers to adhere to its demands. A key element in supplier management is supplier evaluation – determining the capabilities of suppliers. Existing suppliers are periodically evaluated and potential suppliers are evaluated for future purchases. Over time, poor-performing suppliers may be dropped and relationships with the remaining top-performing suppliers may be strengthened. The purchasing firms will benefit from making larger purchases from the remaining suppliers, i.e., larger volumes per supplier typically result in lower cost per purchased unit to the purchaser. Also, better service (e.g., faster delivery time) is expected from top-performing suppliers. This strategic partnership will also benefit the suppliers, e.g., long-term, high-volume sales.

How many suppliers should a firm have? Closer relationships can be established between a manufacturing firm and a single or a few suppliers. However, by relying on a single supplier, the manufacturing firm increases its risk of the supplier not being able to satisfy its needs, e.g., in not providing enough raw materials so that the firm can satisfy a significant increase in consumer demand.

Distribution is the management of the flow of end-product from the manufacturer to the customer. Planning and cooperation are required among the end-product firms, their customers, and various logistics providers, e.g., transportation carriers and warehouse firms, so that end-products are delivered in the correct quantities, at the correct time, and to the correct locations.

In just-in-time production supply chains, in particular, transportation service is critical to their success. Several modes of transportation may be involved. Modal selection decisions will be based upon the trade-offs between the prices charged by the modes and the quality of the modes' services (e.g., speed of movement, reliability, and frequency of service).

Supply chain integration

When individual firms in the supply chain ignore the interests of other chain member firms, the chain's system-wide costs will be higher (resulting in higher end-product prices, thereby decreasing the quantity demanded for end-products) and the supply chain service levels will be lower (e.g., from increases in transportation waiting and travel times). Supply chain management recognizes the interdependent behavior among interdependent firms. In not recognizing such behavior, firms may duplicate their activities and not respond rapidly to changes, other than through price changes.

The supply chain will emerge when it provides solutions to the problems of duplication and responsiveness among interdependent firms. Supply chain integration occurs when interdependent firms realize that supply chain management must become part of their strategic planning processes in which their objectives are jointly determined. "Ultimately, firms act together to maximize total supply chain profits by determining optimal purchase quantities, product availabilities, service levels, lead times, production quantities, and technical and product support at each tier within the supply chain" (Wisner *et al.* 2005: 16).

The goal in managing a supply chain is to achieve sustainable competitive advantage for the supply chain by creating value for its members (Li 2007). However, difficulties may arise in attempting to do so. Actions in one part of the supply chain may affect the actions in other parts, thus making it difficult for supply chain managers to disentangle the cause and effect of their actions on the supply chain and consequently to optimize the supply chain system. Furthermore, chain members may have conflicting objectives and supply chain relationships may change over time. Also, chain members may be reluctant to share information and technologies in integrating the supply chain. Further, a firm may be a member of more than one supply chain.

Transportation demand by shippers

The demand for transportation service by shippers is a derived demand. Transportation is a means to an end and not an end in itself, i.e., there is no demand for transportation by shippers unless there is a demand for the product that is being transported. Transportation creates value to shippers by creating (1) place utility, i.e., moving product to a place where it can be consumed, and (2) time utility, i.e., the product arrives at the right time to be consumed.

Two parties must be in agreement for a freight transportation service to occur – the shipper must be willing to provide the product to be transported and a transportation carrier must be willing to transport the product. Consequently, the shipper incurs two prices for a freight trip where its product is transported by a carrier from origin A to destination B. The shipper pays a price (or rate) to the carrier for transporting the shipment. The shipper also pays a price related to the product being shipped, i.e., the shipment itself. If the shipper retains ownership of the shipment, the shipper will incur logistics costs (e.g., inventory carrying costs such as obsolescence, depreciation, and insurance costs) for the shipment while it is in transit. These logistics costs represent the shipper's logistics price for the freight trip. The sum of the rate and the logistics price is the full (or total) price for the freight trip to be incurred by the shipper.

When logistics costs include only inventory costs, the logistics price for a freight trip has been referred to as the shipper's inventory price (Talley 1983: 105). The inventory price for a freight trip will depend upon the levels of the carrier's operating options (see Chapter 4) and the value of the shipment. The greater the carrier's quality of service, the lower will be the shipper's inventory price for the freight trip. For example, the greater the carrier's speed of movement, the less time the shipment will be in transit and thus the lower the shipper's in-transit inventory costs will be with respect to the shipment. When carrier service is more reliable and less susceptible to cargo damage, the shipper will also incur lower inventory costs from maintaining a lower level of inventory. The value of the shipment affects the inventory price for a freight trip, since inventory costs such as inventory depreciation and insurance costs are positively related to this value, i.e., the higher the value of the shipment, the higher the inventory price for the freight trip, all else held constant.

In Figure 5.4, the full or total price, $P_{FS} = P_R + P_I$, for a freight trip appears on the vertical axis, where P_R is the carrier's rate and P_I is the shipper's inventory price for the freight trip. The number of freight trips for a shipper from origin A to destination B for a given time period appears on the horizontal axis. For the sake of simplicity, it is assumed that the shipper transports a homogenous shipment in each freight trip. The number of freight trips demanded by the shipper at various full prices is represented by the shipper's derived demand curve D_{FS}. At lower full prices, a greater number of freight trips will be demanded, and conversely for higher full prices. At full price P^*_{FS}, Q^*_{FS} freight trips are demanded by the shipper.

A carrier is generally expected to incur greater costs from improving the quality of its service and thus charges a higher price (or rate). However, if the decline in the shipper's inventory price (from the improvement in the quality of service) more than offsets the increase in the carrier's price, the full price for the freight trip to the shipper will be lower. This explains why a shipper may demand transportation service from a carrier that charges a higher rate but provides a higher quality of service as opposed to a carrier that charges a lower rate and provides a lower quality of service.

Greater insight into the demand for a freight trip is gained with the help of Figure 5.5. The right-hand side has the same horizontal axis as in Figure 5.4. The left-hand-side has the delivery time (in hours) for a freight shipment on its horizontal axis. Delivery time is the time interval between the pickup of the shipment at origin A and delivery at destination B. The inventory

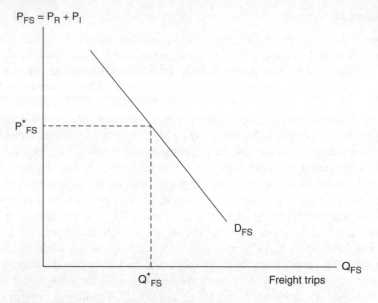

Figure 5.4 Shipper transportation demand at full prices

price per trip for the shipper is the product of the in-transit inventory costs per unit of delivery time (C_I) and delivery time (T), i.e., $P_I = C_I*T$. In Figure 5.5, the inventory price P_I and the rate per freight trip P_R are plotted on the common vertical axis. The vertical sum of the two prices is the full price $P_{FS} = P_R + P_I$ per trip (as found in Figure 5.4).

Assume that the delivery time of a freight trip is OA hours. The slope of line $AP*_I$ is C_I. If the delivery time of the trip increases to OA' and C_I remains constant, there will be a parallel shift to the left of line $AP*_I$, i.e., to line $A'P'_I$, thereby increasing the trip's inventory price (from $P*_I$ to P'_I) and the trip's full price (from $P*_{FS}$ to P'_{FS}). If the in-transit inventory cost C_I

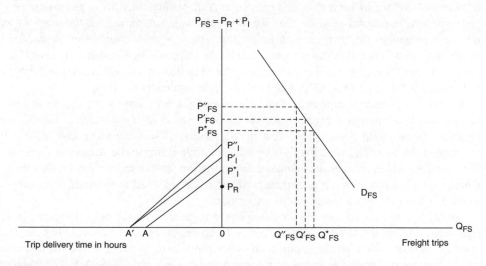

Figure 5.5 Full price, delivery time, and shipper transportation demand

increases to C''_I and delivery time remains constant at OA', the trip's inventory price will increase from P'_I to P''_I and the trip's full price will increase from P'_{FS} to P''_{FS}. If these prices are for different carriers (as opposed to price changes for the same carrier), the carrier with the lower full price will be selected over the carrier with the higher full price by the shipper.

Shipper demand in port

In order for a port shipper service (i.e., a service to a shipper in port) to occur, the shipper or its agent must be willing to provide cargo to the port and the port must be willing to service this cargo. If so, there will be two prices for the port shipper service, a money price to be paid by the shipper or its agent and a time price to be incurred by the shipper (Talley 2006). The money price for the service is the money price (per unit of service) charged by the port for the service. The time price for the service is the time price (per unit of service) incurred by the shipper's cargo that was involved in the provision of the port shipper service. Specifically, the time price is found by multiplying the cargo's value or cost of time per unit of time in port and the time that the cargo was involved in the provision of the port shipper service. An example of cargo time cost is the inventory cost incurred by the cargo while in port. An example of a port shipper service is the stripping and stuffing (from and to) of a container of the shipper's cargo.

In Chapter 2 the shipper demand for a port service was considered only from the perspective of the money price for the port service (see Figure 2.2). The shipper demand for a port service from the perspective of the full price for this service appears in Figure 5.6, where the full price is the sum of the money price and the shipper time price for the port shipper service. Specifically, the shipper demand for a port service with respect to the full price is represented by the demand curve D_{FSH}. At lower full prices, more port service is demanded by shippers and less service at higher prices, other things remaining the same. The full price is $P_{FSH} = P_{SH} + P_{TSH}$, where P_{SH} is the port money price for the port shipper service and P_{TSH} is the time price to be incurred by the shipper's cargo in the provision of the port shipper service.

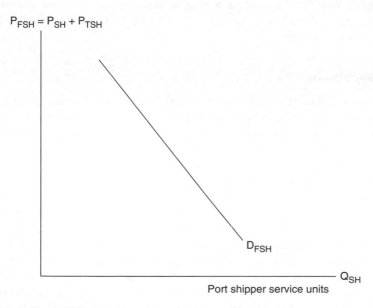

Figure 5.6 Shipper demand for port services at full prices

Port choice and shippers

The choice of ports by shippers is influenced by port money prices, port characteristics, and ship-schedule characteristics of ships that call at a port. It is assumed that shipping lines charge port-to-port rates in transporting cargo to and from ports (see Chapter 4). The higher the money prices that are charged to a shipper by the port, the less likely the port will be chosen by this shipper. Time prices incurred by a shipper at a port are affected by port and ship-schedule characteristics.

Port characteristics that are likely to be important to a shipper in choosing a port through which to ship its export cargo include (1) the distance between the origin inland location of the cargo and the location of the port (the greater this distance and thus the higher the expected logistics price for the freight trip to the port, the less likely the port will be chosen); (2) the oceanic or water distance from the port to the cargo's destination port (the greater this distance and the higher expected logistics price for the freight trip, the less likely the port will be chosen); and (3) the time that cargo remains in port (the longer the time in port and thus the higher expected port time for the cargo, the less likely the port will be chosen). Thus, shippers are generally expected to choose nearby ports with respect to both the origins and destinations of cargoes.

Ship-schedule characteristics at a port that are likely to be important to a shipper in choosing an origin port through which to ship its export cargo include (1) the frequency of ship calls (greater the frequency and the expected lower port time price, the more likely the port will be chosen) and (2) the number of destination ports served by ships calling at the port, i.e., the greater the spatial accessibility of the port, the more likely it will be chosen.

The location that a port has in a ship's schedule along a given range of ports is also an important ship-schedule characteristic of the port to a shipper. A shipper of discretionary cargo (cargo originating in a region that does not contain a port or is not located in a port's hinterland) can reduce ship transit time to a destination port by having its cargo shipped through the last port of call by a ship in a given range of ports.

Port choice decisions for import cargo are similar to those for export cargo, except in regard to storage space. Importers have a stronger preference than exporters for ports that have distribution warehouses nearby.

Port choice and supply chains

Traditionally, the focus of ports has been to increase their throughput of cargo and/or passengers in providing services to their users. Consequently, port performance evaluation has been based on how well (e.g., in terms of quality of service) ports provide throughput. Today, it is clear that ports, in particular container ports, are important links in supply chains. In this role, container ports are part of a group of organizations that bring value to end consumers by coordinating the activities of supply chains.

In a competitive environment, ports not only compete on the basis of operational efficiency and location, but also on the basis of the fact that they are embedded in the supply chains of shippers (Robinson 2002). For example, consider an exporting firm in country X that plans to ship cargo to an importing firm in country Y. The exporting firm in country X has the option of shipping cargo through three possible ports, A, B, and C, to port D in country Y, and then having the cargo transported from this port to the importing firm (see Figure 5.7). The exporting firm has a choice of routes and inland transportation, e.g., truck and rail, carriers that link it to the three exporting ports; shipping lines that link each of these ports

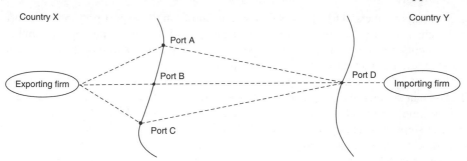

Figure 5.7 Shipper supply chains

to importing port D in country Y; and routes and inland transportation carriers that link the importing port to the importing firm – thus generating a number of possible supply chains over which the cargo may move.

The particular supply chain that is chosen by the shipper or its representative (e.g., a freight forwarder and a third-party logistics provider) may be that supply chain for which shipments incur the least logistics costs, e.g., transportation and inventory costs. The selected supply chain may also provide greater competitive advantage to the shipper, not only in terms of lower logistics costs, but also in terms of enhancing its market value, e.g., by allowing the shipper to differentiate itself from its competitors and thereby increasing sales. Improvements in the supply chain management operations of the shipper also give the port (as a member of the chain) a competitive advantage. A port's competitive advantage is a derived advantage, e.g., derived from the advantage created for shippers.

Port choice is also a derived choice from the choice of supply chains by shippers, shipper representatives, shipping lines, and others (Magala and Sammons 2008). That is to say, if the decisions of many parties, e.g., shippers and shipping lines, determine the choice of a supply chain that contains a port, it therefore follows that the port choice is a supply chain port choice as opposed to a shipper port choice or a shipping-line port choice (see Chapter 4).

Ports can add value to supply chains by (1) sharing information with upstream and downstream supply chain partners, (2) undertaking long-term planning with supply chain partners, e.g., shipping lines, inland transportation carriers, and shippers, (3) providing the flexibility to accommodate changes in the needs of port users, e.g., to launch new tailored services, and (4) planning and organizing activities beyond their boundaries that improve the performance of the supply chain as a whole (Panayides and Song 2006). Firms involved in demand-pull chains will have a low tolerance to value-eroding port activities and port inefficiency. "Port planning simply on the basis of freight volumes or cargo tonnages (which is essentially the current practice) is likely to be much less adequate in planning which has an understanding of the dynamics of chain structures and the way component firms do business in port-oriented supply chains" (Robinson 2008: 11).

Supply chain shipping capacity

The shipping capacity of a supply chain in Figure 5.7 may be described in terms of the chain's port-to-port shipping capacity and network shipping capacity (Staff 2006). In the shipment of containers, the port-to-port shipping capacity of a given chain is the maximum number of containers (TEUs) that shippers can ship from the export port to the import port of the chain for a given time period. This capacity will be determined by the number and size of containerships that call at the exporting port, the cruise speed of the containerships, and ship turnaround times at the exporting port.

The network shipping capacity of a given chain is the maximum number of containers (TEUs) that shippers can ship from their export sites to their consignee sites in the chain for a given time period. This capacity will be constrained by the chain's link or node with the smallest shipping capacity. The network links of a chain in Figure 5.7 consist of the port-to-port (water) link (e.g., port A to port D), the exporter inland link (e.g., exporter site to port A) and the importer inland link (e.g., port D to the importer site). The nodes in the chain are the ports (e.g., ports A and D). If the flow of containers over the links and through the ports of the chain is inefficient, then this flow of containers will be less than the chain's network shipping capacity. The network shipping capacity for a given chain will be determined by the port-to-port shipping capacity of the chain, the number and size of inland carriers utilized in the network, the cruise speed of these carriers, and their turnaround times at the exporting and importing ports.

Summary

In addition to incurring transportation costs in the carriage of their cargo, shippers also incur various logistics costs related to this carriage – e.g., inventory and warehousing costs. Business logistics management is the management of the integration of the business logistics activities of a firm. Supply chain management extends the latter by considering the decisions of other firms on a given firm's operations. Supply chain management is the management of the complete process in the movement of products and raw materials to a firm's production sites and the movement of the firm's products from these sites to end-customers. The supply chain is both a network and a system. The goal of supply chain management is to achieve sustainable competitive advantage for the supply chain by creating value for its members.

A shipper incurs two prices for a freight trip – the price paid to the carrier for transporting a shipment and a logistics price related to the shipment itself. The latter arises because the shipper incurs logistics costs (e.g., inventory carrying costs) for the shipment while it is in transit. A shipper also incurs two prices for a port shipper service – the price paid to the port for providing the service and a time price related to the shipment itself while in port.

The choice of ports by shippers is influenced by port money prices, port characteristics, and ship-schedule characteristics of ships that call at a port. In a competitive environment, ports not only compete on the basis of operational efficiency and location, but also on the basis of the fact that they are embedded in the supply chains of shippers. The chosen supply chain by a shipper may be that supply chain with the least logistics costs while enhancing the shipper's market value. If the choice of a port is derived from the choice of a supply chain, then the port choice is a supply chain port choice. The shipping capacity of a supply chain that contains a port may be described in terms of the chain's port-to-port shipping capacity and network shipping capacity.

Note

1 The interest rate that is often used in determining this cost is the interest rate that the firm would be charged in borrowing from a financial institution.

Bibliography

Bichou, K. and Gray, R. (2004) "A Logistics and Supply Chain Management Approach to Port Performance Measurement", *Maritime Policy and Management*, 31: 47–67.

Carbone, V. and de Martino, M. (2003) "The Changing Role of Ports in Supply-Chain Management: An Empirical Analysis", *Maritime Policy and Management*, 30: 305–320.

Henesey, L. E. (2006) *Multi-Agent Systems for Container Terminal Management*, Karlskrona, Sweden: Blekinge Institute of Technology.

Lam, J. S. L. (2006) "Managing Container Shipping Supply Chains", a paper presented at the 2006 International Association of Maritime Economists Conference, Melbourne, Australia.

Li, L. (2007) *Supply Chain Management: Concepts, Techniques and Practices – Enhancing Value through Collaboration*, Hackensack, NJ: World Scientific Publishing Company.

Magala, M. and Sammons, A. (2008) "A New Approach to Port Choice Modelling", *Maritime Economics and Logistics*, 10: 9–34.

Malchow, M. B. and Kanafani, A. (2001) "A Disaggregate Analysis of Factors Influencing a Port's Attractiveness", *Maritime Policy and Management*, 28: 361–373.

—— (2004) "A Disaggregate Analysis of Port Selection", in M. G. Kuvussanos and W. K. Talley (eds) *Shipping Finance and Port Issues*, a special issue of the journal, *Transportation Research Part E: Logistics and Transportation Review*, 40: 317–337.

Nir, A.-S., Lin, K., and Liang, G.-S. (2003) "Port Choice Behaviour – From the Perspective of the Shipper", *Maritime Policy and Management*, 30: 165–173.

Notteboom, T. and Rodrigue, J.-P. (2008) "Containerization, Box Logistics and Global Supply Chains: The Integration of Ports and Liner Shipping Networks", *Maritime Economics and Logistics*, 10: 152–174.

Panayides, P. M. (2006) "Maritime Logistics and Global Supply Chains: Towards a Research Agenda", *Maritime Economics and Logistics*, 8: 3–18.

—— (2007) "Global Supply Chain Integration and Competitiveness of Port Terminals", in J. Wang, D. Olivier, T. Notteboom, and B. Slack (eds) *Ports, Cities and Global Supply Chains*, Aldershot, UK: Ashgate, 27–39.

—— and Song, D.-W. (2006) "Port Supply Chain Orientation and Performance", a paper presented at the 2006 International Association of Maritime Economists Conference, Melbourne, Australia.

Pope, J. and Talley, W. K. (1988) "Inventory Costs and Optimal Ship Size", *Logistics and Transportation Review*, 24: 107–120.

Robinson, R. (2002) "Ports as Elements in Value-Driven Chain Systems: The New Paradigm", *Maritime Policy and Management*, 29: 241–255.

—— (2006) "Regulating Efficiency into Port-Oriented Chain Systems: Export Coal through the Dalrymple Bay Terminal, Australia", a paper presented at the 2006 International Association of Maritime Economists Conference, Melbourne, Australia.

—— (2008) "Efficient Ports in Efficient Supply Chains: New Strategic Perspectives", a paper presented at the 2008 International Conference on Shipping, Port and Logistics Management, Kainan University, Taiwan.

Schary, P. B. and Skjott-Larsen, T. (2001) *Managing the Global Supply Chain*, Copenhagen, Denmark: Copenhagen Business School Press.

Staff (2006) "Containerized Trade Ocean Forecast", *American Shipper*, 48, July: 39–42, 44, 46.

Talley, W. K. (1983) *Introduction to Transportation*, Cincinnati, OH: South-Western Publishing Company.

—— (1996). "Determinants of Cargo Damage Risk and Severity: The Case of Containership Accidents", *Logistics and Transportation Review*, 32: 377–388.

—— (2006) "An Economic Theory of the Port", in K. Cullinane and W. K. Talley (eds) *Port Economics: Research in Transportation Economics*, 16, Amsterdam: Elsevier, 43–65.

Tiwari, P., Itoh, H., and Doi, M. (2003) "Shipper's Port and Carrier Selection Behaviour in China: A Discrete Choice Analysis", *Maritime Economics and Logistics*, 5: 23–39.

Wang, J. and Olivier, D. (2007) "Chinese Port-Cities in Global Supply Chains", in J. Wang, D. Olivier, T. Notteboom, and B. Slack (eds) *Ports, Cities and Global Supply Chains*, Aldershot, UK: Ashgate, 173–186,

Wisner, J. D., Leon, G. K., and Tan, K.-C. (2005) *Principles of Supply Chain Management: A Balanced Approach*, Mason, OH: Thomson-Southwestern.

6   Passengers

Introduction

In 2005, 14 million passengers worldwide sailed on cruise passenger vessels (Staff 2006a). The worldwide growth in cruise passengers in the foreseeable future is expected to be 9 percent per year (Speares 2005); worldwide cruise vessel capacity is expected to increase 75 percent by 2015 (Staff 2006b). In North America the annual cruise passenger growth was 8.2 percent for the years 1980–2004, increasing from 1.4 million passengers in 1980 to 9.1 million passengers in 2004 (Cruise Lines International Association 2005).

In the U.S., 134 million passengers travel annually on ferry vessels (Stoller 1999). Ferry vessels may transport passengers or individuals and their vehicles (autos and trucks). Ferries that transport vehicles are roll on-roll off ferries. For ferries that transport passengers, 60 percent have a passenger-carrying capacity of 200 passengers or fewer; 16 percent have a capacity of over 500 passengers (Wieriman 2003).

Public interest in expanding existing or starting new ferry services in coastal urban regions has increased in countries where there is significant highway congestion at bridges and tunnels and the construction of the new bridges and tunnels has become increasingly cost-prohibitive or politically infeasible (Corbett and Farrell 2002). Ferry service is a less costly alternative to bridge and tunnel construction for adding urban water-crossing capacity. Also, ferry service is able to be more time responsive to increases in transport demand than fixed crossings. Specifically, it takes less time to add ferry service to meet increases in transport demand than to add bridge and tunnel capacity.

The interest in expanding ferry services has also been spurred by the deployment of high-speed (exceeding 30 knots) ferries, known technically as high-speed craft (HSC). The HSC come in a variety of shapes and sizes from small hovercraft to large HSC that can carry the same number of passengers and vehicles as a conventional ferry. The hovercraft is supported by a cushion of air, having boundaries defined by the rubber skirt in which the craft sits. Lift is provided by a fan system that blows air into the cushion, and propulsion is provided by engines. The catamaran is the most commonly used HSC by passenger ferry operators. A catamaran is a twin-hull vessel with slender hulls or pontoons. Its advantage is its stability – it is not as susceptible to adverse sea conditions as single-hull HSC.

This chapter discusses the transportation demand by passengers in general, the demand by ferry passengers in particular, and transportation choice by ferry passengers. In addition, passenger demand in port and port choice by passengers are discussed.

Passenger time prices

As for a freight transportation trip, two parties must be in agreement in order for a passenger transportation trip to occur. For a passenger trip an individual must be willing to provide himself or herself as a passenger to be transported and a transportation carrier must be willing to transport the individual as a passenger. Consequently, an individual incurs two prices for a passenger trip when he or she is transported by a carrier from origin A to destination B. The individual pays a price or fare (P_E) to the carrier for the transportation service provided. The individual also incurs a price related to himself or herself. That is to say, while in transit, an individual incurs an opportunity cost – the cost of an opportunity foregone while in transit (e.g., income that could have been earned if the time had been spent at work). In addition to opportunity cost, the individual may also benefit from the in-transit time (e.g., from the sights seen while in transit).

The price incurred by a passenger for a passenger trip that is related to his or her time incurred in taking the trip is the passenger's time price for the trip. A passenger's time price (P_T) for a passenger trip is the product of the individual's value of time per unit of time for the passenger trip (V) and the elapsed time of the trip (T), i.e., $P_T = V*T$. The elapsed time of a passenger trip is the total time incurred by an individual in taking the trip – i.e., the difference between the arrival time at the final destination and the starting time at the origin of the trip. An individual's value of time (V) per unit of time for a passenger trip is the individual's opportunity cost (K) minus his or her money equivalent of the direct level of satisfaction (S) per unit of time for the trip, i.e., $V = K - S$. The opportunity cost K is often measured by the passenger's wage rate per unit of time, i.e., the opportunity cost of non-work time is the wage forgone in not being at work.

The greater the passenger's opportunity cost of time, the greater will be his or her value of time per unit of time for a passenger trip and thus the greater the time price for the trip, all else held constant. Alternatively, a negative relationship exists between a passenger's value of time and the satisfaction received from the passenger trip. Thus, the greater the satisfaction received from a passenger trip, the lower will be the passenger's value of time per unit of time for the trip and thus the lower the time price for the trip.

The elapsed time for a passenger trip (T) includes walking, waiting, and vehicle (or vessel) in-transit time. Walking time (T_l) is that time incurred by an individual in taking a passenger trip for which he or she must walk in order for the passenger trip to occur, e.g., walking from one's front (home) door to one's automobile for an automobile trip or walking in a cruise marine terminal to reach the cruise vessel's berthing gate. Waiting time (T_a) is that time incurred by an individual in taking a passenger trip for which he or she must wait in order for the passenger trip to occur, e.g., waiting at a cruise or a ferry marine terminal to board a cruise or ferry vessel. Vehicle (or vessel) in-transit time (T_t) is the travel time incurred by an individual while onboard a vehicle (or vessel), e.g., a ferry vessel. The elapsed time for a passenger trip is thus $T = T_l + T_a + T_t$. Hence, an individual's time price P_T for a passenger trip may be expressed as the sum of his walking time price (P_{Tl}), waiting time price (P_{Ta}), and vehicle in-transit time price (P_{Tt}) for the passenger trip, i.e., $P_T = P_{Tl} + P_{Ta} + P_{Tt}$, where $P_{Tl} = V_l*T_l$, $P_{Ta} = V_a*T_a$, and $P_{Tt} = V_t*T_t$, and V_l, V_a, and V_t are the values of time per unit of time for the passenger trip related to walking, waiting, and vehicle in-transit times, respectively.

A passenger's hourly value of time (V) is a fraction of his or her hourly wage rate if $S > 0$. This fraction ranges from 25 percent for low-income individuals to approximately 50 percent for middle- and upper-income individuals (Talley 1983). A passenger's walking (V_l) and waiting (V_a) values of time per unit of time, range from two to three times greater than his or her vehicle in-transit value of time (V_t) per unit of time, due to the discomfort associated with these times (Talley 1983).

Transportation demand by ferry passengers

As for freight transportation, the demand for transportation service by passengers is also a derived demand. Transportation creates value to passengers by transporting them to places where they desire to be (e.g., restaurants, work, and home) and at the time desired, thereby, creating place and time utilities.

In Figure 6.1, the full price, $P_{FP} = P_E + P_T$, for a ferry passenger trip appears on the vertical axis. The number of ferry passenger trips for a passenger from origin A to destination B for a given time period appears on the horizontal axis. The number of ferry passenger trips demanded by an individual at various full prices is represented by the individual's derived demand curve D_{FP}. At lower full prices, a greater number of ferry passenger trips will be demanded; at higher full prices, a smaller number of ferry passenger trips will be demanded. At the full price P^*_{FP}, Q^*_{FP} ferry passenger trips will be demanded by the individual.

Greater insight into the demand for a ferry passenger trip by an individual is gained with the help of Figure 6.2. The right-hand side is the same as in Figure 6.1. The left-hand side has the trip times (in hours) incurred by a ferry passenger trip on the horizontal axis. The times T^*_l, T^*_a, and T^*_t in Figure 6.2 represent the walking, waiting, and vessel in-transit times incurred by an individual in taking a ferry passenger trip. The time prices for the trip incurred by the passenger that correspond to these times are P^*_{Tl}, P^*_{Ta}, and P^*_{Tt}, respectively. Thus, $P^*_T = P^*_{Tl} + P^*_{Ta} + P^*_{Tt}$. The slopes of the lines $T^*_l\,P^*_{Tl}$, $T^*_a P^*_{Ta}$, and $T^*_t\,P^*_{Tt}$ in Figure 6.2 are the passenger's values of time per unit of time V^*_l, V^*_a, and V^*_t (not shown in Figure 6.2) for the walking, waiting, and vehicle in-transit times, respectively, for a ferry passenger trip. The ferry fare charged by the ferry carrier for the passenger trip in transporting the passenger is the price P^*_E. The full price for the ferry passenger trip is thus $P^*_{FP} = P^*_E + P^*_{Tl} + P^*_{Ta} + P^*_{Tt}$ at which Q^*_{FP} ferry passenger trips will be demanded by the individual.,

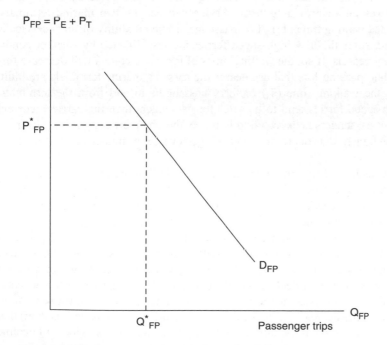

Figure 6.1 Passenger transportation demand at full prices

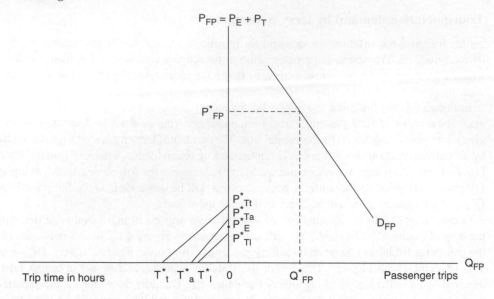

Figure 6.2 Full price, trip time, and passenger transportation demand

Suppose the ferry carrier improves the quality of its service by increasing the speed of movement of its ferry service between its two marine terminals by replacing its current ferry vessel fleet with high-speed ferry vessels, thereby decreasing the vessel in-transit time (T_t) of its passengers. Also, the carrier increases its frequency of its service by employing a greater number of vessels in providing ferry service between its two marine terminals, thereby decreasing the waiting time (T_a) of its passengers. The reliability of ferry service is expected to improve, since the new high-speed ferries are less affected by weather conditions than the current vessels. If so, the waiting times of ferry passengers will decrease further. Also, automobile parking lots that are nearer the carrier's marine terminals are built, thereby decreasing the walking time (T_l) of ferry passengers to and from the terminals. Since the new high-speed ferries tend to be safer for passengers than the carrier's current vessels, the safety of passengers is expected to improve, thereby increasing ferry passenger satisfaction while in transit, thus decreasing a passenger's vessel in-transit value of time per unit of time (V_t).

In contrast to the decline in walking, waiting, and vehicle in-transit times for ferry passenger trips, the fare charged by the ferry carrier is expected to increase. This expectation is due to the fact that the ferry carrier will have experienced higher costs from the purchase of high-speed ferry vessels and in the construction of new automobile parking lots.

The decreases in the walking, waiting, and vessel in-transit times and vessel in-transit value of time per unit of time of ferry passengers will result in decreases in ferry passenger walking, waiting, and vessel in-transit time prices for ferry vessel service. However, whether the full price for ferry service will decline will depend upon the magnitude of the decrease in the sum of the time prices versus the increase in the magnitude of the fare for ferry service. If the magnitude of the decrease in the sum of the time prices exceeds (is less than) that of the increase in the magnitude of the fare, then the full price for ferry service will decline (increase).

Transportation choice and ferry passengers

Suppose an individual has two ferry carriers from which to choose for passenger trips from origin A to destination B. The transportation service of one carrier is slower than that of the other carrier. Further, the fare price of the "slow carrier" is less than that of the "fast carrier." Other than speed of movement, the levels of the operating options of both carriers are assumed to be the same. What impact will passenger income have on which service, that of the "slow carrier" or that of the "fast carrier," will be chosen? Figure 6.3 is used to provide an answer to this question.

Figure 6.3 is similar to Figure 6.2 except that the trip time (T) horizontal axis in Figure 6.2 is replaced in Figure 6.3 with the value of passenger in-transit time per unit of time (V_t) horizontal axis. In order to simplify the discussion, the vertical axis in Figure 6.3 is represented by $P_{FP} = P_E + P_{Tt}$, i.e., only the time price P_{Tt} is considered. As the individual's income increases, his or her value of passenger in-transit time per unit of time V_t in taking a ferry passenger trip will also increase, since the opportunity cost component of V_t is increasing. The vessel in-transit time for the "slow carrier" is T_{ts} and T_{tf} for the "fast carrier," where $T_{ts} > T_{tf}$. The slope of line sP_{Es} is T_{ts} and the slope of line fP_{Ef} is T_{tf}. The fare for the "slow carrier" is P_{Es} and P_{Ef} for the "fast carrier," where $P_{Es} < P_{Ef}$. The demand for ferry passenger trips provided by the "slow carrier" is represented by the individual's derived demand curve D_{FPs}. The demand for ferry passenger trips provided by the "fast carrier" is represented by the individual's derived demand curve D_{FPf}.

Note that at a relatively low value of passenger in-transit time per unit of time such as V_{t1} (in Figure 6.3), reflecting low income, the individual will choose the transport service of the "slow carrier" and pay the full price $P_{FPs1} = P_{Es} + P_{Tts1}$, where $P_{Tts1} = V_{t1}*T_{ts}$. If the individual's level of income increases so that his or her value of passenger in-transit time per unit of time is now V_{t2}, the individual will be indifferent between using the "slow carrier" or the "fast carrier" in taking a ferry passenger trip from origin A to destination B. At the value of time V_{t2}

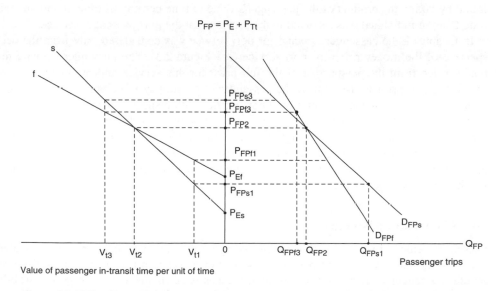

Figure 6.3 Full price, value of passenger in-transit time, and passenger transportation demand

the individual will pay the same full price for the ferry passenger trip whether it is provided by the "slow carrier" or the "fast carrier." If the individual's level of income increases even further so that his or her value of passenger in-transit time per unit of time is now V_{t3}, the individual will choose the transportation service of the "fast carrier" and pay the full price of $P_{FPf3} = P_{Ef} + P_{Ttf3}$, where $P_{Ttf3} = V_{t3} * T_{tf}$.

Note that at the full price of P_{FPs1} the individual will demand Q_{FPs1} ferry passenger trips to be provided by the "slow carrier." At the full price of P_{FP2} the individual will be indifferent between using the "slow carrier" and "fast carrier," which is revealed by the intersection of the demand curves at this price. At the full price of P_{FPf3} the individual will demand Q_{FPf3} ferry passenger trips to be provided by the "fast carrier."

Rather than using the value of passenger in-transit time per unit of time V_t in Figure 6.3, the value of passenger walking time per unit of time V_l or the value of passenger waiting time per unit of time V_a could have also been used. If there are differences in an individual's walking or waiting times related to the transportation service provided by the two ferry carriers, similar results would follow for walking and waiting values of time as an individual's income increases. Thus, the discussion reveals that higher income individuals are likely to choose less time intensive and higher fare transportation service. Conversely, lower income individuals are likely to choose more time intensive and lower fare transportation service.

Passenger demand in port

In order for a port passenger service to occur (i.e., a service provided by a port to a passenger), an individual must be willing to provide himself or herself as a passenger at the port and the port must be willing to provide passenger service to this individual. If so, there will be two prices for the port passenger service, a port money price to be paid by the individual to the port and a port time price to be incurred by the individual as a port passenger. The port money price is the price (per unit of service) charged by the port for the service. The port time price is the time price (per unit of service) incurred by the individual that was involved in the provision of the port passenger service. Specifically, the port time price is found by taking the product of the passenger's value of time per unit of time in port and the time that the individual was involved in the provision of the port passenger service.

In Chapter 2 the passenger demand for port service was considered only from the perspective of the money price for port service (see Figure 2.3). The passenger demand for port service from the perspective of the full price for this service appears in Figure 6.4, where the full price is the sum of the passenger's port money price and port time price. Specifically, the passenger demand for a port service with respect to the full price is represented by the demand curve D_{FPA}. At lower full prices, more port service is demanded by the passenger and less service at higher prices, other things remaining the same. The full price is $P_{FPA} = P_{PA} + P_{TPA}$, where P_{PA} is the port money price (per unit of service) for the port passenger service and P_{TPA} is the time price (per unit of service) incurred by the individual for the port passenger service.

Port choice and passengers

Passenger demand for a port will be influenced by whether the passenger port is a dedicated port (i.e., utilized by only one passenger carrier) or a common-user port (i.e., utilized by several passenger carriers). For the former, the passenger demand for the port is wholly subsumed within the preference for and choice of the carrier that offers passenger service

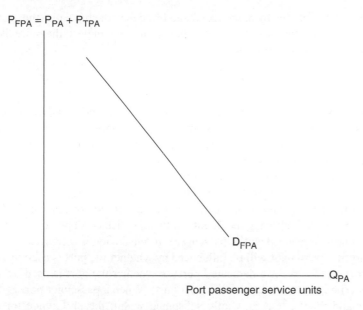

Figure 6.4 Passenger demand for port service at full prices

to the port. That is to say, the port demand by passengers is wholly subsumed within the transportation demand by passengers. The port is a resource under the control of the carrier and used in conjunction with its other resources to provide transportation service. The use of the port is considered by the carrier in determining its level of operating options in providing passenger transportation service. For common-user ports, the passenger demand for these ports is not wholly subsumed within the transportation demand by its passengers. At these ports, passengers will have more than one carrier from which to choose. If no carrier is chosen, the passenger will demand an alternative passenger port or an alternative mode of passenger transportation.

Whether a passenger will choose a port will depend upon the port prices charged by the common-user port, the port's characteristics, and the ship-schedule characteristics of the ships that call at the port. The higher the port prices, the less likely passengers will be to choose the port.

Port and ship-schedule characteristics will affect a passenger's time prices for passenger trips. If these characteristics result in higher time prices for passenger trips, the less likely the port will be chosen. Port characteristics include the distance from the individual passenger's home to the port (the greater the distance and the higher the vehicle in-transit time price for the land vehicle trip, the less likely the port will be chosen) and the oceanic or water distance from the port to the passenger's destination port (the greater the distance and the higher the vessel in-transit time price for the water trip, the less likely the port will be chosen). Greater inland and oceanic distances are also expected to be positively correlated with higher inland and oceanic passenger fares. Thus, passengers are generally expected to choose nearby as opposed to more distant ports.

Ship-schedule characteristics that are expected to affect the port choice of passengers include the number of destination passenger ports served by ships calling at the port (the greater the number, the more accessible the port will be to distant locations, and the more likely the port will be a port of choice by passengers) and frequency of ship calls (the greater the frequency and thus the lower the expected passenger waiting time in port, the more likely the port will be a port of choice by passengers).

Summary

Transportation passengers incur two prices for a passenger trip – a money price and a time price. The full price for a passenger trip is the sum of these two prices. The individual passenger pays a fare to the passenger carrier, e.g., a ferry or cruise vessel carrier, for the transportation service that it provides and incurs a time price that is related to himself or herself – i.e., the opportunity cost of the trip minus any satisfaction received from the trip per unit of time multiplied by the trip time incurred by the passenger. The total time price for a passenger trip is the sum of the passenger's walking, waiting, and vessel (or vehicle) in-transit time prices. Carriers can reduce passenger time prices by improving the quality of their service (via operating options) so that passenger trip times are reduced and/or passenger trip satisfaction is increased.

The choice of a port by a passenger will be influenced by whether the port is used by only one passenger carrier (i.e., the port is a dedicated port) or whether the port is used by several passenger carriers (i.e., the port is a common-user port). When a passenger port is dedicated, passenger demand for the port is wholly subsumed within the preference for and choice of the carrier. Passenger demand for common-user ports is not wholly subsumed within the transportation demand by passengers, since passengers will have more than one carrier at the port from which to choose. Whether a passenger will choose a port will depend upon the port prices that are charged, the port characteristics, and the ship-schedule characteristics of the ships that call at the port.

Bibliography

Cartwright, R. and Baird, C. (1999) *The Development and Growth of the Cruise Industry*, Oxford: Butterworth/Heinemann.

Coleman, M.T., Meyer, D.W., and Scheffman, D. T. (2003) "Economic Analyses of Mergers at the FTC: The Cruise Ships Mergers Investigation", *Review of Industrial Organization*, 25: 93–109.

Corbett, J. J. and Farrell, A. (2002) "Mitigating Air Pollution Impacts of Passenger Ferries", *Transportation Research Part D: Transport and Environment*, 7: 197–211.

Cruise Lines International Association (2005). Available online at http://www.cruising.org/press/overview (accessed 7 November 2005).

Ebersold, W. B. (2004) "Cruise Industry in Figures", *Global Cruise 2004*, Burr Ridge, IL: Business Briefings.

Gossard, H. W. (1995) "Marine Safety on Board Cruise Ships", *World Cruise Industry Review*, London: Sterling Publications.

McIntire, M. (2003) "History of Human Error Found in Ferry Accidents", *New York Times*, November 1.

Marti, B. E. (2004) "Trends in World and Extended-Length Cruising (1985–2002)", *Marine Policy*, 28: 199–211.

Speares, S. (2005) "Cruise Lines Urged to Build New Vessels to Meet Demand", *Lloyd's List*. Available online at http://www.lloydslist.com, November 3.

Staff (2005) "Cruise Industry Worth More Than $30bn to US Economy", *Lloyd's List*. Available online at http://www.lloydslist.com, September 9.

—— (2006a) "Cruise Conventions Ride Tide of Passenger Growth", *Lloyd's List*. Available online at http://www.lloydslist.com, January 17.

—— (2006b) "Positive Outlook for Passenger Shipping as Capacity Comes Online", *Lloyd's List*. Available online at http://www.lloydslist.com, January 17.

Stoller, G. (1999) "When the Bow Breaks", *USA Today*, January 11: 1B–3B.

Talley, W. K. (1983) *Introduction to Transportation*, Cincinnati, OH: South-Western Publishing Company.

—— (1995) "Safety Investments and Operating Conditions: Determinants of Accident Passenger-Vessel Damage Cost", *Southern Economic Journal*, 61: 819–829.

—— (2002) "The Safety of Ferries: An Accident Injury Perspective", *Maritime Policy and Management*, 29: 331–338.

—— (forthcoming) "Ferry Services", in K. Button, P. Nijkamp, and H. Vega (eds) *Transportation Dictionary*, Cheltenham, UK: Edward Elgar.

Talley, W. K., Jin, D., and Kite-Powell, H. (2008a) "Determinants of the Damage Cost and Injury Severity of Ferry Vessel Accidents", *WMU Journal of Maritime Affairs*, 7: 175–188.

—— (2008b) "Determinants of the Severity of Cruise Vessel Accidents", *Transportation Research Part D: Transport and Environment*, 13: 86–94.

Wieriman, J. (2003) "New Practices in the Collection of Ferry Passenger Data", presentation at the Annual Transportation Research Board Conference, Washington, DC.

7 Port operator operating options, production, and cost

Introduction

The port operator (as stated in Chapter 2) is the primary service provider of a port. If the port has more than one terminal, there may be a separate terminal operator for each terminal. A port operator is a firm that is responsible for moving cargo and/or passengers through a port, i.e., creating port throughput. Cargo may arrive at a port by land (rail and truck) and inland waterway (barge) carriers and then depart from the port on a ship, or conversely. For transshipment cargo, the cargo arrives at a port by ship and then departs from the port on another ship. Passengers may arrive at a port by automobile or for-hire transportation service (e.g., taxi) and then depart from the port on a ship, or conversely.

The port operator may be a port authority that operates a government-owned port or a private firm (e.g., a shipping line or a terminal operator) that contracts with the port authority to perform the daily operations of the government-owned port. If the port is owned by a private firm, the same firm may operate the port or it may enter into a contract with another firm to perform the daily operations of the port.

If a port is in competition with other ports, the port operator will be under pressure to allocate port resources technically and cost efficiently. Technical efficiency occurs when the port's throughput is the maximum throughput obtainable given the levels of resources utilized by the port operator. Cost efficiency occurs when the port's throughput is provided at the least cost given the resource prices to be paid by the port operator.

This chapter discusses technical and cost efficiency in the provision of port throughput by a port operator. The following sections discuss the operating options that are available to the port operator for varying the quality of port services, port resource utilization and congestion, port production and capacity, port cost, and costing port throughput.

Operating options

An operating option of a port operator (similar to that of a carrier) is the means by which the port operator can differentiate the quality of its port service. Operating options that are used by carriers to differentiate their service include speed of movement, frequency of service, reliability of service, spatial accessibility, and susceptibility of cargo to loss or damage and passengers to fatal or nonfatal injuries (see Chapter 4). The port operator has similar operating options with which to differentiate the quality of its service (Talley 2006).

Operating options of a port operator that are analogous to a carrier's speed of movement are port vehicle loading and unloading service rates. If the vehicle is a ship, the port ship loading service rate is the amount of cargo (e.g., tons and TEUs) loaded on to a ship per hour of loading time; the port ship unloading service rate is the amount of cargo unloaded from a ship per hour of unloading time. There are similar operating options whether the vehicle is a truck, rail car, or barge. The greater these service rates, the higher the quality of service provided by the port operator.

A port operator operating option that is similar to a carrier's frequency of service is port vehicle turn-around time (i.e., the difference between departure and arrival times for a port vehicle). For instance, how long does it take the port to turn around a ship, truck, rail car, or barge once it enters the port? Port vehicle turn-around time is analogous to headway time for an urban transit vehicle, i.e., headway time is the reciprocal of frequency of service on a scheduled transit route. For example, if a transit vehicle arrives every 20 minutes at a stop on a transit route, the headway time of transit vehicles arriving at the stop is 20 minutes, but the reciprocal of 20 minutes is the frequency of service at the stop or three transit vehicles every hour. The lower the port vehicle turn-around time, the higher the quality of service provided by the port operator.

Port operator operating options that are analogous to carrier reliability of service are port channel reliability and port berth reliability. The former may be measured as the percent of time that the port's channel is open to navigation for a given period of time, the latter as the percent of time that the port's berth is open to the berthing of ships. Port reliability operating options with respect to gates include entrance gate reliability and departure gate reliability. The former may be measured as the percent of time that the port's entrance gate is open for vehicles for a given time period, the latter the percent of time that the port's departure gate is open for vehicles for a given time period. The greater these percentages, the higher the quality of service provided by the port operator.

Port operator operating options that are similar to carrier spatial accessibility are port channel accessibility and port berth accessibility. The former may be measured as the percent of time that the port's channel adheres to authorized depth and width dimensions for a given time period, the latter the percent of time that the port's berth adheres to authorized depth and width dimensions for a given time period. The greater these percentages, the higher the quality of service provided by the port operator.

Port operator operating options that are analogous to carrier susceptibility of cargo to loss or damage are probability of port cargo loss and probability of port cargo damage. If port operators are responsible for damage to ships and inland carrier vehicles and loss to their property while in port, port operating options that relate to this damage and loss include probability of ship damage, probability of ship property loss, probability of inland carrier vehicle damage, and probability of inland carrier vehicle property loss. For ports that have passenger throughput, the port operating options, probability of a port fatal injury and probability of a port nonfatal injury, may be used by port operators. The lower these probabilities, the higher the quality of service provided by the port operator.

Resource utilization and congestion

A port operator may seek to improve the quality of its service, e.g., by increasing its port ship loading and unloading service rates. However, in order to do so, the container port will have to employ a greater amount of resources, e.g., employ a greater number of ship-to-shore cranes to work ships and a greater number of yard cranes to stack and unstack containers in storage areas (see Chapter 3), assuming no crane excess capacity. The positive relationship between the minimum amount of a resource employed by a port operator and the level of its operating options and cargo (provided by shipping lines and shippers) and passengers (provided by individuals who are willing to be passengers) to be handled by the port is the port operator's resource function for the resource (Talley 1988, 2006), i.e.,

Minimum Port Resource = j(Port Operating Options; Amount of Cargo,
Number of Passengers)   (7.1)

While the levels of the operating options are under the control of the port operator (i.e., the port operator can decide what these levels should be and take appropriate actions for their attainment), cargo and passengers to be handled are not. The port operator cannot make shippers and passengers use their ports. Hence, the cargo and passengers handled by the port are beyond the control of the port operator, i.e., determined outside the port operator's decision-making domain.

Port congestion occurs when port users (carriers, shippers, and passengers) interfere with one another in the utilization of port resources, thereby increasing their time in port. Port congestion may be unintentional or intentional. Unintentional interference occurs in the normal utilization of port resources, e.g., when the berthing of a ship is delayed because of the unberthing of another ship. Intentional port congestion may arise from preemptive priority, e.g., when a port operator gives priority to one port user for port services over that of another. The berthing (unberthing) of ships of one carrier may be delayed to allow for the berthing (unberthing) of incoming (departing) ships of another carrier.

Port resources such as cranes and labor may not be sufficient to prevent ship work congestion, e.g., congestion that arises when a ship has to wait at the berth to be loaded/unloaded (or worked) until another ship has been worked. Port resources also may not be sufficient to allow for the simultaneous loading/unloading of vehicles, i.e., to prevent vehicle work congestion. Congestion may also occur at a port's inland gate. For example, railcars (trucks) transporting bulk cargo to the port may have to wait at the gate's entrance for railcars (trucks) transporting containers to enter the gate.

Production and capacity

A port is technically efficient when its throughput is the maximum throughput obtainable given the levels of resources utilized by the port operator. The functional relationship between this maximum throughput and the levels of resources utilized by the port operator is the port's economic production function, i.e.,

Maximum Port Throughput = f(Port Resources)   (7.2)

where throughput may be the number of containers (measured in 20 foot equivalent unit, TEUs) or tons of cargo handled and port resources include labor, immobile capital (e.g., wharfs and buildings), mobile capital (e.g., cranes and vehicles), fuel, and ways (e.g., port roadways and railways). If the port achieves the maximum throughput in utilizing given levels of resources, then it is technically efficient; otherwise it is technically inefficient.

The port's economic production function with respect to the resource, port labor, is plotted as curve PT in Figure 7.1. Any point on the curve is technically efficient. At any point below the curve, the port is technically inefficient with respect to the corresponding amount of labor. At point X, for example, the port is technically inefficient, since the labor at that point is providing less throughput than that for which it is capable (i.e., at point Y). Throughput points above the curve are not obtainable by the port.

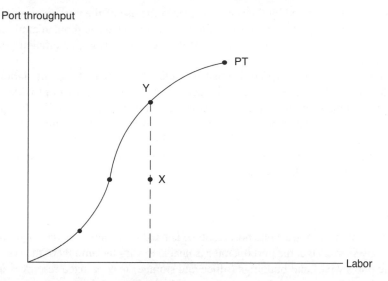

Figure 7.1 Port throughput and labor

The maximum throughput (from an engineering perspective) that a port can physically handle under certain conditions is the port's capacity. The latter has been classified as (1) design capacity, (2) preferred capacity, and (3) practical capacity (Chadwin *et al.* 1990). A port's design capacity is its maximum designed utilization rate. For example, the design capacity of the storage area of a container port is the maximum number of containers that can physically be stored in the storage area. A port's preferred capacity is the utilization rate beyond which certain utilization characteristics or requirements cannot be obtained, e.g., the utilization rate beyond which port congestion occurs. A port's practical capacity is its maximum utilization rate under realistic working conditions. For example, the practical capacity for a container port's ship-to-shore crane is the maximum number of containers that the crane can load and unload from a ship per hour under realistic working conditions.

A port's capability is the choke-point maximum throughput of a port under normal port working conditions. A modular method for estimating a port's capability is found in the port handbook by Hockney and Whiteneck (1986). Estimates of the following port modular capabilities (i.e., the maximum throughputs for various components of the port under normal port working conditions) for a given time period are found: ship-to-apron transfer capability, apron-to-storage transfer capability, yard storage capability, storage-to-inland transport transfer capability, and inland transport processing capability. The port's capability estimate is the lowest throughput value among the five estimates. This lowest throughput estimate is the constraining capability of the port or its choke-point throughput.

Cost

A port operator is cost efficient when the port's throughput is provided at the least cost given the resource prices that are paid by the port operator. A port's economic cost function represents the relationship between the port's minimum costs to be incurred in handling a given level of throughput, i.e.,

Minimum Port Costs = g(Port Throughput) (7.3)

where the costs are those incurred by the port operator in the use of the port resources, e.g., wages paid to labor and vehicle fuel expenses. If the port provides throughput at a minimum cost (given the unit costs or resource prices to be paid), then the port is cost efficient; otherwise it is cost inefficient.

In order for a port to be cost efficient, it must be technically efficient, i.e., the latter is a necessary condition for the former. If a port is technically inefficient, it can provide additional throughput with the same resources by becoming technically efficient. Further, given the same resources and thus the same resource prices, the average cost per unit of throughput will decline with the port becoming technically efficient. Alternatively, if the port is technically inefficient, it must also follow that it is cost inefficient. For further explanation, see the appendix at the end of this chapter.

Short-run cost

For the short-run time period, at least one port resource is fixed in amount, i.e., the length of the period is sufficiently short so that the port operator is unable to vary the amount of the resource. For example, the port's wharf and buildings (office and storage) may be fixed resources in the short run. For the long-run time period, the port operator has sufficient time to vary the amounts of all resources, e.g., to expand the wharf as well as office and storage buildings.

Port costs related to fixed resources are the port operator's fixed costs (FC_{PO}) incurred in the operation of the port. These costs do not vary with the port's throughput. Costs that are incurred by variable resources and thus vary with changes in port throughput are the port operator's variable costs (VC_{PO}). The port operator's short-run total cost, $STC_{PO} = FC_{PO} + VC_{PO}$, for various amounts of port throughput Q_{PO} is plotted in Figure 7.2a. Unit costs with respect to the above costs are determined by dividing these costs by their corresponding amounts of port throughput Q_{PO} to obtain $SATC_{PO} = AFC_{PO} + AVC_{PO}$. Short-run average total

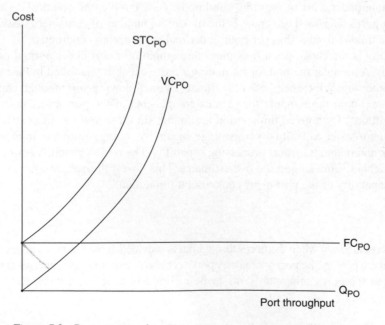

Figure 7.2a Port operator short-run costs

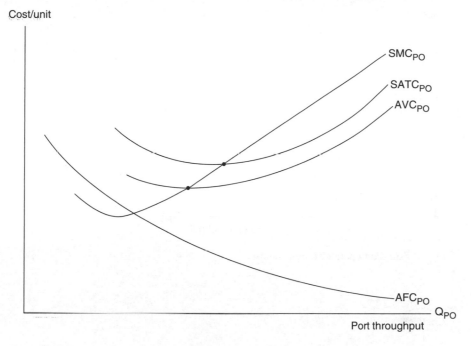

Cost/unit

SMC$_{PO}$

SATC$_{PO}$

AVC$_{PO}$

AFC$_{PO}$

Q$_{PO}$

Port throughput

Figure 7.2b Port operator short-run unit and marginal costs

cost SATC$_{PO}$ is STC$_{PO}$/Q$_{PO}$, short-run average fixed cost AFC$_{PO}$ is FC$_{PO}$/Q$_{PO}$, and short-run average variable cost AVC$_{PO}$ is VC$_{PO}$/Q$_{PO}$. Port operator unit costs are graphed in Figure 7.2b.

In Figure 7.2b, AFC$_{PO}$ declines continuously as throughput increases, since a fixed (or constant) cost is divided by larger and larger amounts of port throughput. As throughput increases, AVC$_{PO}$ and SATC$_{PO}$ decline initially, reach a minimum, and then increase. The addition to the port operator's short-run variable cost in providing an additional unit of throughput is the operator's short-run marginal cost (SMC$_{PO}$), i.e., SMC$_{PO}$ = ΔVC$_{PO}$/ΔQ$_{PO}$. Note that in Figure 7.2b, the SMC$_{PO}$ curve intersects the AVC$_{PO}$ and SATC$_{PO}$ curves from below at their minimum unit costs.

Long-run cost

In the long run, all costs of the port operator are variable. The long-run total cost (LTC$_{PO}$) incurred by the port operator for various amounts of port throughput appears in Figure 7.3a. The long-run average total cost LATC$_{PO}$ for a port operator is LTC$_{PO}$ divided by Q$_{PO}$. The operator's long-run marginal cost is the addition to the port's long-run cost in providing an additional unit of throughput, i.e., LMC$_{PO}$ = ΔLTC$_{PO}$/ΔQ$_{PO}$ (see Figure 7.3b).

In Figure 7.3b, the LATC$_{PO}$ curve is negatively sloped over a range of port throughput. Within this range the port operator exhibits "economies of scale" in the provision of port throughput. As throughput increases by a certain percentage, the operator's long-run costs increase by a smaller percentage. Economies of scale may arise from the use of larger ship-to-shore cranes for the loading/unloading of containers for a wide range of containership sizes.

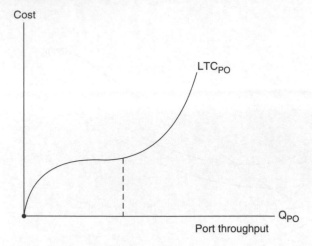

Figure 7.3a Port operator long-run costs

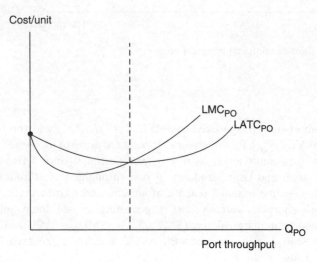

Figure 7.3b Port operator long-run unit and marginal costs

The port operator exhibits "diseconomies of scale" in the provision of port throughput when the $LATC_{PO}$ curve in Figure 7.3b is positively sloped. If port throughput increases by a certain percentage, the port operator's long-run costs will increase by a larger percentage. Diseconomies of scale may arise when the port operator incurs greater difficulty in managing (i.e., coordinating and controlling) the port's operations of a larger sized port.

In Figure 7.4, the port operator exhibits "constant returns to scale" in the provision of port throughput. The port operator's long-run average total cost remains constant over a range of port throughput. That is to say, if throughput increases by a certain percentage, the port operator's long-run costs will increase by the same percentage.

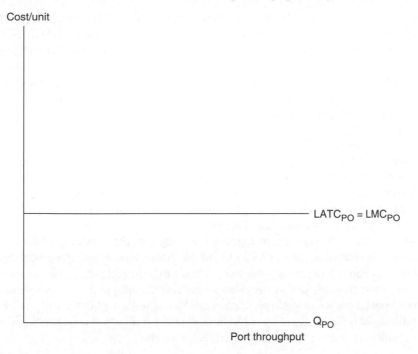

Figure 7.4 Port constant returns to scale

The empirical literature suggests that ports exhibit economies of scale, i.e., as throughput increases by a certain percentage, the operator's long-run costs increase by a smaller percentage (Tovar *et al.* 2007). Alternatively, a port's long-run unit cost decreases as port throughput increases.

Long-run cost: multiple throughputs

If a port handles more than one type of cargo, e.g., container and dry bulk, how would the port operator determine whether the port exhibits economies of scale, diseconomies of scale, or constant returns to scale in the provision of its throughputs? How would the port operator determine the unit costs of these throughputs?

For a one-throughput port, economies of scale exist if $S = LATC_{PO}/LMC_{PO} = LTC_{PO}/Q_{PO}*LMC_{PO} > 1$; if $S < 1$, diseconomies of scale exist; and if $S = 1$, constant returns to scale exist. (See Chapter 4 for a similar discussion but with respect to carriers.) By similar reasoning, S for a two-throughput port may be expressed as $S = LTC_{PO}/[Q_{PO1}*LMC_{PO1} + Q_{PO2}*LMC_{PO2}]$, where Q_{PO1} represents the throughput of cargo type one and Q_{PO2} represents the throughput of cargo type two (Talley 1988). If $S > 1$, the two-throughput port exhibits economies of scale; if $S < 1$, it exhibits diseconomies of scale; and if $S = 1$, it exhibits constant returns to scale.

For a one-throughput port, long-run average total cost is obtained by dividing long-run costs by the amount of the throughput that incurred this cost, i.e., to obtain $LATC_{PO}$. However, for a two-throughput port, the throughputs will share one or more resources, e.g., administrative labor and the roadway of the port. Hence, the division of LTC_{PO} by Q_{PO1} will not be the long-run average total cost for the throughput of cargo type one, since part of

LTC_{PO} costs includes costs to be borne by the throughput of cargo type two. This problem is addressed by computing the long-run average incremental total cost (LAITC) for each throughput. The long-run average incremental total cost for throughput of cargo type one may be expressed as $LAITC_{PO1} = [h(Q_{PO1}, Q_{PO2}) - h(0, Q_{PO2})]/Q_{PO1}$, where $LTC_{PO} = h(Q_{PO1}, Q_{PO2})$ and $[h(Q_{PO1}, Q_{PO2}) - h(0, Q_{PO2})]$ is the incremental cost for the throughput of cargo type one, given the throughput of cargo type two Q_{PO2}. Similarly, the long-run average incremental total cost for throughput of cargo type two may be expressed as $LAITC_{PO2} = [h(Q_{PO1}, Q_{PO2}) - h(Q_{PO1}, 0)]/Q_{PO2}$, given the throughput of cargo type one Q_{PO1}.

Economies of scope exist for a multiple-throughput port when it has a long-run cost advantage over a one-throughput port. Specifically, economies of scope exist for a multiple-throughput port if it can provide its throughputs at less cost than if each throughput (at the same level) were provided by single-throughput ports. Our two-throughput port above will exhibit economies of scope if $h(Q_{PO1}, Q_{PO2}) < h(Q_{PO1}, 0) + h(0, Q_{PO2})$. If the inequality sign is reversed, i.e., ">," then diseconomies of scope exist.

The empirical literature suggests that multiple throughput ports exhibit economies of scope. For example, Jara-Diaz *et al*. (2002) found that Spanish ports providing such multiple throughputs as liquid bulk, solid bulk, and general cargo throughputs exhibit economies of scope. Thus, these throughputs are provided at less cost at multiple-throughput ports than if each throughput (at the same level) were provided by single-throughput ports – i.e., when the liquid bulk, solid bulk, and general cargo throughputs are provided only at a liquid bulk port, a solid bulk port, and a general cargo port, respectively.

Types of costs

Costs incurred by port operators in the provision of port throughput may be classified (in addition to being short-run versus long-run costs) as accounting versus economic costs, non-shared versus shared costs, and internal versus external costs (Talley 2001). Since accountants are primarily concerned with measuring costs for financial reporting purposes, port accounting costs reflect the recorded payments for resources. Economists, on the other hand, are concerned with measuring costs for decision-making purposes. Thus, port economic costs reflect the opportunity costs of resources in their current use, i.e., the earnings of these resources in their next best alternative. The prices of resources in competitive resource markets reflect the opportunity costs of these resources.

Port non-shared (shared) costs are costs than can (cannot) be traced to a particular unit of port throughput, e.g., a TEU. The time incurred by a port worker in checking in a container (being hauled by a trucker) at the entrance gate of a container port can be traced to that particular container; hence, the cost of the port worker's time in doing so is a cost that is not shared with other port containers. A joint (common) shared cost arises when one container movement at a container port, for example, does (does not) unavoidably result in the creation of another container movement (Talley 1988). If the repositioning of empty containers in a port involves a straddle carrier moving an empty container from location A to location B in the port, but then must return to location A, the straddle carrier's round trip cost is a joint cost to be shared between the straddle carrier's front-haul and back-haul trips. The cost of a wharf (or quay) at a container port that is shared by containers is a common cost, since the use of the wharf by one container does not unavoidably result in the use of the wharf by another container.

Internal (external) costs generated by port operators in the provision of port throughput are borne (not borne) by these operators and therefore enter (do not enter) into the decision-making processes of these operators. External costs generated by port operators include air, noise, water, and esthetic (appearance) pollution costs. If port operators are forced by government regulation to internalize these costs, then they will become internal rather than external costs. For example, containerships may be forced to eliminate air pollution while in port by cutting off their engines; the port operator, in turn, may require the ships to hook up to a port auxiliary power source, i.e., cold ironing.

Costing port throughput

There are a number of reasons for determining (or estimating) the total costs incurred by a port operator in providing port throughput. First, these costs are required for determining the port's financial status, i.e., is the port making a profit, loss, or at break-even when compared to revenue received? Second, these costs may be used by a port regulatory agency for evaluating the reasonableness of the port's level of rates with respect to profits and losses. Are the rates too high or too low? Third, these costs may be analyzed for decision-making purposes by the port operator, e.g., to investigate whether the port exhibits economies of scale and economies of scope. If the former is found, an expansion of the port will be expected to result in lower unit cost from increases in port throughput. If economies of scope are found, the port operator has evidence that it is incurring less cost as a two-or-more-throughput port than if each throughput at the same level is provided by separate one-throughput ports.

There are also a number of reasons for determining (or estimating) the unit or marginal cost of a port's throughput. First, the unit costs of throughput for particular port services may be compared with their specific rates (or prices) for these services, i.e., for determining whether the revenue from these services is covering their costs. Second, the unit cost or marginal cost for throughput may be used for determining the rate structure (i.e., specific rates) for the port's throughput. That is to say, unit costs for various port services may be used by the port operator (in a non-competitive environment) to determine unit-cost prices for these services; marginal costs for various port services may be used by the port operator to determine marginal-cost prices for these services.

Resource costing

Resource costing may be used by a port operator to determine (or estimate) the costs to be incurred in the provision of various levels of port throughput. Specifically, resource costing involves the port operator determining the amount of various resources that it utilizes (or will utilize) in providing various levels of port throughput at given quality-of-service levels and then determining the costs of these resources. If the amounts of resources are the minimum amounts to be utilized, then the port operator will have utilized its resource functions (explicitly or implicitly) in determining these amounts. The costs of the resources utilized by the port operator will also be the costs that it incurs for the throughputs provided by these resources.

In a study by Vanelslander (2006), resource costing was used to estimate the costs to be incurred by 210,000 and 600,000 TEU (capacity) marine terminals. Short-run resources required for each of the two TEU-sized container terminals were determined. The determined variable costs included costs for labor (management, administration, operations, and equipment maintenance), maintenance of cargo-handling equipment, and container handling. A distinction between buying used and new equipment was considered in determining capital (or fixed) costs for equipment. The total short-run (sum of variable and fixed) costs for each TEU-sized marine terminal was then divided by the terminal's TEU capacity (i.e., 210,000 or 600,000 TEUs) to determine cost per TEU. The cost per TEU for the

600,000 TEU terminal was found to be smaller than that for the 210,000 TEU terminal, thus suggesting that there are cost economies in the short run in the operation of larger container terminals.

Information on port resources utilized by individual containers may be retrieved from RFID (radio frequency identification) sensors attached to containers. That is to say, RFIDs can be used to record the locations of containers in the port and the port's resources, e.g., infrastructure, equipment, and labor, and resource times utilized by containers. The costs of these resources and resource utilization times incurred by a particular container can be used to determine the cost that the port incurs in providing service to the container. The shared cost of port infrastructure (e.g., berth and storage areas) may be allocated among containers based upon their time in use of the infrastructure relative to that of other containers. A port's equipment costs and the time incurred by a particular container in using this equipment (e.g., in lifting, lowering, and moving the container) may be used to determine the port's equipment cost to be borne by the container. The cost of the labor time incurred by the container would also be assigned to the container.

Cost-center costing

A cost center is defined as a service area in a port, where costs accumulate. For a container port, these cost centers are the entrance/departure gates for trucks and trains where containers enter and depart from the port; container storage areas; container staging areas where containers are moved from storage to these areas for loading on a ship, or once unloaded from a ship are moved to these areas to await movement to storage; and loading/unloading areas. The latter areas are ship, truck, and railcar loading/unloading areas where containers are loaded to and from ships, trucks, and railcars, respectively.

The cost-center costing process allocates the port's total costs incurred for a given time period among the port's cost centers. For a container port, the cost allocated to each center is then divided by the TEU throughput of that center for the given time period to obtain the unit cost (i.e., the cost per TEU throughput) for that center. These unit costs may then be used by a port operator in a future time period to estimate the costs to be incurred by each center for various levels of port throughput – i.e., by multiplying the levels of throughput by the corresponding unit costs. The sum of the centers' cost estimates with respect to a given level of TEU throughput will be an estimate of the port's total cost in handling the TEU throughput.

Cost-equation costing

Cost-equation costing uses historical cost and throughput data to obtain an estimated cost equation for the port. The specific functional form of the cost equation may be linear or non-linear. The estimation is usually performed using statistical regression analysis. If estimated using variable-cost, time-series data, the estimated equation will be an estimated short-run variable cost equation, where short-run variable costs are a function of port throughput. Times series data are historical data for a single port for many time periods.

If the short-run cost equation is linear, then $STC_{PO} = a + bQ_{PO}$, where "a" and "b" are the intercept and slope parameters, respectively, to be estimated. However, "a" is also a measure of FC_{PO} and bQ_{PO} is a measure of VC_{PO}. Thus, the port can obtain estimates of its short-run variable costs for various levels of throughputs by substituting these throughputs into bQ_{PO} (once "b" is estimated) and solving. In dividing VC_{PO} by Q_{PO}, we obtain short-run average variable cost AVC_{PO} = b. In addition to being an estimate of the port's short-run average variable cost, the estimate of "b" will also be an estimate of the port's short-run marginal cost with respect to its throughput, i.e., SMC_{PO}.

If it can be assumed that several ports (with the same type of cargo) have the same specific cost equation, then cross-section cost data from these ports can be used to estimate the ports' long-run cost equation. Cross-section data are historical data for two or more ports for the same time period. The estimated cost equation would be interpreted as a long-run cost equation, since the levels of all resources for the ports (from which the data were obtained) are expected to differ. If the equation is linear, then $LTC_{PO} = bQ_{PO}$, where in this case b = $LATC_{PO} = LMC_{PO}$. With the latter two being equal, it follows by assumption of the specific form of the long-run cost equation that each port exhibits constant returns to scale. Also, each port can obtain estimates of its long-run costs for various levels of throughputs by substituting these throughputs into bQ_{PO} (once "b" is estimated) and solving.

If it can be assumed that several two-throughput ports (with the same types of cargoes) have the same specific cost equation, then their cross-section cost data can be used to estimate their long-run cost equation. The estimated cost equation can then be used by each port to estimate its long-run costs to be incurred for various levels of the two types of cargoes. Also, the equation can be used to investigate whether the ports exhibit economies of scale and economies of scope.

Port output measures

It is common practice in the port industry to measure port output in terms of port throughput, i.e., in terms of the total tons or TEUs of cargo and the total number of passengers that move through a port. However, a container port, for instance, does not produce TEUs, but rather provides interchange service to the TEUs that it receives. In order for TEU interchange service to occur, shipping lines must be willing for TEUs to be loaded and unloaded to and from their ships in port and the port must be willing to provide interchange service for these TEUs.

It is thus reasonable to argue that a container port's output measure should reflect the interchange service provided by the port and the number of TEUs to which it provides this service (Talley 2008). One such output measure is the number of TEUs that pass through the port per unit of TEU time in port (TEU ratio). For a given time period, the TEU ratio would be determined by dividing the number of TEUs that pass through a port (or are interchanged) by the total time that these TEUs are in port. The latter reflects the interchange service provided by the port measured in time. Since the TEUs that pass through a port are the port's TEU throughput, the TEU ratio may also be described as TEU throughput per unit of TEU time in port.

The TEU ratio is analogous to the ton-mile output measure used in the U.S. by land carriers, where a ton-mile is a ton of cargo that is received from a shipper by a carrier and is transported one mile by this carrier. A rising TEU ratio over time is consistent with the concept of technical efficiency in that a rising TEU ratio suggests that a port is becoming less technically inefficient, since more TEUs are interchanged per unit of interchange time. The container port output measure, TEU ratio, is also consistent with the actions that have been undertaken by port managers for reducing technical inefficiency at their ports. For example, increases in the operating options, TEUs loaded on to and unloaded from ships per hour of loading and unloading time, will result in an increase in the TEU ratio, all else held constant. The TEU ratio will also increase when there are reductions in the dwell times of containers in storage. Further, the TEU ratio is consistent with the uses of the productivity measures, TEUs per acre of land and TEUs per foot of berth length, that have been used by container ports to evaluate the productivity of their storage areas and berths, respectively. That is to say, increases in the values of these productivity measures for a container port are expected to result in increases in the port's TEU ratio.

Summary

A port operator's operating option (e.g., a port's loading service rate) is the means by which it can differentiate the quality of its port service. The positive relationship between the minimum amount of a resource employed by the port operator and the level of its operating options and cargo and passengers to be handled is the port operator's resource function for that resource. Port congestion occurs when port users (carriers, shippers, and passengers) interfere with one another in the utilization of port resources, thereby increasing their time in port.

A port is technically efficient when the port's throughput is the maximum throughput obtainable given the levels of resources utilized by the port. The maximum throughput that the port can physically handle under certain conditions is the port's capacity. In the short run, ports incur variable (fixed) costs that vary (do not vary) with changes in the port's throughput. In the long run, ports can vary the levels of all of their resources. Hence, all costs are variable costs. The port exhibits economies (diseconomies) of scale when its long-run costs increase by a smaller (larger) percentage than the percentage increase in throughput. Economies of scope exist for a multiple-throughput port when it has a long-run cost advantage over one-throughput ports.

There are a number of reasons for determining (or estimating) the costs incurred by a port operator in providing port throughput – determining the port's financial status; evaluating the reasonableness of port prices; investigating whether the port exhibits economies of scale and scope; and estimating port unit and marginal costs. Methods available to ports for determining (or estimating) costs include resource costing, cost-center costing, and cost-equation costing. TEU throughput per unit of TEU time in port appears to be a preferable measure of output for a container port rather than just TEU throughput.

Bibliography

Chadwin, M., Pope, J., and Talley, W. K. (1990) "Costing Terminal Operations and Measuring Capacity", *Ocean Container Transportation: An Operational Perspective*, New York: Taylor & Francis, 35–56.

Cullinane, K. (2002) "The Productivity and Efficiency of Ports and Terminals", in C. T. Grammenos (ed.) *The Handbook of Maritime Economics and Business*, London: Informa, 803–831.

Haralambides, H. E., Cariou, P., and Benacchio, M. (2003) "Costs, Benefits and Pricing of Dedicated Container Terminals", *Maritime Economics and Logistics*, 4: 21–34.

Hockney, L. A. and Whiteneck, L. L. (1986) *Port Handbook for Estimating Marine Terminal Cargo Handling Capability*, Washington, DC: Office of Port and Intermodal Development, Maritime Administration, U.S. Department of Commerce.

Jansson, J. O. and Shneerson, D. (1982) *Port Economics*, Cambridge, MA: MIT Press.

Jara-Diaz, S., Martinez-Budria, E., Cortes, C., and Basso, L. (2002) "A Multioutput Cost Function for the Services of Spanish Ports' Infrastructure", *Transportation*, 29: 419–437.

Kim, M. and Sachish, A. (1986) "The Structure of Production, Technical Change and Productivity in a Port", *Journal of Industrial Economics*, 35: 209–223.

Meersman, H., Monteiro, F., Onghena, E., Pauwels, T., Van de Voorde, E., and Vanelslander, T. (2006) *Social Marginal Cost Calculation for Ports*, unpublished paper.

Talley, W. K. (1983) "Fully Allocated Costing in U.S. Regulated Transportation Industries", *Transportation Research Part B*, 17: 319–331.

—— (1986) "A Rule for Allocating Joint Truck-Carrier Costs", *Transportation Research Part B*, 20: 49–57.

—— (1988) *Transport Carrier Costing*, New York: Gordon and Breach Science Publishers, 159–216.

—— (2001) "Costing Theory and Processes", in M. Brewer, K. Button, and D. Hensher (eds) *Handbook of Logistics and Supply Chain Management*, Amsterdam: Elsevier, 313–323.

—— (2006) "An Economic Theory of the Port", in K. Cullinane and W. K. Talley (eds) *Port Economics: Research in Transportation Economics*, 16, Amsterdam: Elsevier, 43–65.

—— (2008) "Output Measures for Container Ports", a paper presented at the Annual Conference of the International Association of Maritime Economists, Dalian Maritime University, Dalian, China.

Tongzon, J. (2001) "Efficiency Measurement of Selected Australian and Other International Ports using Data Envelopment Analysis", *Transportation Research Part A*, 35: 107–122.

Tovar, B., Jara-Diaz, S., and Trujillos, L. (2007) "Econometric Estimation of Scale and Scope Economies within the Port Sector: A Review", *Maritime Policy and Management*, 34: 203–223.

Vanelslander, T. (2006) "Cost Structures in Container Handling: How About Economies of Scale?", a paper presented at the 2006 International Association of Maritime Economists Conference, Melbourne, Australia.

Appendix

Assume a port's maximum port throughput may be expressed as a function of the amount of capital and labor utilized by the port, i.e., its economic production function may be expressed as

$$\text{Maximum Port Throughput} = f(\text{Port Capital, Port Labor}) \tag{7A.1}$$

For a given level of maximum port throughput, this function can be solved for various combinations of capital and labor that can provide this maximum level of port throughput. These combinations of capital (K) and labor (L) for the provision of maximum port throughput $Q_{PO''}$ are plotted in Figure 7A.1 as isoquant curve $Q_{PO''}$.

The long-run cost (LTC) incurred by the port in the employment of capital and labor resources may be expressed as

$$\text{LTC} = P_K * K + P_L * L \tag{7A.2}$$

Where P_K is the price per unit of capital and P_L is the price per unit of labor incurred by the port in the employment of capital and labor, respectively. In solving equation 7A.2 for K, it follows that

$$K = \text{LTC}/P_K - (P_L/P_K) * L \tag{7A.3}$$

For a given level of cost, this equation plots as an isocost line in Figure 7A.1.

A cost expenditure of amount LTC_1 (exhibited by isocost line LTC_1 in Figure 7A.1) is not sufficient for the port to be able to pay for enough resources to provide for $Q_{PO''}$ level of throughput. Alternatively, cost expenditure LTC_3 is sufficient. At capital intensive point X (i.e., a relatively large amount of capital to labor is being utilized) on isocost line LTC_3, the port is technically efficient but cost inefficient in the provision $Q_{PO''}$ level of port throughput. This is also true for the relatively labor intensive point Y on isocost line LTC_3. Resource combinations at points X and Y are technically efficient but cost inefficient, since there are other combinations of resources on isoquant curve $Q_{PO''}$ that will incur less cost when used in the provision of $Q_{PO''}$ level of port throughput.

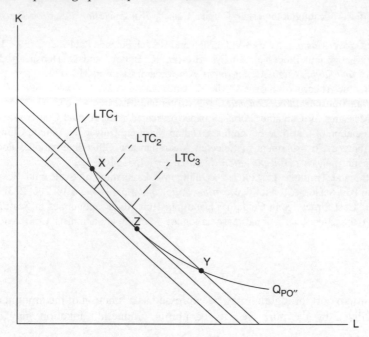

Figure 7A.1 Minimization of port cost for a single port throughput

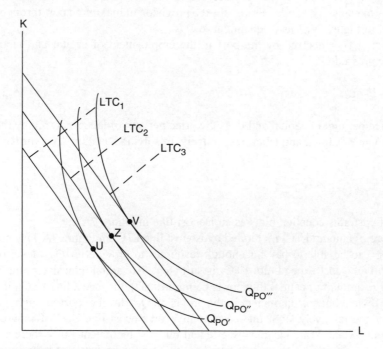

Figure 7A.2 Minimization of port cost for several port throughputs

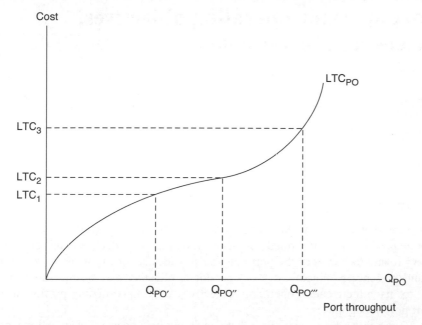

Figure 7A.3 Port operator long-run costs

At point Z, isocost line LTC_2 is just tangent to isoquant curve $Q_{PO''}$. Further, cost expenditure LTC2 is the minimum expenditure to be incurred by the port in the provision of $Q_{PO''}$ level of output. Thus, at the resource combination at point Z, the port is both technically and cost efficient.

Note that the port cannot be cost efficient without being technically efficient. Alternatively, if a port is technically inefficient, it must be cost inefficient. If technically inefficient, the port will utilize at least more of one resource than that found at any point on isoquant curve $Q_{PO''}$. Consequently, the port will incur greater cost in the provision of $Q_{PO''}$ level of port throughput when it is technically inefficient.

At points U, Z, and V in Figure 7A.2, the combinations of resources are both technically and cost efficient in the provision of $Q_{P'}$, $Q_{PO''}$, and $Q_{PO'''}$ levels of port throughput, respectively. At these points the isocost cost curves LTC_1, LTC_2, and LTC_3 are tangent to the isoquants for these levels of port throughput. These points also provide information for the plotting of the port's long-run total cost curve LTC_{PO} as found in Figure 7A.3 (and as also found in Figure 7.3a). In Figure 7A.3, the minimum cost to be incurred by the port in the provision of $Q_{PO'}$, $Q_{PO''}$, and $Q_{PO'''}$ levels of port throughput (given the resource prices P_K and P_L) are LTC_1, LTC_2, and LTC_3, respectively

8 Port operator operating objectives, prices, and investment

Introduction

A port operator should not only be concerned with whether it is technically and cost efficient in the provision of port throughput, but also whether it is effective in this provision. Effectiveness relates to how well the port operator provides service to its users – carriers, shippers, and passengers. Whether a port operator is effective may be measured by its adherence to its effectiveness operating objective, e.g., maximizing profits in the provision of port throughput.

It is well known that a firm cannot be effective without being cost efficient and it cannot be cost efficient without being technically efficient (Talley 1994b, 2006). That is to say, technical efficiency is a necessary condition for cost efficiency and cost efficiency is a necessary condition for profit maximization (or for a firm to be effective). A technically inefficient port by becoming technically efficient (i.e., providing more throughput with the same level of resources) lowers its unit cost, since the cost of the resources is now divided by a larger throughput. A cost-inefficient port by becoming cost efficient lowers its cost for a given level of throughput, thereby allowing the port to make greater profits.

This chapter presents a discussion of port effectiveness operating objectives. Prices charged by ports for services are also discussed, since they play an important role in whether a port is effective. The chapter ends with a discussion of port investment.

Effectiveness operating objectives

A critical component of a port's effectiveness operating objective is the demand for its throughput services. A freight port's throughput demand function represents the relationship between the demand for the port's throughput services by its freight users and the generalized port price (per unit of throughput) incurred by these users, i.e.,

$$\text{Port Throughput} = k(\text{Generalized Port Price}) \tag{8.1}$$

where

$$\begin{aligned}\text{Generalized Port Price} = \text{Port Price} + \text{Ocean Carrier Port Time Price} \\ + \text{Inland Carrier Port Time Price} + \\ \text{Shipper Port Time Price}\end{aligned} \tag{8.2}$$

The Port Price per unit of throughput represents prices charged by the port for various port services, e.g., wharfage, berthing, and cargo handling charges; the Ocean Carrier Port Time

Price per unit of throughput represents the time-related costs incurred by ocean carriers while their ships are in port, e.g., ship depreciation, fuel, and labor costs; the Inland Carrier Port Time Price per unit of throughput represents the time-related costs incurred by inland (rail and truck) carriers while their vehicles are in port, e.g., vehicle depreciation, fuel, and labor costs; and the Shipper Port Time Price per unit of throughput represents the time-related costs incurred by shippers while their shipments are in port, e.g., inventory costs such as insurance, obsolescence, and depreciation costs.

If a port seeks to maximize profits, its profit (or effectiveness operating objective) equation may be written as

Profit = Port Price*Port Throughput − Minimum Port Costs (8.3)

Substituting the port's throughput demand function (8.1) into profit equation (8.3) and rewriting, it follows that

Profit = Port Price*k(Generalized Port Price) − Minimum Port Costs (8.4)

Port effectiveness operating objectives of the port operator will differ depending upon whether the operator is a public port authority in charge of the operations of a government-owned port; is contracted by a public port authority or the port owner to operate its port; owns the private port that it operates; is operating a common-user, dedicated, or transshipment port; or is operating a privately owned versus a government-owned port. That is to say, port effectiveness operating objectives will differ depending upon the management or governance structure of the port.

If the operator is a public port authority operator that is in charge of the operations of a government-owned port, its effectiveness operating objective will likely focus (at least to some extent) on regional economic development, e.g., promoting the export of locally produced products in order to promote employment and economic development in the region. The government-appointed commissioners of the port authority may require that its operator maximize port throughput subject to a zero operating deficit (where port revenue equals cost) or subject to a maximum operating deficit (where port revenue is less than cost) that is subsidized by government.

A private operator under contract to the owner of a port to operate the port will likely seek to maximize profits. The contract, however, may place restrictions on the operator, e.g., requiring that certain stevedore firms be used and a certain percentage of the profits be shared with the port's owner.

If an operator owns a private port, several scenarios arise. First, the operator may be a private terminal operator that is in the business of operating ports. If so, the port will likely be a common-user port at which the operator seeks to maximize profits. If the port is a hub port where there is transshipment cargo, the operator may seek to promote this type of cargo to further increase profits. Second, the owner operator may be a shipping line that operates the port as a dedicated port, where only its ships or those of its alliance partners call. If so, the operator's operating objective might be to operate the port so that the profits of the owner shipping line are maximized (which may not be consistent with maximizing the profits of the port).

In a survey of ports worldwide by the Port Performance Research Network (Baltazar and Brooks 2007), the majority of the ports listed economic performance as a primary operating objective – e.g., maximize profits for shareholders, maximize return on investment for government, maximize throughput, and maximize throughput subject to a maximum allowable operating deficit. It is interesting to note that these operating objectives are effectiveness operating objectives. The second prominent operating objective (although not that of a majority of the ports) is to optimize economic development prospects (local or national) in order to, for example, create jobs and opportunities for business firms.

Port prices

Port prices may be levied on the ship, cargo, and passenger. Port cargo prices are referred to as port rates; port passenger prices are port fares. The publication that quotes port prices is the port's tariff. However, the actual prices charged by a port may not be the same as found in the tariff but rather are contract port prices – prices that arise between the port and a port user from contract negotiation. Contract prices generally arise when port competition exists in a region. A port seeking to entice a shipping line to maintain its port calls or to start new port calls may enter into a price contract with the shipping line, where the contract prices are lower than those found in the tariff.

Port prices are expected to be compatible with its operating objectives. If the operating objective is to promote economic development, port prices may not reflect port costs. For example, port prices may be set to favor exports over imports. If so, port prices may be set higher for imports than for exports for the same port services.

Port prices may also differ with respect to the value of the cargo, i.e., charging what the traffic will bear. Value-of-service pricing occurs when higher-valued cargo is charged a higher rate and lower-valued cargo is charged a lower rate for the same service. Value-of-service pricing is a form of price discrimination. In order for a port to discriminate in this fashion, it must be able to segment cargo according to high- and low-valued cargo. Since high-valued (low-valued) cargo will be less (more) sensitive to port prices, the demand for port services by shippers of high-valued (low-valued) cargo is expected to be price inelastic (price elastic). Thus, the port may charge a higher (lower) price for a port service to the shipper of high-valued (low-valued) cargo. Note further that (from the economic principles of pricing) an increase (decrease) in the price for a port service for which the demand is price inelastic (elastic) will result in an increase in revenue from this port service.

Port prices in practice

Prices charged for servicing a containership and its cargo while in port may include, for example, prices for pilotage, tuggage, wharfage, dockage, line-handling, stevedoring, vessel overtime, rental of terminal cranes, and number of containers moved on to and off the vessel. The price of pilotage is the price for the service rendered by a licensed marine pilot in guiding a vessel in or out of a port or in confined waters (charged to the vessel). The price of tuggage is the price for the service rendered by a tugboat in the towing, tugging, or berthing of vessels (charged to the vessel). The wharfage price is the price charged for renting space on the port's wharf, i.e., for use of the wharf (charged to cargo). The dockage price is the price levied against a vessel for berthing alongside a wharf where the vessel ties up, i.e., the price levied for renting the space alongside the wharf (charged to the vessel). The line-handling price is the price for tying and untying of a vessel to or from a wharf (charged to the vessel). The stevedoring price is the price for the service provided by dockworkers in the loading/unloading of a vessel's cargo (charged to cargo). The vessel overtime price is the price for the time over and above the standard time, for example, for dockworkers in the loading/unloading of a vessel's cargo. The prices for renting terminal cranes and for the number of containers moved on to and off the vessel are charged to cargo.

For an unnamed container port, the above prices are assessed to a containership and its cargo as follows. The pilotage price is based upon the overall length, breadth, and depth of the containership. The tuggage price is based on the net tonnage of the containership. Wharfage and dockage prices are based upon the net tonnage of cargo loaded and unloaded and gross registered tonnage of the containership, respectively. The line-handling price is a fixed price per containership. The stevedoring price is a price per dockworker gang hour. The vessel overtime price is a price for each overtime hour. The rental price for a terminal crane is a price per hour of usage; the price for the movement of containers is a price per container movement.

From the historical records of the above unnamed port, a 2,700 TEU containership on a given day docked at the port at 1900 hours and departed on the following day at 0600 hours. While docked, 223 TEUs of cargo were loaded and 293 TEUs of cargo were unloaded. Three dock cranes (ship-to-shore gantry cranes) and three transtainers (yard gantry cranes) were used to work the ship, i.e., loading and unloading containers on to and from the ship and moving containers to and from storage areas. The charges incurred by the containership and its cargo while in port are as follows: $1,918.54 (pilotage), $3,670.80 (tuggage), $30,600 (stevedore), $13,609.60 (wharfage), $5,460.89 (dockage), $360 (linehandling), $12,112.50 (dock cranes), $2,346 (transtainers), $1,200 (vessel overtime), and $21,334.25 (container movement) or a total of $92,612.58 port charges during the nine hours while the containership was in port.

Fully allocated cost port prices

If the effectiveness operating objective of a port is to maximize throughput subject to a zero profit constraint, the port prices for which this operating objective is satisfied will be fully allocated cost prices. Such prices generate sufficient revenue to cover (no more, no less) the costs incurred by the port in providing services for a given level of port throughput. In theory, the fully allocated cost price to be borne by a given unit of port throughput equals the cost attributable to this unit plus a fraction of the port costs that it shares with other units of port throughput. Attributable (or direct) costs can be traced to a particular unit of throughput. Shared costs cannot be traced to a particular unit of throughput and are common costs if the throughput that shares these costs is not jointly determined – one unit of throughput does not unavoidably create another. At a container port, the depreciation costs of the various cranes used in the movement of containers within the port are common shared costs to be allocated among the containers that utilize these cranes.

A major difficulty in determining fully allocated cost prices for particular units of port throughput is how to allocate the costs that these units share i.e., selecting the rule or formula to be used in allocating common cost. If the units of throughput are homogenous, the fractional share of the common cost to be borne by a given unit of throughput may be determined by dividing this unit by the number of units of throughput that share this cost. Thus, the fully allocated cost price to be charged for a unit of throughput equals the cost that is attributable to it plus its share of port common costs (for those port resources that it shares with other units of throughput).

If the fractional formulae for allocating common costs are based upon stand-alone costs (explained below), the port may be able to detect whether its resources that are shared (e.g., its cranes) are cost inefficient, i.e., not of the proper size to handle various levels of port throughput at the least cost (Talley 1994a). Suppose 1,000 containers of various sizes (e.g., 20-, 40-, and 45-foot containers) are loaded and unloaded on to and from a ship while in port by a given dock crane. The 1,000 containers share the common cost (e.g., the depreciation cost) of the crane. If each container did not share a dock crane, but had its own assigned dock crane that was the least costly crane in loading or unloading the container on to or from the ship, the cost related to this dock crane for the loading or unloading of the container would be the container's stand-alone dock crane cost.

Suppose the fractional share of the shared crane's common cost to be borne by a given container is the ratio of the container's stand-alone dock crane cost to the sum of the stand-alone dock crane costs for all 1,000 containers. Note that this fractional formula requires stand-alone dock cranes costs for only three types of containers – the 20-, 40-, and 45-foot container. A container's cost share of the crane's common cost (shared by the 1,000 containers) based upon stand-alone costs would be determined by multiplying its stand-alone fractional cost share (as determined above) by the dock crane's common cost. If the container's dock crane cost share (in sharing a crane) exceeds the container's stand-alone dock crane cost, then the port crane that handled the container (along with other containers) is cost inefficient with respect to this container. That is to say, the cost to be borne by the port in loading or unloading the container on to or from the ship would be lower if the stand-alone dock crane (rather than the share dock crane) were used instead.

Marginal-cost port prices

Suppose a government-owned port is operated by its public authority. Further, suppose the authority's board of commissioners adopts the port effectiveness operating objective of maximizing the net benefits of its port services, i.e., in their consumption (by port users) and provision (by the port authority). What pricing scheme should the port adopt to achieve this objective? The well-known pricing structure found in the economics literature for maximizing the net benefits in the consumption and provision of a given good or service is marginal-cost pricing, i.e., set the price of the good or service equal to the marginal cost of the last unit of the good produced or service provided.

An explanation for why marginal cost pricing maximizes net benefits follows. Let $NB = B - STC$ represent the net benefits of a given port service to a given type of port user, where NB represents net benefits, B represents the total benefits of the port service to the user, and STC represents the short-run total cost incurred by the port authority in providing the service. A necessary condition for net benefits to be maximized is that the change in net benefits with respect to a change in the amount of port service (Q) equals to zero, i.e., $\Delta NB/\Delta Q = \Delta B/\Delta Q - \Delta STC/\Delta Q = 0$ or $\Delta B/\Delta Q = \Delta STC/\Delta Q$, where $\Delta B/\Delta Q$ represents the marginal benefit of the last unit of port service consumed by a given type of port user and $\Delta STC/\Delta Q$ represents the short-run marginal cost of this last unit incurred by the port authority. Support for the fact that the price paid for the last unit of service consumed by a user is the marginal benefit of that unit to the user is found in the economics literature (see Layard and Walters 1978). Thus, a necessary condition for maximizing the net benefits of a given port service is for its price to be equal to its marginal cost.

In Figure 8.1 the demand for a port service for a given type of port user (e.g., carrier, shipper, or passenger) is represented by demand curve D_P and the short-run marginal cost by curve SMC. The marginal cost price P^*_P is the price at which the curves D_P and SMC intersect. At this price, Q^*_P is the amount of the port service at which the net benefits of the service are at a maximum. Note that the area under the demand curve between zero and Q^*_P service units represents the total benefits of Q^*_P (since this area is the sum of all prices or marginal benefits from zero to Q^*_P amount of port service) to the port user and the area under the SMC curve for this same service range represents the total variable cost incurred by the port authority in providing Q^*_P amount of the port service. The short-run total cost incurred by the port authority in provision of Q^*_P is the sum of this variable cost and the port authority's fixed cost.

In Figure 8.1 the area between the demand and SMC curves at Q^*_P service level represents net benefits (minus the port authority's fixed cost which is not shown). Note that at price P^*_P the net benefit area is at a maximum; at a price higher than P^*_P the net benefit area is smaller than at P^*_P. At a price lower than P^*_P the net benefit area between SMC and D_P for a service amount greater than Q^*_P is negative. When this area is subtracted from the positive net benefit area between zero and Q^*_P, it thus follows that net benefits with respect to a price lower than P^*_P are less than those net benefits with respect to P^*_P. Since fixed cost does not affect the marginal cost price in the short run, the above discussion is not affected by the fact that fixed costs are not explicitly considered in Figure 8.1.

Port prices and external costs

Suppose a port operator adopts the effectiveness operating objective of maximizing the net benefits of its port services and subsequently adopts a port tariff for which port prices are marginal cost prices. However, if the port incurs external costs in the provision of port services, its marginal cost prices will not result in the maximization of the net benefits of port services.

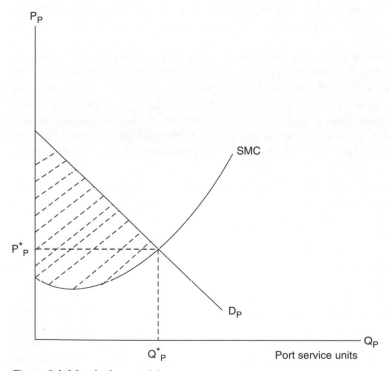

Figure 8.1 Marginal cost pricing

A port generates an externality when its activities affect nonusers of the port. If the externality is a negative externality, the nonusers will bear the costs (i.e., the external costs) of this externality and not the port operator. An example of port external costs is port pollution cost, e.g., from port air and water pollution. Ships docked in port pollute the air when they run their engines to provide electricity to the ship. They pollute the water when they dump toxic ballast water into the port's harbor. The air pollution affects the health of those that live near the port. The ballast water may contain non-indigenous species from foreign ports that may harm local species. Therefore, the pollution costs borne by the port nonusers (individuals that live near the port and local species in the port's waters) are external costs of the port.

In order for marginal cost prices to maximize the net benefits of port services, the marginal costs must reflect all (variable) costs generated by the port, i.e., marginal cost prices must reflect marginal social costs (internal plus external marginal costs). Thus, a port will be able to achieve its effectiveness operating objective of maximizing the net benefits of its port services if government requires the port operator to internalize the port's external costs or port polluters to stop polluting and thus incur the cost in doing so. Internalization of external cost by a port operator may occur when it places a pollution tax, for example, on polluting ships that equals the marginal external cost of the pollution.

Port congestion prices

Port congestion arises when port users interfere with one another in the utilization of port resources, thus increasing their time in port. Port congestion may be intentional or unintentional. Intentional port congestion may arise from preemptive priority, e.g., when a port gives priority to ships or vehicles transporting a certain type of cargo over ships or vehicles transporting another type of cargo. Unintentional port congestion arises in the normal operation of a port.

Port queuing (or waiting time) costs are extreme congestion costs that arise when the demand for port resources exceeds its supply. Ship berth congestion arises when a ship has to wait for a berth that is currently occupied by another ship. Ship work congestion arises when a berthed ship has to wait to have its cargo loaded/unloaded (given the port's limited ship loading/unloading resources) until another ship has had its cargo loaded/unloaded. Vehicle gate congestion may also arise at the entrance and departure gates of container ports as well as vehicle work congestion within the port in the loading/unloading of containers on to and from trucks and trains.

Port congestion prices have been levied by ports for the purpose of increasing the utilization of fixed resources when queuing (or waiting time) congestion occurs, e.g., when trucks queue up at entrance gates at container ports. At the Ports of Los Angeles and Long Beach, the Pier Pass program was initiated, whereby trucks hauling loaded containers to the port are charged a fee per container during the peak hours and no fee during the off-peak hours. The objective of the Pier Pass program is to shift container truck traffic from the peak to the off-peak hours, thereby improving the utilization of the ports' gates over a 24-hour period.

The Pier Pass program was launched on July 23, 2005. A $40 per-TEU (or an $80 per-FEU) traffic mitigation fee was placed on loaded containers that entered the ports' gates during the peak hours. The fee provides an incentive for cargo owners to move cargo to the ports during off-peak hours when there is no fee. This time shift in cargo will reduce (1) congestion at port gates, (2) truck traffic congestion on the local highways, and (3) air pollution from idling trucks during peak hours. The official off-peak Pier Pass gate days and times are Monday through Thursday, 6 p.m. to 3 a.m., and Saturday, 8 a.m. to 6 p.m. On April 24, 2006, the Pier Pass fee was increased to $50 per TEU (or $100 per FEU).

During the first six months of Pier Pass, 30 to 35 percent of all gate activity at the Ports of Los Angeles and Long Beach occurred during off-peak hours. Alternatively, the peak-hour traffic at the ports declined, thereby decreasing the demand for investment for port gate expansion. The Pier Pass program may also be described as a peak-hour pricing program, even though it was established to address gate congestion.

The incidence of port prices

The incidence of port prices refers to who bears the burden of port prices. Although a port price may initially be placed on a port user by a port service provider, part of this initial price may be shifted backward onto the port service provider. If so, both the port user and the port service provider will bear the burden of the port price. Will the port user or the service provider bear a greater share of the burden?

If a competitive market exists for port services, the market price and quantity of port services will be P^*_P and Q^*_P, where the market demand and supply curves D_{PI} and S_P for these services intersect (see Figure 8.2a). Suppose the providers of port services incur an increase in resource costs, thereby resulting in a shift upward (to the left) in their market supply curve to supply curve S'_P in Figure 8.2a. The increase in resource costs per unit of port service is $P^{**}_P - P^*_P$. The demand for port services by port users in Figure 8.2a is assumed to be price inelastic, noted by the steeply sloped market demand curve D_{PI}. At the intersection of market demand and supply curves D_{PI} and S'_P, the market price is P'_P. Since this price is less than P^{**}_P, it follows that port users do not bear the entire burden of the increase in resource costs incurred by service providers. However, they bear a very large fraction of this burden with service providers bearing a relatively small fraction.

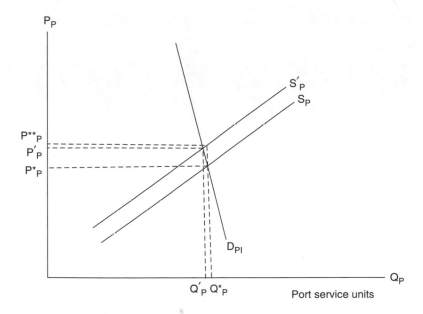

Figure 8.2a Market for port services, price inelastic demand, and price incidence

Suppose the market demand for port services is now price elastic, noted by the less steeply sloped or flatter market demand curve D_{PE} in Figure 8.2b. Suppose further that the market supply curve after an increase in resource costs remains the same, i.e., S'_P, as found in Figure 8.2a. At the intersection of market demand and supply curves D_{PE} and S'_P in Figure 8.2b, the market price is P''_P. With $P''_P < P'_P$ as found in Figure 8.2a, it follows that port users bear a smaller fraction (and port service providers bear a larger fraction) of the increase in resource costs than in Figure 8.2a. Thus, when the demand for port services is price elastic as opposed to being price inelastic, the smaller the fraction of the increases in resource costs that port service providers can shift forward to port users in the form of higher port prices.

Port taxes versus user fees

Prior to 1986, U.S. government-sponsored programs for the deepening and maintenance of port channels were financed 65 percent from the federal general tax fund, with state and/or local governments financing the remainder. The U.S. Water Resources Development Act of 1986 established the Harbor Maintenance Trust Fund (HMTF) as the federal revenue source for financing channel deepening and maintenance costs. This trust fund receives its funding from the harbor maintenance tax (HMT), an *ad valorem* tax placed on the value of exported, imported, and some domestic (coast and lake, but generally excluding inland waterway) cargo moving to and from U.S. ports. The tax rate was originally set at 0.04 percent of the value of the cargo, eventually increasing to 0.125 percent (effective January 1, 1991).

The HMT was declared unconstitutional in 1998 by the U.S. Supreme Court – in violation of the export clause of the U.S. Constitution that prohibits taxes or duties being placed on exports. On April 25, 1998, HMT revenues from exports were discontinued, but

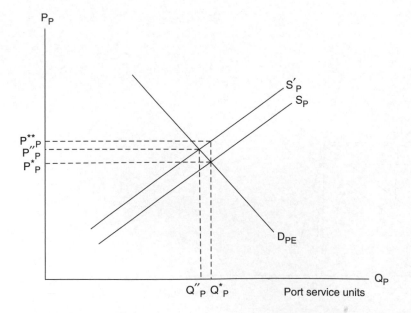

Figure 8.2b Market for port services, price elastic demand, and price incidence

remain for HMT revenues collected on imports and certain domestic and foreign trade zone cargoes. The Supreme Court, however, in the same opinion, ruled that exporters were not exempt from user fees to defray dredging costs. As opposed to having a national tax (the HMT) and therefore the federal government to finance U.S. port dredging costs, these costs can also be financed by local port dredging user fees.

There are two types of dredging costs, construction and maintenance. Construction costs are those incurred in the initial dredging of a waterway, e.g., when a waterway of a natural depth of 25 feet is dredged to a depth of 35 feet. Construction costs for this same waterway will also be incurred at a subsequent time period if the waterway is dredged to 40 feet. Maintenance dredging costs are incurred when dredging is done to maintain the dredged waterway at a given depth, e.g., at 40 feet.

Local port construction dredging user fees can be determined by allocating the construction dredging costs of a waterway among certain vessels that utilize the port waterway. It has been argued that in order to determine the cost-efficient waterway depths for ports that only those vessels for which the dredging of the waterway is necessary (i.e., dredging deeper than the natural depth or dredging a dredged waterway at a deeper depth) should share in the construction dredging costs and thus pay the local port construction dredging user fees (Talley 2007). For example, only those vessels that require that the waterway be dredged from an initial natural depth of 25 to 35 feet should share in the dredging construction cost. If larger vessels in the future wish to use the waterway but require a deeper waterway depth of 40 feet, only these vessels would share in this construction cost. Those vessels for which the natural depth of the waterway at 25 feet is sufficient would not be allocated a share of the dredging construction costs.

Local port maintenance dredging user fees can be determined by allocating the maintenance dredging costs of a waterway among certain vessels that utilize the port's waterway. If without maintenance dredging the waterway returns to its natural depth (or a steady-state dredged depth greater than the natural depth), only those vessels that require water depths greater than the natural depth (or the steady-state dredged depth) should share in the maintenance dredging costs and thus pay the local port maintenance dredging user fees.

Port-specific user dredging fees will allow lower-dredging-cost ports in a country to take advantage of their comparative advantage in dredging, i.e., to dredge to lower waterway depths in order to attract larger vessels. By comparison, higher-dredging-cost ports will be at competitive disadvantage (given their higher dredging costs) in dredging their waterways to lower depths in order to attract larger vessels.

Port investment

In the economics literature, capital is defined as a human-created resource that is used in the production of goods or provision of services. Investment is the creation of capital. Investment is a flow (i.e., for a given time period), while capital is a stock (i.e., at a point in time). Port investment is the creation of port capital that is used in the provision of port services. Port investment may be additions to the port's terminal as well as to the port's way access, e.g., waterways and highways. Investments may be made in a port's immobile capital such as its wharf, apron, and interchange gates and mobile capital such as cranes. Port investments may include investment in (1) the port's seaway access such as dredging of its harbor and provision of navigational aids; (2) its highway access such as pavement and traffic lights; and (3) its rail access such as building of rail tracks.

Port investment decisions

Whether to change port prices is a short-run decision for the port operator, but whether to change its capital stock through investments is a long-run decision. The criteria for whether a port should invest in mobile/immobile capital and way access will depend upon whether the decision is a private (nongovernment) or a public (government) decision. If the decision is to be made by an operator of a for-profit port, i.e., by a private operator, the expected revenue (R) and the cost (C) of the investment to the operator over the investment's anticipated life of N years would need to be known or estimated. Also, the market interest (or discount) rate (r) reflecting the cost of borrowing money for the investment would need to be known. This information would then be used to determine the net present value (NPV) of the investment to the private port operator, i.e.,

$$NPV_p = \sum_{t=1}^{N} [R_t - C_t / (1 + r)^t] \tag{8.5}$$

where t refers to the tth year. If NPV_p is positive (negative), the investment is justified (not justified) on profitability grounds; if zero, the operator is indifferent to undertaking or not undertaking the investment.

In order to gain insight into an understanding of NPV_p, consider the following example. Suppose a port operator has $1,000,000 to invest in a port crane or to purchase a financial instrument that pays an annual interest of r = 0.10. If the operator invests in the financial instrument, it will have available at the end of the first year the initial investment of $1,000,000 plus the interest income of $100,000 or a future value (FV_p) of $1,100,000, i.e., $FV_p = (1 + r)*\$1,000,000$ or $\$1,000,000 = FV_p/(1 + r)$. Note that the $1,000,000 in the latter equation is the NVP_p of the future value of $1,100,000.

Suppose an investment decision is to be made by a port authority that operates a publicly (or government) owned port. It will consider the NPV of the investment as well. However, unlike the situation for the private port operator, the port authority will consider all (i.e., social) benefits (SB) – not only those benefits accruing to users of the capital from the investment but also benefits accruing to nonusers. In addition, social costs (SC) are considered – not only those costs to be incurred by users of the capital from the investment but also costs to be incurred by nonusers. The NPV_u of a port investment from the perspective of the port authority (or public operator) may be expressed as

$$NPV_u = \sum_{t=1}^{N} [SB_t - SC_t / (1 + r)^t] \tag{8.6}$$

If NPV_u is positive (negative), the investment is justified (not justified) on social grounds; otherwise the operator is indifferent to undertaking the investment.

The benefits accruing to users of port capital from an investment are reflected in the demand by the users of the port service(s) provided by the capital, e.g., a dock crane. Recall that the price paid for the last unit of service consumed by a user is the marginal benefit of that unit to the user. Hence, it follows that the area under the user's demand curve for the service between zero and the actual amount of the service consumed represents the total benefit to the user of this amount of service.

The benefits to nonusers of port capital are external benefits. For example, the widening of a highway (by local government) that connects the port with a nearby interstate highway may benefit not only truckers calling at the port but also individuals (or nonusers of the port) that are calling at retail stores in the vicinity of the port. These individuals may benefit specifically from having their travel times reduced due to a reduction in highway congestion from the widening of the highway.

The greater the external benefits of port capital, the greater the likelihood that the investment in the port capital will be publicly (or government) financed. Where external benefits do not exist or are quite small, the greater the likelihood that the investment will be financed from port user revenues or borrowed funds.

In Figure 8.3, NPV_u and NPV_p for a given port investment are plotted. In quadrant I the port investment is both socially desirable and profitable, since $NPV_u > 0$ and $NPV_p > 0$. Thus, a public–private partnership should be considered in financing the investment, e.g., government financing from tax revenues and user financing from port user prices. In quadrant III the port investment is neither socially desirable nor profitable and therefore should not be undertaken. In quadrant IV the port investment is profitable but not socially desirable and therefore should be financed entirely from port user prices. In quadrant II the port investment is socially desirable but not profitable. Hence, it should be financed entirely by government.

Port investment, costs, and prices

In Figure 8.4 a port operator's short-run average total cost $SATC_1$ for a port service, where the port's capital stock is at level K_1, is plotted. Suppose the port operator's pricing policy is

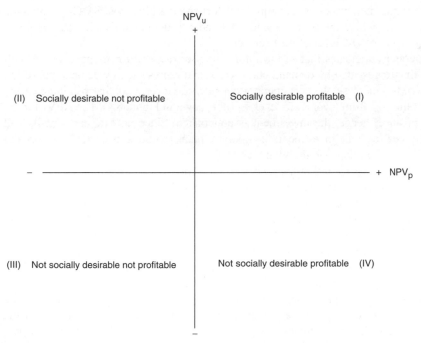

Figure 8.3 Net present value for port investment

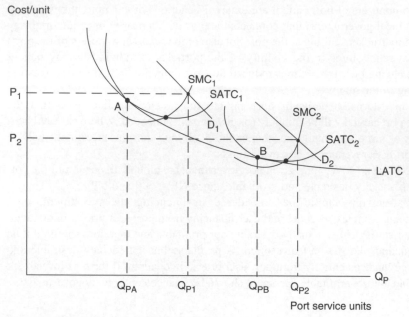

Figure 8.4 Port investment, costs, and prices

marginal cost pricing, i.e., prices are set equal to short-run marginal cost SMC_1. Hence, the port price will be P_1, where the user demand (D_1) and marginal cost (SMC_1) curves intersect for the provision of Q_{P1} level of port service.

The port operator anticipates that in the future the user demand for its port service will increase from that represented by demand curve D_1 to that represented by demand curve D_2. In anticipation of this increase, the port operator considers an investment that will increase the capital stock of the port from level K_1 to level K_2 (not shown in Figure 8.4). The NPV_p for the investment is positive; hence, the investment is undertaken. Since no external benefits and costs are anticipated from the investment, the operator plans to utilize its current port pricing policy – marginal cost pricing – in the future as well.

With the availability of capital stock level K_2, the short-run average total and marginal cost curves shift downward in Figure 8.4 to $SATC_2$ and SMC_2, respectively. These cost curves represent short-run costs for which the capital stock is at level K_2. With respect to port user demand curve D_2, the port price will decline to P_2 (where the D_2 demand and SMC_2 marginal cost curves intersect). At this price, port users demand Q_{P2} level of port service. Note that the investment and thus the increase in port capital stock have lowered the price of the port service, increased the level of service provided by the port, and lowered the short-run unit costs for this service.

The shift downward in the short-run cost curves in Figure 8.4 is explained by the fact the port exhibits economies of scale in the provision of the port service, i.e., its long-run average total cost curve LATC is negatively sloped or LATC declines as the provision of port service increases. When Q_{PA} (Q_{PB}) level of port service is provided, the port's long-run unit cost is minimized when capital stock is at level K_1 (K_2).

Port investment and macroeconomic effects

If a port is publicly owned and operated by a public port authority, it is likely (as stated previously) that its effectiveness operating objective will focus (at least to some extent) on regional economic development. Studies that investigate the impact of such a port on the economic development of its region are often described as port economic impact studies. These studies investigate the jobs created by the port (direct and indirect) and the wages generated by the port (direct and indirect). These effects are the macroeconomic effects of the port on its region.

The direct jobs of a port are those of port workers and workers in port-related jobs in the region. Hence, the direct wages of the port are those received by port workers and workers in port-related jobs in the region. If these wages are spent in the region, e.g., on consumer goods and services such as food and medical care, these expenditures will become (at least in part) wages to those employed in the consumer goods and services industries in the region. These individuals, in turn, may also spend their wages (at least in part) in the region. This re-spending has multiplier effects (see pp. 7–9). Specifically, the re-spending will increase wages in the region by a multiple of the initial spending, i.e., from the spending of wages by port workers and workers in port-related industries (or direct wages). The wages from the re-spending are the indirect wages generated because of the existence of the port in the region. The jobs created from the re-spending are the indirect jobs generated by the port because of its existence in the region.

Port economic impact studies may have many purposes. By determining the direct and indirect wages and jobs generated by publicly owned ports, these studies provide evidence of the ports' macroeconomic contributions to regions. Thus, they can be used to educate the regions' populations about the ports' contributions to the regions. The primary purpose, however, for these studies is for public port authorities to use them to obtain public support for their publicly owned ports, e.g., in order to obtain public financing of port operations and investment and/or public financing of port way-access (highway and seaway) investments.

Summary

Whether a port operator is effective will depend on how well it provides services to its users. Port effectiveness operating objectives include, for example, maximizing profits in the provision of port throughput (for a private operator) and maximizing port throughput subject to a zero profit constraint (for a public operator).

Port prices are generally levied on the ship, cargo, and passenger for the port services that they receive. The port operator is expected to set its port prices based upon its operating objective(s), unless they are set by port competition. If a zero profit constraint is to be satisfied, the port prices will be fully allocated cost prices, where a particular unit of throughput or port service is assigned the cost attributable to it plus a share of the port costs that it shares with other port units. Marginal-cost port prices maximize the net benefits of the port, assuming no port externalities. Port prices may reflect external costs that have been internalized and congestion costs. Port congestion arises when port users interfere with one another in the utilization of port resources, thus increasing their time in port. The incidence of port prices refers to who bears the burden of port prices, the provider and/or users of port services. Port-specific user dredging fees will allow lower-dredging-cost ports in a country to take advantage of their comparative advantage in dredging.

Port investment is the creation of port capital. The investment may create (in total or as an addition) immobile port capital such as the wharf, apron, and interchange gates and mobile capital such as cranes. An investment in a port's way access such as waterways and highways may also occur. An investment proposed by a port operator should be undertaken if the net present value of the investment is positive. If a port exhibits economies of scale in the provision of throughput, an investment in port capital is expected to lower the unit cost of throughput. Studies that measure the macroeconomic effects (e.g., in terms of wages and employment) of a port on its regional economy are described as port economic impact studies.

Bibliography

Baltazar, R. and Brooks, M. (2007) "Port Governance, Devolution and the Matching Framework: A Configuration Theory Approach", in M. Brooks and K. Cullinane (eds) *Devolution, Port Governance and Port Performance: Research in Transportation Economics*, 17, Amsterdam: Elsevier, 379–403.

Bennathan, E. and Walters, A. A. (1979) *Port Pricing and Investment Policy for Developing Countries*, Oxford: Oxford University Press.

Chadwin, M., Pope, J., and Talley, W. K. (1990) "Costing Terminal Operations and Measuring Capacity", *Ocean Container Transportation: An Operational Perspective*, New York: Taylor & Francis, 35–56.

Frankel, Ernst G. (1987a) "Port Pricing", *Port Planning and Development*, New York: John Wiley & Sons, 57–81.

—— (1987b) "Port Investment Criteria", *Port Planning and Development*, New York: John Wiley & Sons, 81–117.

Gripaios, P. and Gripaios, R. (1995) "The Impact of a Port on Its Local Economy: The Case of Plymouth", *Maritime Policy and Management*, 22: 13–24.

Haralambides, H. E. and Veenstra, A. (2002) "Port Pricing", in C. T. Grammenos (ed.) *The Handbook of Maritime Economics and Business*, London: Informa, 782–802.

Haralambides, H. E., Cariou, P., and Benacchio, M. (2002) "Costs, Benefits and Pricing of Dedicated Container Terminals", *Maritime Economics and Logistics*, 4: 21–34.

Layard, P. and Walters, A. (1978) *Microeconomic Theory*, New York: McGraw-Hill Book Company.

McCarthy, P. S. (2001) "Transportation Investment", *Transportation Economics: Theory and Practice – A Case Study Approach*, Malden, MA: Blackwell Publishers, 355–386.

Meersman, H., Van de Voorde, E., and Vanelslander, T. (2003) "Port Pricing: Considerations on Economic Principles and Marginal Costs", *European Journal of Transport and Infrastructure Research*, 3: 371–386.

Musso, E., Ferrari, C., and Benacchio, M. (1999) "On the Global Optimum Size of Port Terminals", *International Journal of Transport Economics*, 26: 415–437.

—— (2006) "Port Investment: Profitability, Economic Impact and Financing", in K. Cullinane and W. K. Talley (eds) *Port Economics: Research in Transportation Economics*, 16, Amsterdam: Elsevier, 171–218.

Strandenes, S. P. (2004) "Port Pricing Structures and Ship Efficiency", in W. K. Talley (ed.) *The Industrial Organization of Shipping and Ports*, a special issue of the journal, *Review of Network Economics*, 3: 135–144.

Talley, W. K. (1982) "Determining Fully Allocated Cost Prices for Regulated Transportation Industries", *International Journal of Transport Economics*, 9: 25–43.

—— (1988) "Allocating Shared Costs", *Transport Carrier Costing*, New York: Gordon and Breach Science Publishers, 159–216.

—— (1989) "Joint Cost and Competitive Value-of-Service Pricing", *International Journal of Transport Economics*, 16: 119–130.

—— (1994a) "Port Pricing: A Cost Axiomatic Approach", *Maritime Policy and Management*, 21: 61–76.

—— (1994b) "Performance Indicators and Port Performance Evaluation", *Logistics and Transportation Review*, 30: 339–352.

—— (1996) "Linkages Between Transportation Infrastructure Investment and Economic Production", in D. Gillen and W. Waters, II (eds) *Transport Infrastructure Investment and Economic Development*, a special issue of the journal *Logistics and Transportation Review*, 32: 145–154.

—— (1998) "Vessel Traffic Service Systems: Cost-Recovery Alternatives", *Maritime Policy and Management*, 25: 107–115.

—— (2006) "An Economic Theory of the Port", in K. Cullinane and W. K. Talley (eds) *Port Economics: Research in Transportation Economics*, 16, Amsterdam: Elsevier, 43–65.

—— (2007) "Financing Port Dredging Costs: Taxes Versus User Fees", *Transportation Journal*, 46: 53–58.

Tongzon, J. (1993) "The Port of Melbourne Authority's Pricing Policy: Its Efficiency and Distribution Implications", *Maritime Policy and Management*, 20: 197–205.

UNCTAD Secretariat (1975) *Port Pricing*, New York: United Nations.

9 Port governance and agglomeration

Introduction

Port governance refers to the ownership, management, and control of the operations of a port. A port may be owned by government or a private entity, i.e., a port may be a public or a private port. A public port is normally managed by a port authority – established by the owner government to manage the port on its behalf. Members of the port authority's governing board are appointed by the owner-government's legislative body or representative. The day-to-day activities of the port authority are managed by its staff. A private port is managed by its private owner, specifically a board of directors or an administrative board of the private owner (e.g., a shipping line, a port terminal operating company, or an investment group). The day-to-day operations of the private port are managed by the staff of the private owner. The control over a port's operations, i.e., the movement of cargo and/or passengers through the port, may be in the hands of the port owner, its representative, or a company to which the operations of the port are leased.

Ports are centers of economic activity. Not only are port users and service providers attracted to a port and its vicinity, but also those who indirectly derive income from the port from providing food, clothing, housing, education, entertainment, etc. to the port's users and service providers. The port stakeholders are willing to locate near one another and in the vicinity of a port because of agglomeration economies – benefits derived by individuals and firms locating near another.

The chapter presents port governance as described in the World Bank Port Reform Toolkit (2001), the privatization of ports, and port governance in practice in European, Asian, and North American ports. Then, port agglomeration is discussed, followed by a discussion of ports and cities.

Port governance

The World Bank Port Reform Toolkit (2001) describes port governance in terms of four types of ports: (1) the service port, (2) the tool port, (3) the landlord port, and (4) the private port. The service port is owned, i.e., its land and all assets (fixed and mobile), by government and managed by a port authority (established by the government) that controls the port's operations. Cargo-handling activities are executed by labor directly employed by the port authority. The strength of the service port is that one agency, the port authority, is responsible for the port's development and operations and thus potentially may provide for a relatively fast port decision-making process. A weakness of the service port is that there is little or no private involvement in the port's services. The lack of private competition for services may result in inefficient provisions of port services. Also, the dependence of the port authority on investment funds from government may result in over- or under-funding of port investments. Many ports in developing countries are service ports (e.g., India and Sri Lanka).

As for the service port, land and all assets (fixed and mobile) of the tool port are owned by government and the port is managed by a port authority. The port authority's staff operates the port-owned equipment. However, other cargo-handling activities such as moving cargo to and from vessels may be carried out by private cargo-handling firms (e.g., stevedoring companies) contracted by shipping lines, ship agents, or other principals licensed by the port authority. A strength of the tool port (as for the service port) is that one agency, the port authority, is responsible for port development. A weakness is that conflicts may arise between the port authority's staff and private service providers that may impede efficiency in the operation of the port.

As for the service and tool ports, the landlord port is owned by government and managed by a port authority. However, the port authority gives up its control over port operations by leasing the port's infrastructure to private terminal operators for their operation of the port. The port authority is the landlord to which lease payments are made. It is responsible for the maintenance of basic port infrastructure such as berths, quays, and access roadways. Private terminal operators may provide and maintain their own buildings, purchase and install their own equipment on the port's grounds, and hire dockworkers. The strength of a landlord port is that private terminal operators are likely to be more responsive to changing market conditions than the port authority, since their survival depends upon commercial success, e.g., making profits. A possible weakness is duplication in the marketing of the port to potential customers by the port authority and the private terminal operator (Brooks 2004). Examples of landlord ports include those found in Rotterdam, Antwerp, and Singapore.

The private port is one for which its land and infrastructure are privately owned and its operations are under the control of the private owner or a private operator to which the operations of the port are leased. The strength of the private port is that it has greater flexibility than a public port in making port investments and controlling port operations, especially in regard to changing market conditions. A weakness is the loss of government involvement in developing port economic policies. Also, where there is little or no port competition, the private port may become monopolistic in behavior. Private ports are found in the United Kingdom and New Zealand.

Port privatization

The number of service ports worldwide has steadily diminished as governments have sought to increase the efficiency of port operations through privatization. Privatization consists of (1) asset privatization, the transfer of assets from a public port to the private sector, for example, to a private port terminal operator, and (2) service privatization, the transfer of a public port service (but not public port assets) to the private sector for its provision.

The United Kingdom (UK) is one of the few countries in the world, where port privatization has been asset privatization – a sale of port assets, including port land, to the private sector. Thus, public ports have been turned into private ports. In most other countries, port privatization has been service privatization.

Service privatization includes contracting-out, franchising, and privatization competition. Port contracting-out occurs when a government or the port authority transfers public port services to private providers, e.g., in the case of tool and landlord ports. The government or public authority, however, maintains control over the contracted-out service via its contract (or lease) with the private provider. Contracting-out privatization can be described in terms of the principal-agency theory. The principal is the port authority that contracts out the service, the agent is the private provider to which the service is transferred, and the contract is the mechanism by which the principal induces the agent to act in its interests.

Franchising occurs when a designated franchising agency (rather than the current public provider) transfers a public service. If the current public provider of the service in addition to private firms are allowed to participate in this franchising, i.e., allowed to provide the auctioned service, the franchising is referred to as privatization competition (Snyder *et al.* 2001). Privatization competition has also been referred to as devolution (Brooks and Cullinane 2007). If a private firm is the lowest bidder and the service is transferred to this bidder, the service is franchised. If the current public provider (or port authority) is the lowest bidder and thus is authorized to provide the service, privatization competition occurs. However, cost savings will still occur if the cost bid is lower than the cost currently incurred by the public provider in the provision of the service.

The model of public ownership and private operations of a port (i.e., contracting-out privatization) is widespread in the worldwide port community. A landlord port authority enters into a contract (e.g., a long-term operating lease) with a private company (say a private port terminal operator) to allow the latter to operate a given marine terminal for a specific period of time. The port authority retains the property rights to the terminal during the concession period for which it receives lease payments. The contract or lease agreement may include stipulations on construction, financing, and operations of the leased terminal.

Examples of port public-ownership and private-operation lease arrangements (Notteboom 2007) include build-lease-operate (BLO), build-operate-transfer (BOT), and build-operate-share-transfer (BOST). Under the BLO arrangement, the private company constructs port facilities and operates them throughout the concession period. The port authority retains the property rights to the port and receives lease payments during this period. The BLO arrangement is popular in China.

Under the BOT arrangement, a private company agrees to build/modernize and operate a terminal. The private company is responsible for all commercial risks, receiving revenues from its port operations during the concession period. At the end of the concession period, the government takes ownership of the terminal. The Port of Tanjung Pelapas in Malaysia, a major competitor of the Port of Singapore, was constructed under a BOT arrangement.

The BOST arrangement is similar to the BOT arrangement except commercial risks and revenues are shared with the port authority during the concession period. As under the BOT arrangement, the government takes ownership of the terminal at the end of the concession period.

Port governance in practice

European ports

Public ports in the United Kingdom have experienced asset privatization, i.e., the sale of assets (including land) to the private sector. Two distinct privatization phases have occurred: (1) the sale of state-owned ports and state-owned railway ports in the early 1980s, and (2) the sale of trust public ports following the passage of the UK Ports Act of 1991. Trust ports are major independent ports, established by an Act of Parliament and governed by a Board of Trustees. Trust ports were privatized at a sales price of between 5 percent and 25 percent of their real market value (Baird 2000). The UK port industry is more concentrated than in the past – the 20 largest ports, 15 of which are privately owned, handled 85 percent of all UK port traffic in 2003 (Baird and Valentine 2007).

Belgian ports, due to their national economic importance, are publicly owned and publicly managed. Belgium has a decentralized port governance structure. For example, the ports of Antwerp and Ghent are autonomous municipal port companies. As such, port services are subject to municipal regulation. Regional governments are the primary financier of port investments. There are no private ports in Belgium.

The three largest ports in the Netherlands – the ports of Rotterdam, Amsterdam, and Zeeland – are public ports that are managed by port authorities. They account for over 90 percent of the total port throughput of the Netherlands (de Langen and van der Lugt 2007). The country's fourth largest port, Velsen/Ymuiden, is a privately owned, single user port. The public ports are generally managed by municipal and regional port authorities. The national government is not directly involved in their management. The one exception is the Port of Rotterdam, where in 2004, the status of its port authority changed from a municipal status to a public corporation. The municipality of Rotterdam, rather than being the only port-authority shareholder, became the majority shareholder and the national government became the minor shareholder – in order to provide investment funds for the port expansion project Second Maasvlakte (de Langen and van der Lugt 2007).

Greek ports have been owned, maintained, and operated by state port authorities. In the early 1990s, the deficiencies of Greek ports became apparent – "absence of long-term vision, the insensitivity towards users' demands, absence of port facilities and inland connections, and lack of investment" (Pallis 2007). In 1999 the Greek government undertook port reform. The ports of Piraeus and Thessaloniki were listed on the Athens Stock Exchange; the Greek state, however, retained 75 percent of their ownership. In 2003 they were converted to limited companies, having one share owned by the state, and were to operate as private businesses. The remaining Greek ports are managed by local authorities. Port reform is still developing and is based upon the desire of the Greek government to overcome years of port inefficiencies.

Commercial ports in Italy are classified into three categories following passage of the Framework Law no. 84 in 1994, the Reorganization of Legislation on Ports: (1) ports of international economic relevance (Class I), (2) ports of national economic relevance (Class II), and (3) ports of regional and interregional economic relevance (Class III). Port authorities replaced state port organizations in the management of the 24 Class I and II ports. Public port authorities own the lands of their ports and have the legal status to lease the port or one or more of its terminals to private operators. Port operations can only be provided by competitive private enterprises; port authorities can provide only ancillary activities (Valleri *et al.* 2007).

Asian ports

The Port of Hong Kong has a three-tiered governance structure (Cullinane and Song 2001): (1) the top tier, the Hong Kong Special Administration Region, leases land to private terminal operators; (2) the second tier, the Marine Department, performs strategic planning and regulatory tasks (similar to that of a port authority); and (3) the third tier, private terminal operators, performs cargo-handling activities. In Hong Kong, the government provides port infrastructure and strategic planning for port development, while private terminal operators finance, develop, and operate the port's terminals. The private terminal operators include Modern Terminals, DP World, Hong Kong International Terminals (a member of the Hutchinson Port Holdings Group), COSCO-HIT Terminals, and Asia Container Terminals.

Prior to 1984, Chinese ports were owned and managed by the central government of China. The Port Law, which came into effect on January 1, 2004, stated that the Chinese central government would no longer own ports. Public ports would be transferred to local provincial or municipal governments. However, the central government must approve all port strategic planning undertaken by local governments. Further, foreign investors without a Chinese partner can invest in and operate ports in China, but no foreign investor can be the predominant investor. The rationale for port reform in China was to free Chinese ports "from the bureaucracy of government, and to increase the competitiveness and efficiency of the port industry, especially with respect to the provision of additional capacity" (Cullinane and Wang 2007).

The Port of Singapore has a strategic advantage in being located on one of the world's busiest shipping lanes, the Malacca Straits. Eighty percent of its container cargo is transshipment cargo. Prior to 1997 the Port of Singapore Authority (PSA) owned, managed, and controlled the operations of the port's marine container terminals. On October 1, 1997, the PSA was reorganized as a public company, the PSA Corporation, a government-owned entity with commercial objectives. The reorganization was done in order to provide the Port of Singapore with the flexibility to compete in a global container market – investing in port infrastructure and responding to port competition (Cullinane *et al.* 2007). In December 2003 the PSA Corporation was reorganized to include only domestic container terminal operations; all international container business was transferred to a new corporation, PSA International. Both corporations, PSA Corporation and PSA International, are owned by the government. In addition to its operations of the container terminals of the Port of Singapore, PSA International is also a major global container port terminal operator (see Chapter 2).

Following passage of the Harbour Act of 1967 and the New Port Construction Promotion Act of 1996, the ports of South Korea are classified as international trading and coastal (or local) ports. The ports are owned by the Korean government. The major container ports, Busan and Gwangyang, are located on the country's southern coast. The port governance of South Korea has both public and private aspects. Container terminal operators are under the supervision of the Korea Container Terminal Authority (KCTA) which in turn is under the control of the Ministry of Maritime Affairs and Fisheries (MOMAF) of the central government. The MOMAF has greatly influenced the management, operation, and development of container terminals in South Korea (Song and Lee 2007). The Busan Port Authority and the Incheon Port Authority were established in 2003 and 2005, respectively, and are responsible for the operations and development of their ports. In 1997 private terminal operators were allowed to operate Korean ports.

North American ports

U.S. general cargo ports have evolved over time from private railroad ports to local and state government-owned ports, managed by port authorities. Container ports are often landlord ports, where port authorities have leased their container operations to private terminal operators. The ports of New York-New Jersey, Philadelphia, Miami, and Los Angeles and Long Beach, for example, have leased their container operations to private terminal operators. Bulk cargo ports are usually private ports. The U.S. Constitution limits the role of the federal government in ports, thus preventing the establishment of a national port policy.

The 1995 Canadian National Marine Policy established three categories of ports in Canada: Canadian Port Authorities (CPAs), Local/Regional Ports, and Remote Ports – with varying ownership and organizational structures. As of January 1, 2004, all but 69 of the 568 Canadian ports were classified according to the 1995 policy (Brooks 2004). The Canada Marine Act of 1998 (which became effective on January 1, 1999) provided for Canadian port reform. Canadian ports were required to become financially self-sufficient.

A decentralized approach to port management replaced a centralized approach. However, appointments to the board of directors of the various Canadian Port Authorities (CPAs) are controlled by the Minister of Transport; thus, government regulation of Canadian ports remains with the Canadian government.

Agglomeration

Ports have always been centers of economic activity. Port users (carriers, shippers, and passengers) and service providers (for example, port operators, stevedores, and ship agents) are obviously part of this economic activity. In addition, the income (or a part thereof) received by port users and service providers and their employees is spent in the port's hinterland, for example, on food, clothing, education, entertainment, and housing. This spending will be income to its receivers, a portion of which is respent (i.e., the multiplier effect) by these receivers in the port's hinterland. Thus, the port also has an indirect effect on the economic activity of the port's hinterland, i.e., from businesses selling goods and services to consumers utilizing their direct and indirect incomes generated by the port (see Chapter 1).

A port exhibits agglomeration economies (or benefits). Agglomeration refers to the concentration of people attracted to one place, because many firms or one large firm are in that place. If the port is that one large firm, the city in which the port is located is often referred to as a port city. In the port literature, port agglomeration has also been discussed in terms of a port cluster, i.e., a port is a cluster of economic activity (de Langen 2002, 2004, 2007; Haezendonck 2001).

The benefits of port agglomeration accrue to port stakeholders – individuals, firms, and government entities that affect or are affected by the operations of the port. The benefits arise from the stakeholders being located close to one another. Port stakeholders have been classified as stakeholders that are (1) internal, e.g., port employees; (2) external, e.g., supporting maritime-related firms; (3) legislative and public policy oriented, e.g., government agencies responsible for transport and port issues; and (4) community based, e.g., community groups, the press, and the general public (Notteboom and Winkelmans 2002).

A retailer's import distribution center located near a port is a specific example of a port external stakeholder. Containerized imports that arrive at major ports by ship are trucked to nearby import distribution centers. These centers operate as traditional distribution warehouses (see Chapter 5), where value-added services such as tagging, bagging, pick-and-pack consolidation, and quality-control inspections are provided. From these centers, merchandise is transported to the retailer's regional distribution centers or directly to its stores. Import distribution centers in the U.S. are a growth market with vacancy rates in Southern California, Seattle-Tacoma, Houston, New Jersey, Savannah, and Norfolk being 2, 5, 7, 7, 4, and 4 percent, respectively (Mongelluzzo 2006). The major factors affecting the location of import distribution centers are (1) the cost of land, (2) the cost and availability of labor, and (3) the logistics efficiencies in serving the target market (Mongelluzzo 2006).

Since there are a large number of port stakeholders, the balancing of their interests and concerns by port managers can be difficult. For instance, the maximization of port throughput by port managers may conflict with the interests of other stakeholders. Stakeholders that seek, for example, to protect the environment or to reduce highway congestion (caused by trucks transporting containers) may prefer less port throughput. "Port managers should give primary consideration to the interests of those stakeholders who are most intimately and critically involved" (Henesey 2006: 104).

One benefit of port agglomeration is transfer economies – the savings in transportation costs to firms in locating near the port (Nourse 1968). For example, importers may store cargo that is imported through the port in nearby distribution warehouses, where cargo is sorted for truckload transport to distant retail sites, thereby reducing importers' inland transportation costs from truckload rather than less-than-truckload transport of cargo. At larger ports, owner-operator truck drivers are expected to be available to provide local drayage and over-the-road hauling of containers to and from the port at a lower cost than that to be incurred by each shipping line utilizing its private fleet of trucks to provide this service.

Agglomeration economies may also arise from external economies of scale, i.e., by firms hiring specialized service providers that exhibit economies of scale (in the provision of services) to provide them with services as opposed to the firms themselves having to provide these services (Bish and Nourse 1975). For example, at larger ports, ship agents (freight forwarders and third-party logistics firms) are expected to be available to provide services to shipping lines (shippers) at a lower cost than that to be incurred by the lines (shippers) themselves in providing these services. The service providers can provide the services at lower cost, since they are providing services to many firms under economies of scale. The degree of agglomeration economies (i.e., from transfer economies and external economies of scale) associated with a port region is expected to be positively correlated with the size of the port.

A port region may also experience agglomeration diseconomies – i.e., firms and individuals in the port region may incur higher costs in being located near one another. Agglomeration diseconomies may arise from external costs that occur when a third party bears the costs of an economic activity in which he or she is not a participant. Port pollution cost is an example of a port external cost. Ships and trucks that call at a port emit emissions that pollute the port's air; ballast water (that contains pollutants) that is dumped by ships into the port's waters will pollute these waters. If the residents of the port region bear the cost of this pollution (e.g., in terms of higher health costs) and not the polluters (ships and trucks), then the pollution cost will be an external cost of the ships and trucks that call at the port. However, governments may force the polluters to bear or internalize this cost through regulation, e.g., governments may require ships to utilize new technology to prevent air pollution while in port. If so, the pollution cost will be internalized by the emitters of the pollution and thus become an internal as opposed to an external cost of the emitters.

Agglomeration diseconomies in a port region may also be attributed to rising congestion costs. Congestion arises in a port region when firms and individuals interfere with one another in the utilization of the region's infrastructure, thereby increasing their time and related cost in this utilization. For example, trucks moving containers to and from a port may utilize the same roads as automobiles. If the truck movements contribute to road congestion, the travel time and related costs of the automobile users of these roads will increase as well as the travel time and related costs of the truckers. At some point, the time and loss in income incurred by truckers (assuming truckers are paid by the number of containers moved) in moving containers to and from the port may become so great that a significant number of truckers may relocate to a less congested port. The subsequent shortage of truck drivers and the decline in the inland movements of containers to and from the port may, in turn, lead to a decrease in number of ship calls at the port.

Ports and cities

During the first half of the twentieth century, ports created cities and big ports created big cities (Norcliffe *et al.* 1996). Settlements appeared on rivers and in sheltered harbors that were accessible to seas and oceans. Port cities were settlements, where cargoes were interfaced between land and ocean and where related businesses (e.g., financing and insuring cargoes) emerged.

Since the first half of the twentieth century, relationships between ports and cities have changed, i.e., a large city does not necessarily have a large port (e.g., London) and vice versa. Large cities without a port (e.g., the U.S. city Atlanta) or having a small port (e.g., the U.S. cities Chicago, Philadelphia, Detroit, Cleveland, St. Louis, Boston, and Buffalo that were developed as port cities) are now more likely to exist. The rationale is that cities can emerge "through agglomeration forces generated by the interaction of increasing returns and transport costs" (Fujita and Mori 1996: 95).

Ports have reasons not to be located in cities. For example, with containerships increasing in size, container shipping lines require container ports to have deeper-draft channels and berths and wider turning basins for the larger containerships. If city ports do not satisfy these requirements, alternative locations for container ports (that satisfy these requirements) will be sought, e.g., the Port of Prince Rupert in Canada. Container ports are more capital intensive and thus less labor intensive than breakbulk ports. Hence, there is less need for container ports to be located in cities, where larger supplies of potential workers are found.

Summary

Port governance refers to the ownership, management, and control of operations of a port. The World Bank classifies port governance in terms of four types of ports: (1) the service port, (2) the tool port, (3) the landlord port, and (4) the private port. The role of government in the World Bank's port governance classification diminishes from a service port, tool port, landlord port, and then to a private port. The privatization of public ports may include the transfer of assets (asset privatization) and the transfer of services (service privatization). The latter includes contracting-out, franchising, and privatization competition (or devolution).

The asset privatization of public ports in the U. K. began in the early 1980s. Belgian ports are publicly owned and publicly managed. The largest ports in the Netherlands are managed by port authorities. Port reform is underway in Greece, where some Greek ports are managed by local port authorities. In Italy, port authorities own the land of their ports and may lease port operations to private operators.

The Port of Hong Kong has a three-tiered governance structure, but private terminal operators operate the port's terminals. Port reform is underway in China, where the ownership of public ports is being transferred from the central government to local governments. The Port of Singapore is owned by the government and PSA International operates the port's container terminals as well as container terminals in other countries. Port governance in South Korea has both public and private aspects; private terminal operators are allowed to operate ports.

Ports in the United States have evolved over time from private railroad ports to local and state government-owned ports, managed by port authorities. In 1995 Canadian ports were classified into three categories – Canadian Port Authorities, Local/Regional Ports, and Remote Ports – with varying ownership and organizational structures. Canadian ports are required to be financially self-sufficient.

Ports exhibit agglomeration economies (or benefits). Agglomeration refers to the concentration of people attracted to one place, because many firms or one large firm such as a port is in that place. The cost savings from agglomeration economies to port stakeholders arise from the stakeholders being located near one another and to the port. Agglomeration economies consist of transfer economies and external economies of scale. Transfer economies are the savings in transportation costs to port stakeholders in locating near the port. External economies of scale occur when a specialized service provider that exhibits economies of scale (in the provision of a service) can provide this service to a port at a lower cost than the cost that would be incurred by the port in providing this service for itself. Ports may also exhibit agglomeration diseconomies, where cost increases rather than cost savings occur for its stakeholders, e.g., from increases in port pollution and congestion costs. Relationships between ports and cities have changed, i.e., a large city does not necessarily have a large port, and vice versa.

Bibliography

Baird, A. J. (2000) "Port Privatization: Objectives, Extent, Process and the UK Experience", *International Journal of Maritime Economics*, 2: 177–194.

—— (2002) "Privatization Trends at the World's Top-100 Container Ports", *Maritime Policy and Management*, 29: 271–284.

—— and Valentine, V. F. (2007) "Port Privatization in the United Kingdom", in M. R. Brooks and K. Cullinane (eds) *Devolution, Port Governance and Port Performance: Research in Transportation Economics*, 17, Amsterdam: Elsevier, 55–84.

Bish, R. L. and Nourse, H. O. (1975) *Urban Economics and Policy Analysis*, New York: McGraw-Hill.

Brooks, M. R. (2004) "The Governance Structure of Ports", in W. K. Talley (ed.) *The Industrial Organization of Shipping and Ports*, a special issue of the journal, *Review of Network Economics*, 3: 168–183.

—— and Cullinane, K. (2007) "Governance Models Defined", in M. R. Brooks and K. Cullinane (eds) *Devolution, Port Governance and Port Performance: Research in Transportation Economics*, 17, Amsterdam: Elsevier, 405–435.

Chang, Y.-C. (2008) "The Impact of Maritime Clusters", a paper presented at the Annual Conference of the International Association of Maritime Economists, Dalian, China.

Cullinane, K. and Song, D.-W. (2001) "The Administrative and Ownership Structure of Asian Container Ports", *International Journal of Maritime Economics*, 3: 175–197.

—— and Wang, T.-F. (2007) "Port Governance in China", in M. R. Brooks and K. Cullinane (eds) *Devolution, Port Governance and Port Performance: Research in Transportation Economics*, 17, Amsterdam: Elsevier, 331–356.

——, Yap, W., and Lam, J. (2007) "The Port of Singapore and its Governance Structure", in M. R. Brooks and K. Cullinane (eds) *Devolution, Port Governance and Port Performance: Research in Transportation Economics*, 17, Amsterdam: Elsevier, 285–310.

de Langen, P. W. (2002) "Clustering and Performance: The Case of Maritime Clustering in the Netherlands", *Maritime Policy and Management*, 29: 209–221.

—— (2004) "Governance in Seaport Clusters", *Maritime Economics and Logistics*, 6: 141–156.

—— (2007) "Stakeholders, Conflicting Interests and Governance in Port Clusters", in M. R. Brooks and K. Cullinane (eds) *Devolution, Port Governance and Port Performance: Research in Transportation Economics*, 17, Amsterdam: Elsevier, 457–477.

—— and van der Lugt, L. M. (2007) "Governance Structures of Port Authorities in the Netherlands", in M. R. Brooks and K. Cullinane (eds) *Devolution, Port Governance and Port Performance: Research in Transportation Economics*, 17, Amsterdam: Elsevier, 109–137.

Fujita, M. and Mori, T. (1996) "The Role of Ports in the Making of Major Cities: Self-Agglomeration and Hub-Effect", *Journal of Development Economics*, 49: 93–120.

Goss, R. O. (1999) "On the Distribution of Economic Rent in Seaports", *International Journal of Maritime Economics*, 1: 1–18.

Haezendonck, E. (2001) *Essays on Strategy Analysis for Seaports*, Leuven: Garant.

Henesey, L. E. (2006) *Multi-Agent Systems for Container Terminal Management*, Karlskrona, Sweden: Blekinge Institute of Technology.

Lee, S.-W., Song, D.-W., and Ducruet, C. (2008) "A Tale of Asia's World Ports: The Spatial Evolution in Global Hub Port Cities", *Geoforum*, 39: 372–385.

Maloni, M. J. and Jackson, E. C. (2007) "Stakeholder Contributions to Container Port Capacity: A Survey of Port Authorities", *Journal of the Transportation Research Forum*, 46: 23–42.

Mongelluzo, B. (2006) "White-Hot Market: Growth of Big-Box Chains and Containerized Imports Create a Boom in Distribution Centers Near Seaports", *Journal of Commerce*, March 27: 14.

Norcliffe, G., Bassett, K., and Hoare, T. (1996) "The Emergence of Postmodernism on the Urban Waterfront", *Journal of Transport Geography*, 4: 123–134.

Notteboom, T. (2007) "Concession Agreements as Port Governance Tools", in M. R. Brooks and K. Cullinane (eds) *Devolution, Port Governance and Port Performance: Research in Transportation Economics*, 17, Amsterdam: Elsevier, 437–455.

—— and Winkelmans, W. (2002) "Stakeholder Relations Management in Ports: Dealing with the Interplay of Forces Among Stakeholders in a Changing Competitive Environment", *Proceedings of the 2002 Annual Conference of the International Association of Maritime Economists*, Panama City, Panama.

Nourse, H. O. (1968) *Regional Economics*, New York: McGraw-Hill.

Pallis, A. A. (2007) "Port Governance in Greece", in M. R. Brooks and K. Cullinane (eds) *Devolution, Port Governance and Port Performance: Research in Transportation Economics*, 17, Amsterdam: Elsevier, 155–169.

Pettit, S. J. (2008) "United Kingdom Ports Policy: Changing Government Attitudes", *Marine Policy*, 32: 719–727.

Snyder, C. M., Trost, R. P., and Trunker, R. D. (2001) "Reducing Government Spending with Privatization Competitions: A Study of the Department of Defense Experiences", *Review of Economics and Statistics*, 83: 108–117.

Song, D.-W. and Lee, S.-W. (2007) "Port Governance in Korea", in M. R. Brooks and K. Cullinane (eds) *Devolution, Port Governance and Port Performance: Research in Transportation Economics*, 17, Amsterdam: Elsevier, 357–375.

Talley, W. K. (1996) "Linkages Between Transportation Infrastructure Investment and Economic Production", in D. Gillen and W. Waters, II (eds) *Transport Infrastructure Investment and Economic Development*, a special issue of the journal, *Logistics and Transportation Review*, 32: 145–154.

Valleri, M. A., Lamonarca, M., and Papa, P. (2007) "Port Governance in Italy", in M. R. Brooks and K. Cullinane (eds) *Devolution, Port Governance and Port Performance: Research in Transportation Economics*, 17, Amsterdam: Elsevier, 139–153.

World Bank (2001) *World Bank Port Reform Tool Kit*. Available online at http://rru.worldbank.org/Documents/Toolkits/ports_fulltoolkit.pdf (accessed 4 March 2009).

10 Port performance and competition

Introduction

Ports have traditionally evaluated their performance by comparing their actual and optimum throughputs (measured in tonnage or number of containers handled). If a port's actual throughput approaches (departs from) its optimum throughput over time, the conclusion is that its performance has improved (deteriorated) over time.

A port may also use performance indicators to evaluate its performance. If the port's economic objective is to maximize profits, port management would select values for the port indicators that would result in the maximization of the port's profits. These indicator values are the port's performance indicator standards (or benchmarks).

Port competition may be interport competition (between ports) or intraport competition (within a given port). Ports may exhibit economic rents in the form of high port prices. A port market is contestable if the threat of competition by potential entrants will force incumbent ports to behave competitively. A port's competitiveness may be evaluated in terms of the growth, market share, and diversification of its traffic volume.

This chapter discusses throughput and indicator port performance evaluation of a single port and performance evaluation from a multiport perspective. Inter- and intraport competition, the roles of economic rent and contestability in port competition, and port competitiveness are also discussed.

Performance evaluation: a single port perspective

A port, especially in a competitive environment, is not only concerned with whether it is technically and cost efficient but also whether it is effective in providing throughput. Effectiveness is concerned with how well the port utilizes its available resources. Specifically, effectiveness is concerned with how well the port provides throughput service to its users – carriers (ocean and inland) and shippers. Economic operating objectives of a port may be classified as either efficiency or effectiveness objectives. For example, port efficiency operating objectives include the technical efficiency objective of maximizing throughput in the employment of a given level of resources (exhibited by the port's economic production function) and the cost efficiency objective of minimizing cost in the provision of a given level of throughput (exhibited by the port's economic cost function).

Port effectiveness operating objectives will differ between privately owned and government-owned ports. If the port is privately owned, its effectiveness economic operating objective might be to maximize profits or to maximize throughput subject to a minimum profit constraint. If the port is owned by government, its effectiveness economic operating objective might be to maximize throughput subject to a zero operating deficit (where port revenue equals cost) or subject to a maximum operating deficit (where port revenue is less than cost) that is to be subsidized by government.

In order for a port to be effective, it must be efficient – i.e., it must be cost efficient which in turn requires that it must be technically efficient. For example, if a port has the effectiveness operating objective of maximizing profits and is cost inefficient, it can obtain greater profits for the same level of throughput service by lowering its costs to become cost efficient. Note that a port can be cost efficient without being effective.

Poorly performing ports that are cost inefficient may have to increase their port prices to cover costs and thus to break even (where revenue covers costs), thereby possibly placing them at a competitive price disadvantage, all else held constant. When ports are technically inefficient, resulting in ships staying in port longer, shipping lines may have to introduce more ships on a given trade route in order to meet their scheduled port calls on the route. Also, when cargoes stay in ports longer, shippers may have to increase their inventories, resulting in higher inventory costs. Ineffective ports may have lower profits as a consequence, thereby having less profit to finance port investments (Marlow and Paixao Casaca 2003).

Throughput performance evaluation

If a port's actual throughput departs from (approaches) its optimum throughput over time, one would conclude that its performance has deteriorated (improved) over time. While a port's optimum throughput may be a technically (or production) efficient, a cost-efficient, or an effectiveness optimum throughput, the technically efficient optimum throughput has typically been utilized in port throughput performance evaluations.

A port's economic optimum throughput is that throughput that satisfies an economic objective or objectives of the port. It may be either an economic (1) technically efficient optimum throughput (based upon the port's economic production function), (2) cost-efficient optimum throughput (based upon the port's economic cost function), or (3) effectiveness optimum throughput (based upon the port's effectiveness operating objective such as maximizing profits). Thus, the economic performance of a port may be evaluated from the standpoint of technical efficiency, cost efficiency, and effectiveness by comparing its actual throughput with its economic: technically efficient optimum throughput, cost-efficient optimum throughput, and effectiveness optimum throughput, respectively.

Indicator performance evaluation

Two contrasting methodologies have appeared in the literature for selecting performance indicators for transportation carriers and ports – the operating objective specification methodology and the criteria specification methodology (Talley 1986). The operating objective specification methodology requires the specification of an operating objective for the purpose of then selecting performance indicators. The criteria specification methodology specifies the criteria that selected performance indicators must satisfy.

With respect to an economics operating objective, a port's performance indicators are those variables whose values are under the control of port management (i.e., choice variables) for optimizing the operating objective. If the operating objective is the port's technical efficiency operating objective, then the port's operating options discussed in Chapter 7 are the port's performance indicators for this operating objective. The values of these variables that optimize the economic objective are the indicators' standards (or benchmarks). If the actual values of the indicators approach (depart from) their standards over time, the port's performance with respect to the economic objective will have improved (deteriorated) over time.

The criteria specification methodology for selecting port performance indicators may include the following selection criteria: (1) conciseness, (2) consistency with objectives, (3) data availability, (4) data-collection time and cost, (5) measurability, (6) minimization of uncontrollable factors, and (7) robustness (Talley 1994). The conciseness criterion requires that the redundancy and overlap among selected indicators be limited. The consistency-with-objectives criterion requires that the indicators be consistent with the port's operating objectives, i.e., they affect these objectives when their values change. In addition to the availability of data, the time and cost to be incurred in the collection of the indicator data should be considered in the selection of port performance indicators. The measurability criterion requires that the selected indicators be measurable, i.e., having a continuous as opposed to a discrete unit of measurement. The minimizing–uncontrollable–factors criterion requires that the values of the port's selected indicators be under the control of port management. The robustness criterion requires that the selected indicators allow for the port to be evaluated under various scenarios. Port performance indicators selected from an economic operating objective specification perspective (i.e., choice variables for optimizing the given economic objective) in general satisfy the selection criteria of the criteria specification methodology.

Port performance indicators selected by the economic operating objective approach, where the port's operating objective is an effectiveness operating objective such as to maximize the port's annual throughput (in tons) subject to a profit constraint, are found in Table 10.1. These indicators are the operating options for ports found in Chapter 7 with respect to port technical efficiency as well as port prices (assuming that the port does not face competition, where the market sets port prices) with respect to port effectiveness (Talley 1994). However, since a port must be technically efficient in order to be effective, all of the indicators in Table 10.1 are also effectiveness indicators.

Table 10.1 Port performance indicators

Vehicle/ship loading and unloading service rates
Vehicle/ship turn-around times
Channel reliability – the percent of time that the port's channel is open to navigation
Berth reliability – the percent of time that the port's berth is open to the berthing of ships
Entrance gate reliability – the percent of time that the port's entrance gate is open for vehicles
Departure gate reliability – the percent of time that the port's departure gate is open for vehicles
Channel accessibility – the percent of time that the port's channel adheres to authorized depth and
  width dimensions
Berth accessibility – the percent of time that the port's berth adheres to authorized depth and width
  dimensions
Probability of cargo loss in port
Probability of cargo damage in port
Probability of ship damage in port
Probability of ship property loss in port
Probability of vehicle damage in port
Probability of vehicle property loss in port
Port prices

Source: Talley, W. K. (1994) "Performance Indicators and Port Performance Evaluation", *Logistics and Transportation Review*, 30: 339–352; Talley, W. K. (2006a) "An Economic Theory of the Port", in K. Cullinane and W. K. Talley (eds) *Port Economics: Research in Transportation Economics*, 16, Amsterdam: Elsevier, 43–65.

Evaluation in practice

If the specific form of a port's economic objective function is not known (or a reliable estimate is not available), the port's performance over time with respect to the economic objective can still be evaluated by means of performance indicators – i.e., it can be evaluated by just knowing the actual values of its performance indicators. Specifically, if the direction of movement in these values over time moves the port nearer to (away from) achieving its economic objective, the conclusion is that the port's performance has improved (deteriorated) over time. For one indicator, a rising trend over time in its actual values might move the port nearer to achieving its economic objective; for another indicator, it might be a declining trend in its actual values.

An advantage to a port having individual performance indicators to evaluate its performance over time is that the performance of its various services and service areas (e.g., the wharf, entrance and departure gates, and the port channel) can be evaluated, thereby allowing for the detection of port activity centers where performance is improving or declining. However, a disadvantage is the problem of how to evaluate the net impact of changes in these indicators on the port's overall performance – given that the changes in some indicators may improve performance and changes in other indicators may negatively affect performance. What is needed is an overall (or single) port performance indicator that captures the net impact of the changes in the individual performance indicators on the port's performance.

In a study by Talley (2006a), where the port's economic objective is to maximize annual throughput subject to a profit constraint, this overall performance indicator is the port's annual throughput per profit dollar. If this overall indicator is rising (declining) over time, it follows that the port's performance has been improving (declining) over time – furthermore, the net impact of the changes over time in the individual performance indicators on port performance has been positive (negative).

Performance evaluation: a multiport perspective

Although it is tempting to compare the performance of one port to that of another, such comparisons may be misleading. Ports operate in different economic, social, and fiscal environments. For example, even if ports have the same economic objective of maximizing annual throughput subject to a profit constraint, the profit constraint is likely to differ among the ports. Also, one port may have a negative profit (or deficit) constraint that is to be subsidized, while another port may have a positive or break-even profit constraint. Ports may also have different economic objectives (Suykens 1986). Thus, in a multiport performance evaluation approach, where the performance of one port is compared to that of another, similar ports should be used.

In the literature, multiport performance evaluations of the technical efficiency of ports have generally been conducted by using frontier statistical models. These models are used to investigate the relative technical inefficiency of ports. Specifically, they relate the throughputs (or outputs) to the resources (or inputs) utilized by a group of ports to investigate which of these ports are technically efficient or inefficient relative to each other. If technically efficient, the ports' throughputs are the maximum throughputs for the levels of resources utilized, i.e., the ports' throughputs are on the ports' production frontiers; if technically inefficient, the ports' throughputs lie below their production frontiers.

The frontier statistical technique, data envelopment analysis (DEA), has often been used in multiport technical performance evaluations. DEA is a mathematical programming technique for deriving estimates of the production frontier (or function) for a group of ports, from which the relative technical efficiency ratings for the ports are derived. Based upon these ratings, each port can be described as being technically efficient or inefficient within the group of ports. DEA techniques make no assumptions about the stochastic properties of the data. When such assumptions are made, frontier statistical models are referred to as stochastic frontier models. An in-depth discussion of frontier models is found in Cullinane (2002).

The Tongzon (2001) study used DEA to investigate the relative technical efficiency of sixteen international (including four Australian) container ports for the year 1996. Initially, the investigation considered two output and six input variables. The output variables were the total number of TEUs loaded and unloaded (cargo throughput) and the number of TEUs moved per working hour (ship working rate). The input variables were (1) the number of cranes, (2) the number of container berths, (3) the number of tugs, (4) the ship delay time, (5) the terminal area, and (6) the number of port authority employees. Two versions of the DEA model were used in the investigation – the Charnes, Cooper, and Rhodes (CCR) version that assumes constant returns to scale in production and the Additive version that allows for variable returns to scale (Cullinane 2002).

Because of a small sample, the Tongzon (2001) study used only one output – cargo throughput – in the final analysis. More ports were found to be technically inefficient based upon the CCR version than based upon the Additive version. This is not surprising, since the CCR version has the restrictive assumption of constant returns to scale. For both DEA versions, the ports of Melbourne, Rotterdam, Yokohama, and Osaka were identified as technically inefficient and the ports of Hong Kong, Singapore, Hamburg, Keelung, Zeebrugge, and Tanjung Priok were identified as technically efficient. Since a number of the container ports in the sample are quite different with respect to size and function (e.g., hub versus a nonhub container port), the results suggest that the technical efficiency of ports does not depend only upon port size or function. For example, in the technically inefficient group, Rotterdam is large relative to the port of Melbourne and is a hub container port as opposed to the ports of Melbourne, Yokohama, and Osaka.

Port competition

Port competition may be inter- or intraport competition. The former is competition between ports and the latter is competition within ports. Interport competition is competition between different ports, whereas intraport competition is competition among marine terminals within the same port.

Interport competition

The competitiveness of a port in interport competition is influenced by (1) port performance, (2) port accessibility and location, (3) port tradition, (4) government assistance, and (5) port user preferences (Fleming and Baird 1999). Port performance improvements, e.g., improving the quality of service to port users and reducing technical and cost inefficiencies, increases the port's competitiveness in interport competition. With improvements in quality of service, the port time prices of port users are expected to be lower. By reducing its costs, the port is then able to lower its port prices.

By having superior sea and land accessibilities, a port's competitiveness relative to other ports is enhanced. A ship's transit time and costs such as pilotage and towage costs are less when a port is near the open sea. By having direct connections to highways, rail, and inland navigation systems, a port's land-transportation transit times for its cargoes will be less, all else held constant. The competitiveness of ports is also enhanced if they are located near centers of consumption and production. For example, the Port of New York-New Jersey's top ranking in container throughput among U.S. East Coast container ports is primarily due to the large population and thus the large consumer market of New York City and the surrounding area.

Ports located in cities with a long tradition of supporting port expansion projects give rise to a culture of support for port improvement projects, especially when a competing port appears to be gaining an interport competitive edge. The greater the government assistance to a port, the greater will be the port's competitiveness relative to other ports. That is to say, the port will be in the position to reduce its port prices after receiving government operating assistance. Government assistance includes cash gift payments (subsidies) and in-kind assistance. The latter may include, for example, tax reductions, low-cost loans, guaranteed loans, provision of port infrastructure, and the fallout from government-funded research and development programs that benefit the port. In the United States, public ports do not pay taxes on port property unlike private ports – thus, giving public ports a comparative cost advantage over private ports. If a port has certain characteristics (not mentioned above), such as superior service providers for which port users (carriers and shippers) have a strong preference, its competitiveness relative to other ports will be enhanced.

The U.S. Shipping Act of 1984 allowed shipping lines calling at U.S. ports to charge door-to-door rates as opposed to only port-to-port rates as in the past. Under port-to-port rates, shipping lines charge shippers for the transportation service provided from origin ports to final destination ports. Obtaining inland transportation for cargoes to and from ports is the responsibility of the shipper or its agent. Under door-to-door rates, shipping lines charge shippers for the transportation service incurred for cargoes from their origins to their final destinations. It is the responsibility of the lines to obtain inland transportation for these cargoes to and from ports.

Under door-to-door rates, container shipping lines that call at U.S. ports enter into contracts with inland carriers – railroads, truck carriers, and barge carriers – to provide inland transportation for their cargoes under negotiated lower rates. As a consequence, the lines are able to choose their ports of call; they have their under-contract inland carriers transport containers to and from the chosen ports even though these ports may not be the closest ports for shippers. By doing so, containers can be congregated at a few ports, allowing the lines to use larger containerships to call at these ports. The lines incur cost savings in using the larger containerships, since these ships incur cost savings from economies of ship size at sea and from being able to stay at sea longer by calling at a few U.S. ports. By congregating larger volumes of cargo at fewer ports, the shipping lines (due to the larger cargo volumes at these ports) are able to obtain lower negotiated rates (often not proportional to distance) from inland carriers and thus charge lower door-to-door rates.

Competition among U.S. container ports has increased following the introduction of door-to-door rates. U.S. container port natural hinterlands are disappearing – container cargo to and from regions via the closest port can no longer be guaranteed. Not only has interport competition increased among container ports on the same coast, e.g., among ports on the East Coast and among ports on the West Coast, but also among ports between the two coasts. For example, in 2002 the port congestion problems that arose as a result of a dispute between the West Coast terminal operators and the International Longshore and Warehouse Union (ILWU) resulted in some container cargo being diverted to all-water service – i.e., in being transported by containerships through the Panama Canal to East Coast ports, as opposed to being land-bridged by rail from a West Coast port to the East Coast. However, the introduction of larger containerships in U.S. trades has placed pressure on U.S. container ports to increase (1) water depths in entrance channels and at berths, (2) channel widths to have sufficient vessel turning circles, (3) the size of dock cranes to have longer reach, greater loading capacity, and higher lift height, (4) terminal storage capacity, and (5) truck and railroad facilities.

Intraport competition

There are a number of benefits from intraport competition. First, intraport competition prevents monopolistic pricing. That is to say, the prices charged by terminal operators within the same port are expected to be lower as opposed to when intraport competition does not exist. Second, intraport competition fosters port specialization, innovation, and diversity. Competitors within the same port compete in the same environment, e.g., they face the same regulations, labor market, and suppliers. The specialization of terminal operator services is more likely to occur when operators operate in the same environment as opposed to a different environment (de Langen and Pallis 2005).

In 1993 the federal government of Argentina offered concession contracts to private terminal operators to operate six marine terminals at the Puerto Nuevo Port Authority in Buenos Aires. Five concession contracts were awarded. The award-winning operators had to pay the port authority concession payments of $4 per ton for imports and $2 per ton for exports. They were also prohibited from price collusion, and would have to adhere to environmental and safety legislation. At the same time, a new marine terminal was built in South Dock, just outside the city, under the jurisdiction of the Province of Buenos Aires. The latter granted a 30-year concession for the South Dock terminal to a consortium of local and foreign investors that was of a lower cost than the concession contracts afforded the Puerto Nuevo operators by the federal government. As a consequence, the South Dock terminal operator was able to charge lower port prices (e.g., lower wharfage fees) than the Puerto Nuevo operators, resulting in greater intraport price competition within the region. In response, the Puerto Nuevo operators have sought to renegotiate their concession agreements in order to compete with the South Dock terminal operator.

Port competition, economic rent, and contestability

Economic rent is the reward to a factor of production or resource (e.g., land) whose supply is perfectly inelastic in the long run, i.e., the factor's supply curve is perpendicular to the quantity axis. Economic rent is also the payment to a factor of production over and above what is needed to keep the factor in its current employment. This economics definition of rent differs from contractual rent, where a port tenant, for example, pays the port authority for the use of some or all of the port's facilities.

If the supply of the factor of production is only perfectly inelastic in the short run, then the rent is referred to as quasi economic rents. Such a factor may include ship officers that require several years of training to develop a particular skill. If so, there will be a lag between the increase in demand for ship officers and the increase in their supply. In the long run, the entry to professions may be liberalized, capital equipment may be replicated, and technological advances may reduce the significance of seafarer and port labor skills; if so, quasi economic rents in the long run are competed away.

Economic and quasi economic rents of ports may appear in the form of high financial rewards (e.g., high factor incomes and port prices) and/or higher levels of technical inefficiency (Goss 1999). The economic rent of a port facing intense (little) interport competition is likely to be small (large). Rent seeking (e.g., charging higher prices) by port service providers may lead to vertical integration by port users. For example, a shipping line may own its own marine terminal or operate a dedicated (leased) terminal in order to avoid the abusive market power of the operator of a common-user terminal.

"If we are going to rely on competition to ensure that ports are efficient and that their benefits are widely distributed, then it is necessary to ensure that competition actually exists – within ports and between them" (Goss 1999: 7). Port competition may be in the form of actual or potential competition. Interport (intraport) competition not only increases with the increase in the number of actual port (terminal) competitors but also with the increase in the number of potential port (terminal) competitors.

In a perfectly contestable market, the threat of competition by potential entrants will force incumbent firms to behave competitively, i.e., as if there were a large number of actual firms in the market (Baumol *et al.* 1982). That is to say, competition exists in a perfectly contestable market even if there are only a few firms, as long as entry and exit are costless so that potential entrants exist.

If barriers to entry and exit exist in a market, the market is non-contestable. Examples of port barriers to entry are long-term leases (20–30 years) between landlord ports and private terminal operators that provide for a single private terminal operator to be the only operator of a port or terminal for the term of the lease. Sunk costs are a barrier to exit. Sunk costs are a firm's capital costs that cannot be recovered when the firm exits the market, e.g., the cost of a port's immobile capital such as its quay. Immobile capital is capital that cannot be moved elsewhere for an alternative use.

Port hinterlands have been described as captive and contestable (de Langen and Pallis 2005). A captive port hinterland is a region, where a single port has a competitive advantage (e.g., lower prices for freight trips) over other ports in handling the region's cargo. A contestable hinterland is a region where no single port has a clear competitive advantage over competing ports. Port terminal operators have greater (less) bargaining power versus port users when their ports have captive (contestable) hinterlands; operators are more likely to charge relatively high (low) port prices when port hinterlands are captive (contestable), i.e., high (low) rent extraction. The bargaining position of port service providers versus shippers is generally stronger than that of port service providers versus shipping lines. The rationale for the latter is that shipping lines have large volumes of cargo (from consolidating different origin-destination cargoes) that strengthens their bargaining position in the bargaining process.

Port hinterlands have also been described as captive and overlapping (shared by more than one port) hinterlands. Ports with overlapping hinterlands compete for the overlapping-hinterland market. However, a port with a large hinterland can also compete and be more competitive in competing for the overlapping market (Zhang 2008). Specifically, a port with a large captive hinterland will (1) allow for more frequent services by shipping lines, (2) facilitate the growth of third-party logistics providers and freight forwarders, (3) allow shipping lines to use larger ships, deriving cost economies of ship size at sea, (4) yield higher ship utilization, and (5) allow more value-added clusters to be developed. The higher traffic density at the port will in turn, among other things, lower shipping rates to and from the port, thereby making it more competitive in competing for the overlapping market.

Port competitiveness

A port's competitive position (or its competitiveness) may be evaluated in terms of the growth, market share, and diversification of its traffic volume. An analytical tool that has been used to evaluate the competitiveness of a port (in a port range) that considers these factors is strategic position analysis (SPA). SPA consists of three interrelated analytical components: (1) product portfolio analysis (PPA), (2) shift-share analysis (SSA), and (3) product diversification analysis (PDA).

Four levels of PPA have been used to evaluate the competitive position of ports in a port range (Haezendonck *et al.* 2006). At the first level, the overall market shares and total growth rates of the traffic volumes of ports in the port range are presented (external positioning analysis/portfolio of ports). At the second level, the market shares and the growth rates of various traffic categories in a port's total traffic volume in the port range are described (internal positioning analysis/portfolio of traffic categories). At the third level, the ports' market shares and growth rates of each commodity group in their total commodity groups in their traffic volumes in the port range are described (portfolio of commodity groups). The fourth level differs from the third level in that the shares and growth rates are within a port rather than within the port range.

SSA decomposes the increase or decrease in a port's traffic volume into various components – a share effect, a commodity shift effect, and a competitiveness shift effect. The share effect is the estimated increase or decrease in a port's traffic volume, assuming that the port's volume is a constant share of the port traffic volume in the port range. The difference between a port's actual and estimated traffic volumes is its shift effect in traffic volume. If the difference is positive (negative), the port has evolved more (less) than expected with respect to the share effect. This difference can be further decomposed into traffic volume commodity and competitiveness shift effects.

The commodity shift effect for a port's traffic volume reflects the volume's degree of specialization. A positive (negative) commodity shift suggests that the port has specialized in fast (slow) growing traffic; thus, it has a favorable (unfavorable) traffic structure. A positive (negative) competitiveness shift effect for a port, given its traffic structure, indicates that it has performed relatively better (worse) than its port rivals in the port range in the traffic categories in which it has specialized. A model that decomposes a port's change in traffic volume into the share, commodity shift, and competitiveness shift effects is found in de Lombaerde and Verbeke (1989).

PDA, the third component of SPA, analyzes the diversification of a port's traffic volume for a specific period of time. A product diversification index that has been developed by de Lombaerde and Verbeke (1989) may be used to determine the relative importance of various traffic categories in a port's traffic volume. A high value for the index reflects low traffic diversification (e.g., dominated by one type of cargo), whereas a low value reflects greater diversification or greater balance in traffic categories. An application of SPA to nine ports in the Hamburg–Le Havre port range is found in Haezendonck *et al.* (2006).

Summary

A port in a competitive environment is concerned not only with whether it is efficient but also whether it is effective in providing throughput. A port may be technically efficient (exhibited by the port's economic production function) and cost efficient (exhibited by the port's economic cost function). Effectiveness is concerned with how well the port provides throughput. In the case of a privately owned port, the port may be effective if it maximizes throughput subject to a minimum positive profit constraint. For a publicly owned port, it may maximize throughput subject to a zero profit constraint.

If a port's throughput approaches (departs from) its optimum throughput over time, the port's performance has improved (deteriorated) over time. The optimum throughput is that throughput that satisfies a given operating objective of the port. A port's performance indicators (from the perspective of an economics operating objective) are those variables whose values are under the control of port management (i.e., choice variables) for optimizing the operating objective. The values of these variables that optimize the economic objective are the indicators' standards. If the actual values of the indicators depart from (approach) their perspective standards over time, the port's performance with respect to the given economic objective has deteriorated (improved) over time. In addition to the port evaluation of a single port, the relative performance of ports with respect to technical efficiency in a group of ports may also be evaluated.

Port competition may be interport competition (between ports) or intraport competition (within a given port). Interport competition is influenced by (1) port performance, (2) port accessibility and location, (3) port tradition, (4) government assistance, and (5) port user preferences. Intraport competition prevents monopoly pricing and fosters port specialization, innovation, and diversity within a port. Economic rents of ports may appear in the form of high port prices and higher levels of technical inefficiency. Ports in a port range (or market) are contestable if potential entrants will force incumbent ports to behave competitively. A port's competitive position (or its competitiveness) may be evaluated with respect to the growth, market share, and diversification of its traffic volume in a port range. Strategic position analysis (SPA) has been used to evaluate the competitiveness of ports in a port range.

Bibliography

Baumol, W. J., Panzas, J. C., and Willig, R. D. (1982) *Contestable Markets and the Theory of Industry Structure*, New York: Harcourt, Brace and Jovanovich.

Chadwin, M. L., Pope, J. A., and Talley, W. K. (1990) *Ocean Container Transportation: An Operational Perspective*, New York: Taylor & Francis.

Cullinane, K. (2002) "The Productivity and Efficiency of Ports and Terminals: Methods and Applications", in C. Grammenos (ed.) *The Handbook of Maritime Economics and Business*, London: Informa, 426–442.

De Borger, B., Proost, S., and Van Dender, K. (forthcoming) "Private Port Pricing and Public Investment in Port and Hinterland Capacity", *Journal of Transport Economics and Policy*.

Defilippi, E. (2004) "Intra-Port Competition, Regulatory Challenges and the Concession of Callao Port", *Maritime Economics and Logistics*, 6: 279–311.

de Langen, P. W. and Pallis, A. A. (2005) "Analysis of the Benefits of Intra-Port Competition", a paper presented at the 2005 Annual Meeting of the International Association of Maritime Economists, Limassol, Cyprus.

de Lombaerde, P. and Verbeke, A. (1989) "Assessing International Seaport Competition: A Tool for Strategic Decision Making", *International Journal of Transport Economics*, 16: 175–192.

Fleming, D. K. and Baird, A. J. (1999) "Some Reflections on Port Competition in the United States and Europe", *Maritime Policy and Management*, 26: 383–394.

Goss, R. O. (1999) "On the Distribution of Economic Rent in Seaports", *International Journal of Maritime Economics*, 1: 1–9.

Haezendonck, E. (2001) *Essays on Strategy Analysis for Seaports*, Leuven: Garant.

——, Verbeke, A., and Coeck, C. (2006) "Strategic Positioning Analysis for Seaports", in K. Cullinane and W. K. Talley (eds) *Port Economics: Research in Transportation Economics*, 16, Amsterdam: Elsevier, 141–169.

Lam, J. S. L. and Yap, W. Y. (2006) "A Measurement and Comparison of Cost Competitiveness of Container Ports in Southeast Asia", *Transportation*, 33: 641–654.

—— (2008) "Competition for Transshipment Containers by Major Ports in Southeast Asia: Slot Capacity Analysis", *Maritime Policy and Management*, 35: 89–101.

Marlow, P. B. and Paixao Casaca, A. C. (2003) "Measuring Lean Ports' Performance", *International Journal of Transport Management*, 1: 189–202.

Michalopoulos, V., Pardalis, A., and Stathopoulou, C. (2007) "Estimating Port Competition: The Case of the Mediterranean Sea", a paper presented at the 2007 Annual Meeting of the International Association of Maritime Economists, Athens, Greece.

Notteboom, T. (2002) "Consolidation and Contestability in the European Container Handling Industry", *Maritime Policy and Management*, 29: 257–269.

—— (2007) "Strategic Challenges to Container Ports in a Changing Market Environment", in M. R. Brooks and K. Cullinane (eds) *Devolution, Port Governance and Port Performance: Research in Transportation Economics*, 17, Amsterdam: Elsevier, 29–52.

Perez-Labajos, C. and Blanco, B. (2004) "Competitive Policies for Commercial Seaports in the EU", *Marine Policy*, 28: 553–556.

Slack, B. (1985) "Containerization, Inter-Port Competition and Port Selection", *Maritime Policy and Management*, 12: 293–303.

Suykens, F. (1986) "Ports Should Be Efficient (Even When This Means That Some of Them Are Subsidized)", *Maritime Policy and Management*, 13: 105–126.

Talley, W. K. (1986) "A Comparison of Two Methodologies for Selecting Transit Performance Indicators", *Transportation*, 13: 201–210.

—— (1988a) "Optimum Throughput and Performance Evaluation of Marine Terminals", *Maritime Policy and Management*, 15: 327–331, reprinted in M. Brooks, K. Button, and P. Nijkamp (eds) *Maritime Transport* (2002), Cheltenham, UK: Edward Elgar, 511–515.

—— (1988b) *Transport Carrier Costing*, New York: Gordon and Breach Science Publishers.

—— (1994) "Performance Indicators and Port Performance Evaluation", *Logistics and Transportation Review*, 30: 339–352.

—— (1996) "Determinants of Cargo Damage Risk and Severity: The Case of Containership Accidents", *Logistics and Transportation Review*, 32: 377–388.

—— (2006a) "An Economic Theory of the Port", in K. Cullinane and W. K. Talley (eds) *Port Economics: Research in Transportation Economics*, 16, Amsterdam: Elsevier, 43–65.

—— (2006b) "Optimum Port Throughput", in L. Shuguang and Y. Jinkai (eds) *Approaches to Maritime Industrial Economy*, Beijing, China: Economic Science Press, 21–32.

—— (2007) "Port Performance: An Economics Perspective", in M. Brooks and K. Cullinane (eds) *Devolution, Port Governance and Port Performance: Research in Transportation Economics*, 17, Amsterdam: Elsevier, 499–516.

Tongzon, J. (2001) "Efficiency Measurement of Selected Australian and Other International Ports Using Data Envelopment Analysis", *Transportation Research Part A*, 35: 107–122.

—— and Heng, W. (2005) "Port Privatization, Efficiency and Competitiveness: Some Empirical Evidence from Container Ports (Terminals)", *Transportation Research Part A*, 39: 405–424.

Veldman, S. J. H. and Vroomen, B. L. K. (2007) "A Model of Container Port Competition: An Application for the Transshipment Market of the Mediterranean", a paper presented at the 2007 Annual Meeting of the International Association of Maritime Economists, Athens, Greece.

Yap, W. Y. and Lam, J. L. (2006) "Competition Dynamics Between Container Ports in East Asia", *Transportation Research Part A*, 40: 35–51.

Yap, W. Y., Lam, J. L., and Notteboom, T. E. (2006) "Developments in Container Port Competition in East Asia", *Transport Reviews*, 26: 167–188.

Yeo, G.-T., Roe, M., and Dinwoodie, J. (2008) "Evaluating the Competitiveness of Container Ports in Korea and China", *Transportation Research Part A*, 42: 910–921.

Zhang, A. (2008) "The Impact of Hinterland Access Conditions on Rivalry Between Ports", a paper presented at the International Forum on Shipping, Ports and Airports, Hong Kong Polytechnic University, Hong Kong.

11 Port dockworkers

Introduction

Dockworkers are workers who are involved in the movement of cargo to and from vessels. The number of dockworkers worldwide has been declining. In the U.S., for example, dockworker jobs declined from 80,000 in 1967 to 11,400 in 1986 (Chadwin *et al.* 1990) and declined by 44 percent between 1989 and 1992. In Australia, waterfront reforms introduced in 1989 led to a 42 percent reduction in dockworker jobs; in France, work rule reforms (that were introduced in 1992) led to a 66 percent decline in dockworker jobs at its major ports (Talley 2002). The job losses are attributed to (1) the introduction of port labor-reduction technologies such as containerization, (2) the privatization of ports, and (3) the increasing number of landlord ports, where terminal operators other than the public port authority are operating the ports.

In many countries, dockworkers are members of unions. Dockworker unions have responded to job losses and anticipated job losses from proposed labor-reduction policies by ports and government with strikes, short-term work stoppages, and work slowdowns. At container ports, in particular, such actions by dockworker unions can be highly costly to port users and to the ports themselves. Shipping lines incur opportunity costs at ports when their ships are delayed for servicing and departure due to dockworker work stoppages, i.e., from cargo and its revenue that could have otherwise been transported and received by the lines. Shippers also incur greater logistics costs, e.g., inventory costs, when cargoes are delayed in their departure from ports. The departure-delay costs incurred by shipping lines and shippers, in turn, may result in shipping lines and shippers shifting their port calls and cargoes, respectively, to other ports that are not experiencing such departure-delay problems – thereby having a negative impact on the port itself and the port's local economy. Dockworker employers may reduce or eliminate departure-delay costs for port users by bargaining with dockworker unions for no work-stoppage agreements in return for higher wages.

This chapter presents a discussion of port dockworkers. The next section discusses international unions with which national dockworker unions are affiliated. Then, the EU port services directive, the employment and wages of U.S. union dockworkers, dockworker protests worldwide, and dockworkers in Hong Kong and Germany are discussed.

International unions

An international union with which national dockworker unions are affiliated is the International Transport Workers' Federation (ITF). The ITF is an international union federation of transportation trade unions that was founded in 1896. As of 2005, 600 transportation trade unions in over 140 countries were ITF members, representing five million union workers. Any independent transportation trade union is eligible for ITF membership.

The ITF supports its affiliated unions in defending the interests of their members. The Dockers' Section of the ITF, for example, supports its port-related unions by (1) gathering and disseminating information on workers' interests, e.g., the effects of port reform, privatization, and new technologies on dockworker employment; (2) supporting members in labor disputes; (3) organizing and coordinating international solidarity actions to address anti-union activities; (4) helping members to develop policies that support their interests; and (5) organizing conferences and seminars to develop international trade union policies. The ITF also represents the interests of its transportation trade unions in the International Maritime Organization (IMO) and the International Labour Organization (ILO).

The IMO is a United Nations (UN) agency that is responsible for improving the safety of international shipping and preventing pollution from ships. The IMO has 158 member and two associate member states. In the last 30 years the IMO has promoted the adoption of 30 conventions and protocols and adopted over 700 recommendations and codes for maritime safety, the prevention of pollution, and related matters. IMO conventions normally develop from work undertaken by a committee or subcommittee. A draft instrument is submitted to a conference consisting of invited delegations from all UN (IMO and non-IMO member) states. The final text adopted by the conference, i.e., the convention, is then submitted to governments for their ratification. The convention comes into force (or is ratified) when a specified number of countries have ratified it and fulfilled other requirements. Implementation of the convention is mandatory for countries that have ratified it.

The ILO was created in 1919 under the Treaty of Versailles to advance satisfactory working conditions and pay for workers. In 1946 it became an agency of the UN. Since 1920 the ILO has adopted 32 international conventions (which are mandatory for ratifying states) and 25 recommendations (which are not mandatory) dealing exclusively with maritime labor conditions. Their provisions are primarily concerned with working conditions on board ocean-going ships, addressing such issues as hours of work, minimum age, medical examinations, recruitment and placement, vacation, crew accommodation, pensions, sick pay, occupational safety and health, minimum wages, seafarer identity documents, social security, seafarer welfare in port and at sea, vocational training, certificates of competency, and continuity of employment.

Another international union with which national dockworker unions are affiliated is the International Dockworkers Council (IDC). In July 2000 dockworker union delegates from 85 ports worldwide established the IDC. The delegates, representing 30,000 individual dockworker union members from 13 countries, agreed to adopt article 87 of the ILO Convention – i.e., the Freedom of Association and Protection of the Right to Organize – as the framework with which to establish the IDC. Unlike the ITF, membership in the IDC is restricted to dockworkers. Today, the IDC has 50,000 individual dockworker union members from all over the world. In 2002 the U.S. International Warehouse and Longshore Union joined the IDC. A union representative noted: "The ITF is a good organization, but its focus is mainly on seamen and vessel issues. We thought it was important to be a part of an organization where dockworkers could communicate and share information" (Bartelme 2002).

EU port services directive

In February 2001 the European Union (EU) presented its port services directive to the ITF in Brussels, Belgium. The directive proposed the easing of regulatory constraints on EU port operators in order to create more competition among EU ports. The most controversial provision of the directive is the self-handling provision, whereby ship owners as opposed to just dockworkers would be allowed to handle cargo on their vessels, i.e., to and from vessels while in port (thereby creating "ports of convenience"). Proponents of the directive – ship owners, shippers, and EU port operators – see the directive as a way of decreasing shipping-line costs and improving port efficiency. Union dockworkers, opponents of the directive, see the directive resulting in losses in union dockworker jobs – from the use of seafarer labor and nonunion dockworkers in the loading and unloading of cargo to and from vessels while in port.

The ITF's response to the directive was to organize a number of strikes and work stoppages by EU dockworker unions against the passage of the directive. In January 2003 dockworker strikes blocked entry to ports in Belgium and Finland, contributed to the partial shutdown of the ports of Bremerhaven and Hamburg in Germany, and resulted in worker slowdowns at the Port of Rotterdam. During the first half of 2003, 20,000 dockworkers were involved in directive strikes. In September 2003, 7,000 dockworkers in Belgium, France, Germany, the Netherlands, and Spain were involved in 24-hour strikes at EU ports.

In November 2003, the European Parliament voted 229 to 209 against the directive, a triumph for the ITF. The campaign against the port services directive witnessed the first pan-European strikes and opened a new charter in European labor activism, i.e., resulted in coordinated efforts among national unions and the ITF and IDC (Reyes 2004). National unions from different states also cooperated in their opposition to the directive.

In late 2004, the EU announced its plan to reintroduce the port services directive, which was followed by renewed strike threats by dockworkers. Dockworkers sought the removal of the directive's self-handling clause that allows ship crews and nonunion dockworkers to load and unload cargoes from ships. However, the EU refused to remove this clause. In November 2005, the European Parliament's Transport Committee voted 24:23 against the re-introduced port services directive legislation. Despite this setback, the directive may still be voted on in the European Parliament in the near future, since widespread sentiment for reform of European ports remains.

In March 2008 a port reform law to improve the performance of French ports was presented to the French Parliament. One provision of the law that drew protest from the local ports and docks federation of the CGT union confederation was the division of port labor between the private and public sectors in French ports and the transfer of personnel. An estimated 2,000 employees, e.g., container gantry operators and maintenance personnel, out of a port government workforce of 5,000–6,000 employees would be subject to compulsory transfer to private terminal operating companies (Spurrier 2008). The law was passed by the French Parliament and took its place on the statute book on July 4, 2008. An agreement in principle was reached with the union on July 15, making the transferred workers answerable to a single employer, the terminal operator.

Prior to the July 15 agreement, the union undertook actions that disrupted traffic at France's major ports for three and a half months: (1) weekly 24-hour strikes, (2) a ban on overtime, (3) a ban on exceptional work, and (4) a ban on most night work. Container traffic at France's two leading container ports declined between 40 and 70 percent. In the July 15 agreement, employers agreed to employee protection arrangements: (1) employees dissatisfied with work conditions with the private terminal operating companies may return to their respective port authorities during a transitional three-year period and (2) employees threatened with redundancy on economic grounds may return within up to 10 years to their port authorities.

U.S. dockworkers

The major dockworker unions in the United States are the International Longshoremen's Association (ILA) on the East Coast and the International Longshore and Warehouse Union (ILWU) on the West Coast. In the 1920s there was an excess supply of U.S dockworkers; both union and nonunion dockworkers competed for daily work assignments. In 1937 the West Coast dockworkers broke away from the ILA to form the ILWU. In the following two decades, dockworker employers sought to introduce labor-saving devices such as lift trucks. However, labor resisted with strikes and the threat of strikes. In 1950 there were 100,000 full-time dockworkers in the UnitedStates By 2003 the number had declined to 10,500 (Greenwald 2004).

Employment

In the 1960s containerization – the foremost port labor-saving technology – was introduced at U.S. ports. At breakbulk ports that became container ports, capital replaced labor in many instances, thereby causing a decline in dockworker jobs. The ILA responded to dockworker job losses by negotiating for local guaranteed annual income (GAI) plans and "work preservation" schemes. In 1965 the Port of New York-New Jersey provided ILA GAI agreements of 1,600 paid hours per year to fully registered longshoremen. To qualify, dockworkers had to have worked 700 or more hours in a given fiscal year. In exchange, the ILA agreed to reduce gang sizes and provide greater flexibility in work practices.

The surplus of U.S. dockworkers began to diminish following passage of the U.S. Shipping Act of 1984. This Act amended the U.S. Shipping Act of 1916 to ease the federal government's economic regulation of ocean transportation. The 1916 Act created the U.S. Shipping Board (renamed the Federal Maritime Commission in 1961) to have "jurisdiction over common carriers by water operating in interstate or foreign commerce on the high seas and upon the Great Lakes" (Locklin 1972: 746), but not jurisdiction over inland waterways. The 1916 Act further legalized shipping liner conference agreements by granting them immunity from antitrust legislation. Liner conferences are shipping line cartels that provide scheduled vessel service over specific trade routes and collectively discuss and set rates, usually only port-to-port rates. Liner conferences have immunity from antitrust legislation in most OECD (Organization for Economic Cooperation and Development) countries. (This immunity was eliminated by the EU in Autumn 2008.)

The 1984 Act permitted independent rates (i.e., independent of conference rates), service contracts between shippers and carriers/conferences, and door-to-door (intermodal) rather than just port-to-port rates (Chadwin *et al.* 1990; Cassavant and Wilson 1991). Within 18 months of the effective date of the 1984 Act, service-contract cargoes grew from a negligible amount to over 42 percent, with some shipping trade lanes having over 60 percent of their cargoes under service contracts (Frankel 1986). For cargo moving under port-to-port rates, the shipper (or authorized party) is responsible for hiring inland carriers to transport cargo to and from ports. Under a door-to-door rate, the shipping line has this responsibility.[1]

Door-to-door rates allowed shipping lines to develop more cost-efficient ocean transportation networks. By leaving the port-of-call choice to the shipping line, door-to-door rates have provided shipping lines with the opportunity to utilize larger containerships. These ships provide cost savings (due to economies of ship size at sea) to the shipping lines in that they can stay at sea longer by calling at fewer ports, i.e., at load-center ports where containers are accumulated. Door-to-door rates also enabled shipping lines, given their large volumes of container cargo, to bargain for and obtain lower rates from inland carriers, and thus be able to charge lower door-to-door rates.

The service contract provision of the U.S. Staggers Act of 1980 (which deregulated railroads) and the lower trucking contract rates following trucking deregulation (from passage of the U.S. Motor Carrier Act of 1980) enabled shipping lines to lower their door-to-door rates even further. The rail service contract provision of the Staggers Act allowed U.S. railroads for the first time to enter into contract rates with shipping lines, thus providing the opportunity for these lines to negotiate even lower rail (i.e., contract) rates as well as rail service improvements.

The lower door-to-door shipping line rates, inland carrier rates, and shipper inventory and other logistics costs (from improvements in ocean and inland transportation services) stimulated the growth in containerized trade. U.S. ports and shipping lines responded to the increase in the demand for their services by investing billions of dollars in container terminals and infrastructures and in larger and larger containerships. Also, there was an increase in the demand for U.S. dockworkers. Further, the costs to ports and shipping lines from disruptions in the provision of port services caused by dockworker work stoppages increased.

Dockworker employers became more reluctant to chance a strike – agreeing to settle labor contract extensions much earlier (prior to contract expiration) than in the past and to higher dockworker wage demands than would have occurred under more lengthy negotiations. Also, employers feared that if labor strikes occurred, they might lose ship calls and cargo to port competitors. Further, port capital–labor ratios increased, followed by the decline in port labor costs as a percentage of total port costs – thereby increasing the likelihood that ports would be willing to agree to higher dockworker wages in labor negotiations.

In July 2004, the shortage of ILWU workers at the Port of Los Angeles and Long Beach delayed numerous ships and intermodal rail shipments heading to inland destinations. Subsequently, the Pacific Maritime Association (PMA) hired 5,000 new part-time longshoremen, known as casuals. In addition, 1,750 existing casuals were trained and promoted to the registered ILWU status.

In 2003 the increasing demand for ILA dockworkers (from increasing cargo volumes) and the shrinking supply of dockworkers resulted in a shortage of ILA dockworkers at the Port of New York-New Jersey. The New York Shipping Association responded by expanding its ILA register by 400 to 3,300 registered workers. As of February 2007, the register includes 3,600 ILA members.

Wages

The increase in the demand for dockworkers, the decrease in the likelihood that dockworker employers would chance a strike, and the increase in port capital–labor ratios provided the impetus for the increase in the bargaining power and higher wages of U.S. dockworkers that followed the passage of the Shipping Act of 1984. Although the number of U.S. dockworkers has declined until recent years, the wages, benefits, and productivity of those dockworkers that remained dramatically increased. Since 1984, the hourly wages of union dockworkers (based upon 1973–1997 data) increased by 14.3 percent (Talley 2002). In 2002 the average annual salary of a full-time ILWU worker ranged between $105,278 and $167,122; the average dockworker benefit package was $70,000 (Swoboda 2002).

In the New York City area, there were 35,000 dockworkers in 1954 and 2,700 in 2000. During the same time period, the port cargo tonnage in the area increased from 13.2 to

44.9 million tons; hence, port cargo tonnage per dockworker (i.e., dockworker productivity) increased 4,411 percent (Greenwald 2004). Increases in dockworker productivity at container ports have been attributed to improvements in port communication, information technology, infrastructure, and cranes.

In 2002 a labor dispute between the ILWU and the PMA resulted in a union lockout.[2] The ILWU contract, which was to expire on July 1, 2002, was extended on a day-to-day basis by the ILWU until September 1, 2002. ILWU work slowdowns followed; the productivity at West Coast ports dropped by 50 percent by September 30, 2002.[3] The PMA responded with a lockout of the union. The lockout ended in 10 days when a federal judge, at the request of President George Bush, invoked the Taft-Hartley Act, imposing an 80-day cooling-off period. Under federal mediation, negotiations between the PMA and the ILWU resumed. During the lockout, 200 vessels lay in anchorage at West Coast ports, resulting in a cargo backlog that would require six weeks to clear and in millions of dollars in losses to shippers (U.S. and Asian) and shipping lines.

On November 23, 2002, the ILWU and the PMA agreed to a tentative six-year contract (breaking the traditional three-year contract cycle) that was subsequently ratified by ILWU members, effective February 1, 2003. The new contract expired on July 1, 2008. In return for allowing for the implementation of new information technology (e.g., the right to use optical scanners and other labor-saving devices) by West Coast ports, the ILWU would receive an increase of $3 per hour in its hourly base wage of $27.68 over the six-year contract, job protection guarantees to ensure that no currently registered worker would lose a job as a result of technology, and a 58 percent increase in pension benefits. Four-hundred clerk positions were lost, but the workers would not be unemployed, since they would be retrained for new positions. The mediated contract was "the most lucrative in the union's 70-year history" (Tirschwell 2002: 6) and "more favorable to employers than they could have achieved on their own" (Mongelluzzo 2003: 26).

On June 9, 2004 the ILA on the East Coast voted to accept a six-year master contract, effective October 1, 2004, that runs to September 30, 2010. However, not all the local offices ratified the new contract – objecting to its preservation of a two-tier wage system that prevented new longshoremen from earning as much per hour as veteran longshoremen. However, the difference in the two-tier wages was reduced for workers earning more than $21 per hour as a result of these workers receiving smaller hourly wage increases over time and for workers earning less than $21 per hour as a result of these workers receiving larger hourly wage increases over time.

Dockworker versus seafarer wages

U.S. seafarer unions were established in the late 1800s in response to the harsh treatment of seafarers by shipping lines, e.g., discipline on shipboard was absolute and seafarers on strike could be prosecuted for desertion. The passage of the Seamen Act in 1915 established standards for quarters and food aboard U.S. flag ships and abolished imprisonment for ship desertion.

The bargaining power of U.S. seafarers has declined following passage of the U.S. Shipping Act of 1984 – attributed in part to the continuing decline in the size of the U.S. flag merchant marine fleet. The U.S. merchant marine fleet consists of a fleet of privately owned U.S. flag (or registered) merchant ships that provide waterborne transportation for cargoes moving in domestic and international commerce. In August 1987, the U.S. ocean-going merchant marine fleet consisted of 363 vessels, less than half the number in 1960; by 2003, this number had declined to 221 (U.S. Maritime Administration, various years).

This decline occurred despite the continued growth in U.S. foreign commerce, preference cargoes (cargoes reserved by law, e.g., military cargoes, for U.S. flag vessels), and protected domestic trade – trade between U.S. ports that is reserved by the Jones Act for U.S. registered vessels (Waters 1995; De La Pedraja 1992). Specifically, the Jones Act requires that water-borne cargo that originates at one U.S. port and is destined for another U.S. port must be transported on a vessel that is U.S. built,[4] U.S. crewed, and U.S. owned. In 1986 the U.S. ocean-going merchant marine fleet transported 4.2 percent of the total tonnage of U.S. ocean-borne foreign trade; by 2003, this percentage had declined to 2 percent (U.S. Maritime Administration, various years).

The higher labor costs and more restrictive work rules for U.S. seafarers than those of for-eign seafarers have contributed to the decline in the U.S. flag merchant marine fleet. "Crew costs are high on U.S. ships because crew sizes are larger than competitors' and cost per man is among the highest in the world" (Office of Technology Assessment 1983: 130). U.S. sea-farer costs are high, not only due to high wage rates, but also due to the significant amounts of overtime pay. While at sea, a seafarer typically works eight hours per day (every day) or a 56-hour week and is paid overtime pay. Also, vacation pay is generous, exceeding that of most U.S. industries. Most U.S. seafarer jobs provide 13 days or more paid vacation for each 30 days worked; licensed seafarers' (officers) vacation pay could be one half of total annual earnings. Restrictive work rules limit the flexibility of shipboard management in scheduling work assignments for shipboard personnel. One occupation may not be able to perform the duties of another occupation because of sharp distinctions among occupations due to licens-ing requirements.

The collective bargaining power of and membership in most seafarer unions have declined – not only due to the continuing decline in the size of the U.S. flag merchant marine fleet (from higher labor costs and more restrictive work rules for U.S. seafarers than for for-eign seafarers) but also to union rivalry (e.g., for military cargoes) and the growing reluc-tance by carriers to bargain with multiple unions (Donn 1989). Union rivalry on occasion has been exploited by employers playing one union against another.

For the 1984–1997 period, Talley (2008) found that the union wages of dockworkers were greater than those of seafarer captains/mates and sailors/deckhands; the nonunion wages were comparable for dockworkers and seafarer captains/mates; and the nonunion wages of dockworkers were greater than those of seafarer sailors/deckhands. Positive union hourly and weekly wage gaps of 16.4 and 7.0 percent (39.4 and 31.1 percent) for dockworkers versus seafarer captains/mates (sailors/deckhands) exist; the hourly and weekly wages of nonunion dockworkers are 34.7 and 29.3 percent greater than those of nonunion seafarer sailors/deckhands.

A primary reason for the positive union wage gaps for U.S. dockworkers versus seafarers is the change in the relative bargaining power among the occupations: whereas, the bargain-ing power of union dockworkers has increased, that of union seafarers has decreased (as explained above).

Dockworker versus railroad wages

U.S. government economic regulation of the U.S. railroad industry began with the passage of the Interstate Commerce Act in 1887, establishing the Interstate Commerce Commission (ICC) as the regulatory authority over industry rates, entry, services, and finances. The Act protected railroads from intramodal, but not from intermodal competition. By the 1970s the poor financial status of U.S. railroads prompted the U.S. Congress to deregulate the industry, passing the Railroad Revitalization and Regulatory Reform (the 4-R) Act of 1976 and the Staggers Rail Act of 1980. The former introduced limited industry rate-making freedom and made it easier for railroads to abandon unprofitable lines. The Staggers Act allows service contracts and therefore contract rates, establishes rate floors and ceilings, and expedites the ICC (now the Surface Transportation Board) timetable on merger applications. In the post-deregulation period, railroad rates of return on investment have risen significantly – attributable in part to cost savings and improvements in service and managerial effectiveness.

While shareholders (from higher returns) and shippers (from lower real rates and improved service) have benefited, the impact of railroad deregulation on labor has been negative. Prior to passage of the Staggers Rail Act of 1980, the heavily unionized rail industry operated in a high labor-cost environment, reflecting use of an excessive amount of labor, costly work and pay rules, and high wage rates. Increases in labor costs were typically passed on to customers through higher rail rates. Adhering to this strategy, however, became increasingly difficult as railroads faced competition from an economically deregulated trucking industry.

In order to reduce its labor costs, the railroad industry significantly reduced its workforce. In 1975 the industry had 548,000 (488,000 Class I) employees; by 1985 and 1995 the number had declined to 372,000 (302,000 Class I) and 265,000 (188,000 Class I) employees; and by 2000 the number had declined to 246,000 (168,000 Class I) employees (Association of American Railroads 1994, 2002).[5] By 2003, the number of Class I railroad employees had dropped to 155,000, but increased to 165,000 employees in 2005, reversing decades of job losses brought about by industry restructuring and increased use of technology. The loss of jobs, however, has become more palatable from (1) the railroad industry's willingness to provide generous labor buy-out programs, i.e., paying workers to leave the industry; (2) using attrition rather than layoffs to eliminate jobs; and (3) the potential for retaining a high wage structure for remaining workers through improved productivity.

The bargaining power of rail workers has declined in the post-deregulation period. The settled 1985 industry-wide union contract resulted in a shift in the balance of power from rail labor to management. Before 1985 pay increases were granted at least annually and supplemented by regular cost-of-living adjustments (COLA) payments. In the 1985–1988 contract agreement, pay increases were smaller and certain types of pay were frozen or modified, the COLA provision was less liberal, and a two-tier pay system was introduced. Between December 1987 and July 1991 no changes were made in base pay; the 1991–1995 agreement called for moderate nominal increases in base pay, but no COLA until January 1995.

The union wages of U.S. rail engineers and dockworkers were comparable in the 1970s. After 1984 the union wages of engineers declined relative to those of dockworkers, i.e., a negative union hourly wage gap of 6.9 percent for rail engineers versus dockworkers exists (Talley 2004). The primary reason for the relative decrease in union rail engineer wages versus union dockworker wages is the change in the relative bargaining power among the occupations. For railroads, there has been a shift in the balance of power in wage negotiations from unions to management. For dockworkers, the shift has been from management to unions.

Dockworker versus truck driver wages

The U.S. Motor Carrier Act of 1935 placed truck carriers engaged in intercity, interstate for-hire truck services under the economic regulatory authority of the ICC. By the early 1970s critics of ICC truck regulation noted waste and inefficiency, absence of competition, and high rates in the industry. By the late 1970s ICC administrative deregulation of the for-hire truck carrier industry was underway. In July 1980 Congress passed the Motor Carrier Act of

1980 (1980 MCA) that substantially reduced ICC regulation of the industry, accelerating ICC administrative deregulation. Entry restrictions were eased, contract carriers were permitted to hold common carrier certificates, and the discounting of rates was permitted within a zone of rate freedom.

Following passage of the 1980 MCA the number of truck carriers increased dramatically, more than doubling by 1987. Many of the new entrants were truckload (TL) carriers. Whereas TL carriers are mostly nonunion, less-than-truckload (LTL) carriers have remained highly unionized, but have declined in number. Thus, the industry concentration of TL (LTL) carriers has declined (increased). Union jobs and the membership of the Teamster union (the primary union representing truck carriers) has declined, while the size of the driver work force increased from 1.1 million in 1978 to 1.9 million by 1996 (Peoples 1998).

As for rail workers, truck drivers have lost bargaining power in the post-deregulation period, but occurring much earlier than for the former. The union wages of U.S. truck drivers and dockworkers were comparable in the 1970s. After 1984 the union wages of truck drivers declined relative to those of dockworkers, i.e., a negative union hourly wage gap of 22.7 percent for truck drivers versus dockworkers occurred (Talley 2004). The primary reason for the relative decrease in union truck driver wages versus union dockworker wages is the change in the relative bargaining power among the occupations. For truck carriers, there has been a shift in the balance of power in wage negotiations from unions to management. For dockworkers, the shift has been from management to unions.

Dockworker protests

In addition to the dockworker strikes, work stoppages, and work slowdowns in the EU and the U.S. (as previously discussed), such events have also occurred in other countries. In 2001 dockworker strikes occurred in Bangladesh, Santos (Brazil), Rotterdam (the Netherlands), South Africa, Sri Lanka, and Chile. Dockworkers at the Port of Chittagong (Bangladesh) struck over plans for the construction of a private container terminal at the port. Dockworkers at the Port of Santos struck in an attempt to keep control of how job assignments are handed out. Dockworkers at the P&O North Sea Ferries Rotterdam terminal struck over a plan to have seafarers lash and unlash freight on board ships. In South Africa, dockworkers struck over the value of their performance bonus. The strike has also been referred to as an antiprivatization strike due to the mistrust by dockworkers of the privatization process. A strike at a Sri Lankan marine terminal was in protest at the introduction of three work shifts per day. A work stoppage at the Port of Antofagasta in Chile was part of the dockworkers' program for seeking higher wages.

In 2003 a dockworker strike occurred in Israel to protest the nonadherence by the government of its agreement to curtail further dockworker layoffs until the end of 2004. In January 2004 the government of Israel and the country's largest dockworker union signed an agreement resolving the conflict over the government's plan to reform union pensions. In 2006, Peruvian dockworkers struck over the government's plan to privatize container operations in Caliao, the country's largest port.

Dockworkers in Hong Kong and Germany

Hong Kong recognizes the right of its workforce to join and form trade unions. Following Hong Kong's reunification with China, Hong Kong's trade unions are regulated by the Trade Unions Ordinance and overseen by the Trade Unions Registrar. Hong Kong's trade unions are weak with limited collective bargaining. The wages of dockworkers at the Port of Hong

Kong are low by Western standards. There have been no reported labor strikes at the Port of Hong Kong in recent years and work stoppages are rare.

Dockworkers in Germany are members of national trade unions that are affiliated with the European Federation of Transport Workers and the ITF. These trade unions represent various types of dockworkers, e.g., ship line handlers and checkers, and are members of an umbrella maritime union that represents the dockworker trades in contract negotiations with, for example, the Port of Hamburg. German dockworkers have been active in their opposition to the EU port services directive and their number has declined, primarily due to containerization.

Summary

Dockworkers are workers who are involved in the movement of cargo to and from vessels. The number of dockworkers worldwide has been declining. Dockworker unions have responded to job losses and anticipated job losses from labor-reduction policies (e.g., the substitution of capital and technology for labor and port privatization) by ports and government with strikes, short-term work stoppages, and work slowdowns. Such actions by dockworker unions can be costly to port users (e.g., from ship delays) and to the ports themselves (e.g., from port revenues foregone).

National dockworker unions may be affiliated with the international unions, the International Transport Workers' Federation (ITF) and the International Dockworkers Council (IDC). In 2002, the ITF organized a number of strikes and work stoppages by EU dockworker unions against the passage of the EU port services directive. The directive sought to promote competition among EU ports; its self-handling provision would allow ship owners to use their seafarers as opposed to dockworkers for the loading and unloading of cargo on its ships. In November 2003, the European Parliament voted against the directive.

In the U.S. the primary dockworker unions are the International Longshoremen's Association (ILA) on the East Coast and the International Longshore and Warehouse Union (ILWU) on the West Coast. Membership in both unions had been declining until recent years. However, the increase in the demand for dockworkers (from increases in cargo volumes), the decrease in the likelihood that dockworker employers will chance a strike (due to the cost of such strikes), and the increase in port capital–labor ratios (from the substitution of capital for labor) have attributed to an increase in ILA and ILWU bargaining power and, in turn, an increase in their wages. Following passage of the U.S. Shipping Act of 1984, U.S. ILA and ILWU hourly wages are higher than the wages of U.S. union seafarers, railroad engineers, and truck drivers.

In addition to the EU and the United States, dockworker strikes have also occurred, for example, in Bangladesh, Brazil, the Netherlands, South Africa, Sri Lanka, and Chile. The wages of dockworkers at the Port of Hong Kong are low by Western standards. Dockworkers in Germany are members of national trade unions that are affiliated with the European Federation of Transport Workers and the ITF.

Notes

1 The "independent rate action" and the "intermodal rate-making" provisions of the Shipping Act of 1984 reduced the ability of U.S. liner conferences to set rates. The Ocean Shipping Reform Act of 1998 (which amended the 1984 Act and took effect May 1, 1999) reduced this ability even further and contributed to the further decline of conferences. Its "confidential contract" provision allows,

for the first time, confidential one-on-one contracts by shipping lines, but not conferences, with their customers. Other major provisions of the 1998 Act include (a) shippers remain subject to standard U.S. antitrust law and ocean carriers are still subject to Federal Maritime Commission (FMC) regulation; (b) individual carrier tariff-filing requirements with the FMC have been eliminated, but carriers are required to publish rates via the Internet or other media; (c) contracts must be filed with the FMC for agency oversight; and (d) ocean carriers engaged in confidential arrangements with big shippers must disclose contractual information regarding specific dock and port movements to longshore unions. Between May 1, 1999, and May 31, 2000, 46,035 new service contracts and 95,627 contract amendments were filed with the FMC. During 1999 the number of active conference agreements on file at the FMC dropped from 33 to 22.

2 The PMA represents all major steamship lines and terminal operators on the West Coast and was founded in 1949 to negotiate contracts with the ILWU.

3 In its 1996 and 1999 contract negotiations, the ILWU successfully leveraged its slowdowns to win concessions from employers.

4 There have been exceptions to Jones Act vessels having to be U.S. built.

5 Class I railroads are the largest U.S. railroads.

Bibliography

Association of American Railroads (1994, 2002) *Railroad Facts*, Washington, DC: Association of American Railroads.

Bartelme, T. (2002) "ILWU Joins International Dockworkers Council", *JOC Online*. Available online at http://www.joc.com, March 6.

Barton, H. and Turnbull, P. (2002) "Labor Regulation and Competitive Performance in the Port Transport Industry: The Changing Fortunes of Three Major European Seaports", *European Journal of Industrial Relations*, 8: 133–156.

Bonacich, E. and Wilson, J. B. (2008) *Getting the Goods: Ports, Labor and the Logistics Revolution*, Ithaca, NY: Cornell University Press.

Cassavant, K. L. and Wilson, W. W. (1991) "Shipper Perspectives of the Shipping Act of 1984", *Transportation Quarterly*, 45: 109–120.

Chadwin, M. L., Pope, J. A., and Talley, W. K. (1990) *Ocean Container Transportation: An Operational Perspective*, New York: Taylor & Francis.

De La Pedraja, R. (1992) *The Rise and Decline of U.S. Merchant Shipping in the Twentieth Century*, New York: Twayne-MacMillan.

Donn, C. B. (1989) "Concession Bargaining in the Ocean-Going Maritime Industry", *Industrial and Labor Relations Review*, 42: 189–200.

Frankel, E. G. (1986) "Economic and Commercial Implications of the U.S. Shipping Act of 1984", *Logistics and Transportation Review*, 22: 99–114.

Greenwald, R. A. (2004) "Working the Docks: Labor, Management and the New Waterfront", in S. K. Shah (ed.) *Review of Business*, 25: 16–22.

Hall, P. V. (2004) "We'd Have to Sink the Ships: Impact Studies and the 2002 West Coast Port Lockout", *Economic Development Quarterly*, 18: 354–367.

Locklin, D. P. (1972) *Economics of Transportation*, Homewood, IL: Richard D. Irwin.

Monaco, K. and Olsson, L. (2005) *Labor at the Ports: A Comparison of the ILA and ILUW*, Los Angeles, CA: METRANS Transportation Center, Project 04–02.

Mongelluzzo, B. (2003) "PMA's New Face: Miniace's Team Will be Assertive in Dealing With the ILWU", *Journal of Commerce*, October 13–19: 26–27.

Office of Technology Assessment (1983) *An Assessment of Maritime Trade and Technology*, Washington, DC: U.S. Government Printing Office.

Pallis, A. A. and Vaggelas, G. (2005) "Port Competitiveness and the EU Port Services Directive: The Case of Greek Ports", *Maritime Economics and Logistics*, 7: 116–140.

Peoples, J. (1998) "Deregulation and the Labor Market", *Journal of Economic Perspectives*, 12: 111–130.

—— and Talley, W. K. (2004) "Owner-Operator Truck Driver Earnings and Employment: Port Cities and Deregulation", in J. Peoples and W. K. Talley (eds) *Transportation Labor Issues and Regulatory Reform: Research in Transportation Economics*, 10, Amsterdam: Elsevier, 191– 213.

—— and Talley, W. K. (2007) "Earnings Differentials of Railroad Managers and Labor", in S. Dennis and W. K. Talley (eds) *Railroad Economics: Research in Transportation Economics*, 20, Amsterdam: Elsevier, 259–281.

—— and P. Thanabordeekij (2006) "Shipping Deregulation's Wage Effect on Low and High Wage Dockworkers", in K. Cullinane and W. K. Talley (eds) *Port Economics: Research in Transportation Economics*, 16, Amsterdam: Elsevier, 219–249.

Reyes, B. (2004) "Study Detects Stronger Port Union Links", *Lloyd's List*. Available online at http://www. lloydslist.com, June 25.

Schwarz-Miller, A. and Talley, W. K. (2002) "Technology and Labor Relations: Railroads and Ports", in J. Bennett and D. Taras (eds) *Technological Change and Employment Conditions in Traditionally Heavily Unionized Industries*, a symposium issue of the *Journal of Labor Research*, 23: 513–533.

Spurrier, A. (2008) "The French Solution", *Lloyd's List*. Available online at http://www.lloydslist.com, July 23.

Swoboda, F. (2002) "On the Waterfront, It's Union vs. Tech", *Washington Post*, January 5: E01.

Talley, W. K. (2001) "Wage Differentials of Transportation Industries: Deregulation Versus Regulation", *Economic Inquiry*, 39: 406–429.

—— (2002) "Dockworker Earnings, Containerization and Shipping Deregulation", *Journal of Transport Economics and Policy*, 36: 447–467.

—— (2004) "Wage Differentials of Intermodal Transportation Carriers and Ports: Deregulation versus Regulation", in W. K. Talley (ed.) *The Industrial Organization of Shipping and Ports*, a special issue of the journal, *Review of Network Economics*, 3: 207–227.

—— (2007) "Earnings Differentials of Seafarers", *Journal of Labor Research*, 28: 515–524.

—— (2008) "Earnings Differentials of U.S. Dockworkers and Seafarers", *International Journal of Transport Economics*, 35: 169–184.

—— and Schwarz-Miller, A. V. (1998) "Railroad Deregulation and Union Labor Earnings", in J. Peoples (ed.) *Regulatory Reform and Labor Markets*, Boston, MA: Kluwer Academic Publishers, 125–153.

Tirschwell, P. (2002) "Looking Forward", *Journal of Commerce*, October 21–27: 6.

Tully, S. (1991) "Comeback Ahead for Railroads", *Fortune*, 123: 107–113.

Turnbull, P. (2006) "The War on Europe"s Waterfront – Repertoires of Power in the Port Transport Industry", *British Journal of Industrial Relations*, 44: 305–326.

—— and Sapsford, D. (2001) "Hitting the Bricks: An International Comparative Study of Conflict on the Waterfront", *Industrial Relations*, 40: 231–57.

U.S. Maritime Administration (various years) *Annual Report*, Washington, DC: U.S. Government Printing Office.

Waters, R. C. (1995) "U.S. Maritime: Can It Compete?" *Transportation Quarterly*, 49: 33–44.

Zarocostas, J. (1996) "Port Industry Jobs Worldwide Continue to Decline, Study Says", *Journal of Commerce*, May 12: 8B.

12 Port pollution

Introduction

Ports worldwide are facing environmental challenges while facilitating maritime trade. The negative environmental impacts of ports are increasing with their ever-increasing cargo volumes. Populated port communities, in particular, are placing greater pressure on ports to negate or lessen their environmental impacts. In some cases, ports are seeking to become green ports, e.g., the Port of Seattle. In other cases, ports are waiting the approval of environmental impact studies by environmental regulatory authorities in order to start capital projects. The Ports of Los Angeles and Long Beach in 2007, for example, were waiting for the approval of a number of environmental impact studies in order to start $4 billion worth of capital projects.

Water and air pollution are the major environmental impacts of ports. Port water pollution may be associated with the disposal of vessel ballast water and waste, the use of vessel antifouling paints, vessel oil spillage, and the dredging of waterways to maintain channel depths and/or to increase channel and port berth depths in order to accommodate larger vessels. Port air pollution may arise from emissions from vessels, trucks, cargo-handling equipment, and railroad locomotives while in port.

This chapter discusses the various sources of water and air pollution in ports. Proposals to negate or reduce this pollution are also discussed.

Water pollution

There are numerous ways in which the harbor and berth waters of a port can be polluted. For example, a port's waters can be polluted from vessel ballast water, dredging, vessel waste disposal, vessel antifouling paints, and vessel oil spillage.

Ballast water

It is common practice for vessels while in port to take on and discharge water in order to ballast (or stabilize) the vessels. When cargo is removed, the ballast water may be pumped into specially designed (or cargo) tanks to compensate for the variance in cargo weight distributions. When cargo is loaded, the ballast water is released. Ships worldwide transfer 3 to 5 billion tons of ballast water each year (Staff 2006).

When ballast water is taken in by vessels, microscopic organisms and the larval stages of larger organisms indigenous to the region can be taken in as well. These organisms are then transported to other regions (beyond their natural habitat), where they are released with the discharge of ballast water. The discharged aquatic life may then thrive and disrupt the local ecological system. When there are no natural predators, the non-indigenous aquatic life may alter or destroy the natural marine ecosystem.

The black-stripped mussel was transported in ballast water from South America to Australia. The mussel was a threat to the Australian pearl industry, but early discovery enabled the government to take action to limit its impact at a cost of $2 million. The comb jelly that was transported in ballast water from the United States to the Black and Azov Seas almost wiped out the local anchovy fisheries. The Asian strain of cholera bacterium was likely introduced into Latin American waters through the discharge of ballast water. Invasive species can also cause property damage. The European zebra mussel was introduced via vessel ballast water into the Great Lakes in the mid-1980s, causing $5 billion in damage to water pipes, boat hulls, and other surfaces in the Great Lakes (Loy 1999).

One solution for greatly reducing the discharge of ballast-water nonindigenous aquatic life in port harbors is vessel mid-ocean ballast water exchange. Ballast water taken onboard when vessels are in ocean water depths of 6,600 feet or greater is expected to be nearly free of invasive species. However, the avoidance of nonindigenous species is not expected to be 100 percent, since all of the ballast water is not replaced. The International Maritime Organization (IMO) has promoted mid-ocean ballast exchange as the best short-term solution for avoiding the discharge of ballast-water nonindigenous species. The exchange process, however, is time-consuming (taking at least 48 hours) and can cost up to $25,000 for a large vessel that utilizes its crew for close monitoring. If performed by all ocean vessels calling at U.S. ports, the expected annual cost is $51 million (Mongelluzzo 2000). A benefit to the vessel owner is that the exchange is done while the vessel is underway. Long-term solutions for avoiding the discharge of ballast-water nonindigenous species in port harbors are likely to be treatment innovations that remove or kill non-indigenous species found in ballast waters.

As of January 1, 2000 all vessels calling directly from a foreign port and entering the U.S. California ports of Los Angeles, Long Beach, and Oakland are required to have performed mid-ocean ballast exchange. Also, these vessels are required to pay a $600 fee per vessel call for the purpose of funding research into new methods for preventing foreign aquatic species from entering California waters. More than 200 nonindigenous species have been found in the San Francisco Bay and 46 nonindigenous species have been found in the harbors of the Los Angeles/Long Beach port area.

All vessels calling U.S. ports must report their ballast-water management practices to the U.S. Coast Guard. If not, they will be subject to penalties. As of December 21, 2001 ocean carriers must submit a ballast-water management report at least 24 hours prior to the arrival of their vessels at their first U.S. port of call. In the past, they would report after their arrival. A number of U.S. states such as Washington, Maryland, Oregon, and Virginia also require ballast-water management reports.

The IMO International Convention for the Control and Management for Ships' Ballast Water and Sediments was adopted in 2004. Once ratified, vessels calling at countries that have ratified the convention will be required to have a ballast water and sediments management plan and keep a log of ballast-water management. Further, vessels will only be permitted to discharge clean ballast-water — resulting from sea exchange that was at least 200 miles from the nearest land and in water that was at least 200 meters deep. For vessels having difficulty in conducting ballast-water exchange, the distance is 50 miles from land and in water that is at least 200 meters deep. In February 2007 the Norwegian Parliament authorized the government to begin implementing the rules of the IMO Convention even though the convention had not been ratified.

Dredging

Dredging is the process of removing underwater sediments. A special type of equipment, a dredger, is used to excavate the sediments. Dredgers are generally classified into two groups: mechanical and hydraulic. Mechanical dredgers use a bucket to loosen, raise, and transport underwater materials to the surface. If the materials cannot be discharged close to the dredger, then they must be stored (say on a barge) for subsequent transport. Hydraulic dredgers use water to transport dredged materials. The materials are picked up from the water's bottom by a suction pump for transportation (in the form of slurry) through a pipeline. In addition to dredgers, ancillary equipment such as barges, tugs, work boats, and floating and shore pipelines are used in the removal of underwater sediments. The world's largest dredgers are capable (depending upon the bottom surface) of moving hundreds of thousands of cubic meters of material each week.

Dredging may be undertaken to create greater water depths, recover valuable materials, and remove harmful toxins. Creating greater water depths is associated with the dredging of waterways, port channels, and water bottoms at marine terminal berths. Thus, dredging is vital to maritime navigation and international commerce. A potential side benefit of this dredging is that the dredged material may be used to create new land. For example, the dredging site may be at a port where not only deeper water is needed (so that larger containerships can call) but also new land is needed on which a new marine terminal could be built (to expand the port's throughput capacity).

In addition to the nonsocial costs of dredging, there are also environmental social costs associated with dredging that are borne by nonusers of the port. The environmental costs may occur in the dredging operation and in the disposal of dredged materials. Environmental effects of the dredging operation phase include turbidity plume and other harmful effects to the ecosystem.

Turbidity plume (or elevated suspended solids) emanate when waterways are dredged. Sediments raised by dredging can bury plants near (or away from) the dredged site, thereby reducing their density. The reduction in plant density, in turn, can erode bottom sediments and increase silt. The distance the plume moves from the point of origin is dependent upon the scope of dredging, waterway currents, the nature of the plume, and the preventive measures employed by the dredging contractor. Large quantities of turbidity plume can affect fish species by clogging gills, abrading sensitive epithelial tissues, and reducing light penetration. Light reduction, in turn, reduces the photosynthesis of phytoplankton, reduces water oxygen, and kills submerged vegetation.

The U.S. Environmental Protection Agency (EPA) has shutdown numerous environmental dredging projects for the removal of harmful toxins because of their inability to maintain low levels of turbidity plume. Contaminant removal by dredging has proven to be difficult, costly, and time consuming (Staff 2007).

In addition to removing plants, dredging also changes the biological, chemical, and physical structure of the ecosystem. For example, the removal of bottom sediments frequently kills benthic organisms and disrupts their feeding habitat. Organisms and their habitat are disrupted by the turbulence, noise, and obstructions from dredging operations – taking years in some cases for the recolonization of organisms to occur.

Suspended sediments dredged from waterways may be biologically and chemically active. Dredged spoils from port harbor waterways that are in proximity to industrial and urban centers are often contaminated with heavy metal, organochlorine compound, polyaromatic hydrocarbon, and petroleum hydrocarbon pollutants. Disposal sites for dredged spoils often have high levels of sediment buildup and oxygen depletion that create adverse conditions for biotic communities.

The primary disposal site for dredge spoils from U.S. ocean ports is the ocean. However, because of ocean environmental contamination concerns, there is political pressure to consider alternative sites and to decontaminate the spoils prior to their disposal. A disposal site may not only benefit the depositor of spoils, but the site itself may also benefit. For example, it has been suggested that dredge spoils from the Port of New York-New Jersey be used for coal mine remediation in Pennsylvania. Specifically, acidic seepage from abandoned Pennsylvania mines is posing a threat to the state's drinkable water supply. This seepage may be stopped by depositing port dredge spoils in these mines.

Waste disposal

Vessel waste may include gray water (drainage from laundry, bath, shower, dishwasher, and washbasin drains), garbage (food waste and disposable items such as utensils, plastic cups, bottles, and tins) and sewage (water containing fecal matter and urine). Sewage is also referred to as black water, brown water, or foul water. Gray water may contain high levels of bacteria that are harmful to marine ecosystems. The disposal of food waste has fewer environmental concerns than the disposal of metals and plastics, since organic matter is easier to biodegrade. Waste disposal by cruise ships is especially a concern given that they have greater amounts of waste relative to that of other types of vessels.

Stricter requirements are now in place for the disposal of vessel waste – e.g., more recycling and less sea disposal of waste. Vessel operators face decisions regarding where to store waste onboard and the location of the nearest port reception facilities at which to dump waste.

In 2002, the EU directive 2000/59 on handling vessel waste was passed. By December 27, 2002, all EU member states were required to establish vessel waste reception and handling plans for all of their ports. However, the implementation of the directive among the EU states has not been uniform – EU ports have different waste reception facilities and fees and regulations for handling vessel waste. Directive complaints include (1) port vessel waste communication forms are not uniform, (2) EU port charges for vessel waste disposal are expensive, thereby encouraging vessels to go to non-EU ports for waste disposal, and (3) there are no regulations requiring vessels to use EU port waste-handling facilities, even though EU ports are required to have these facilities. In the UK ports charge vessels for waste reception facilities, whether or not they use them. In Italy, its 25 principal ports are in conformity with the EU directive. In addition to providing vessel waste-handling facilities, Spanish ports also have financial incentives to promote their use.

In October 2005 a California vessel pollution bill was signed into law. The Clean Coast Act went into effect on January 1, 2006. The Act prohibits oceangoing vessels (300 gross tons or larger) from (1) conducting onboard incineration of waste while operating within three miles of the California coast and (2) releasing hazardous waste, gray water, oily bilge-water, and other waste into California waters. If such a release occurs, the vessel owner must, within 24 hours, notify the California Water Resources Control Board. Vessel operators may have to store gray water onboard their vessels until they sail out of California waters, especially if their vessels spend much time in anchorage.

Antifouling paints

Fouling is the unwanted growth of biological material, e.g., algae and barnacles, on the water-immersed surfaces of vessels. When vessel hulls are clean and smooth, i.e., free of fouling, vessels consume less fuel and travel faster through water. When a vessel is dry-docked, its fouling can be removed. Fouling can also be reduced by applying antifouling coatings to vessel hulls. Prior to the 1960s, antifouling coatings such as lime and arsenical and mercurial compounds were applied to vessel hulls. Beginning in the 1960s antifouling paints with metallic compounds, e.g., organotin compounds such as tributyltin (TBT), were painted on vessel hulls. By the 1970s, TBT had been painted on the hulls of most ocean vessels.

Although antifouling TBT paints are effective in killing sea life attached to vessel hulls, they also kill and cause genetic alterations in other sea life, e.g., causing shell deformations in oysters. In the 1970s in the Arcachon Bay on the west coast of France, TBT contamination was linked to the high mortality of oyster larvae. In the 1980s, TBT poisoning was linked to the decline of the dog whelk in southwest England.

TBT is the most toxic substance ever deliberately introduced into the marine environment (Evans *et al.* 1995). Further, it persists in the marine environment: "The half-life of TBT sediments is 10–15 years" (O'Mahony 2006). High concentrations of TBT have been found in the world's coastal waters, especially in port harbor waters where vessels are concentrated.

In response to TBT's environmental problems, the IMO has sought to limit the use of TBT in antifouling paints. In 1990 the IMO's Marine Environment Protection Committee (MEPC) adopted a resolution, Measures to Control Potential Adverse Impacts Associated with Use of Tributyltin Compounds in Anti-Fouling Paints, for the elimination of TBT antifouling paint on nonaluminum hulled vessels of less than 25 meters in length.

In October 2001 the IMO International Convention on the Control of Harmful Anti-Fouling Systems on Ships was adopted. Its implementation requires ratification from 25 countries that represent 25 percent of the world's vessel tonnage. Parties to the Convention are required to prohibit and/or restrict the use of harmful antifouling systems on vessels flying their flag. The Convention also established a "technical group" to review proposals for other substances used in antifouling systems to be prohibited or restricted. As of January 1, 2008 an EU regulation will require that all vessels, irrespective of flag, entering a port of a member state must not be coated with organotin compounds or must have a second topcoat of paint that prevents the leakage of organotin compounds from the undercoat.

Oil spillage

A vessel may intentionally or accidentally spill oil into a port harbor. Intentional spillage is typically operational dumping that involves ballast water – e.g., after discharging its oil cargo, a tanker vessel will likely take on ballast water into its cargo tanks to ensure stability on the return trip, but then dumps the dirty ballast-in-oil-water mixture on or before arrival at the loading port. Accidental spillage may result from a vessel accident or during oil transfers, i.e., during the loading and unloading of oil cargo and fueling while in port. Vessels may spill oil from oil-cargo tanks as well as from fuel tanks.

It is difficult to extrapolate the nature and extent of the environmental damage that follows a vessel oil spill. Because of the interactions of a great number of factors, two spills in the same place will have very different environmental consequences depending, for example, on weather conditions, the time of year, and success of the clean-up (Dicks 1998). If the oil spill occurs in the season when fish and shellfish are spawning and birds and mammals are congregating, the damage to these species from an oil spill can be considerable. High temperatures and wind speeds increase the evaporation of oil, decreasing the toxicity of the oil remaining in the water.

The environmental impact of a vessel oil spill will also depend on the speed of recovery and the type of the oil that is spilt. The speed of oil recovery is affected by the type of oil spilt, the climate and season of year, and the physical and biological characteristics of the area.

Light oils, e.g., gasoline, are more toxic than heavy oils and thus more likely to penetrate and disrupt cell membranes of organisms. Alternatively, heavy oils that spill on shorelines may blanket organisms and kill them from the physical effect of smothering rather than from toxic effects. Bunker fuel in the fuel tanks of oceangoing vessels is a viscous liquid that when released into cold water congeals into a sticky substance and adheres to anything with which it comes into contact.

Air pollution

Oceangoing vessels are significant air polluters in port when they run their engines to generate on-board electricity, e.g., for pumps and lights. The fossil-fuel burning engines of railroad locomotives and trucks while in port and the port equipment itself also contribute to the air pollution of ports. The levels of air pollutants at ports worldwide are a growing concern and thus the impetus of the environmental port movement for their reduction. In December 2005 the ports of Los Angeles and Shanghai, two of the world's largest container ports, signed the Letter of Intent for Collaboration on Air Quality Issues for the promotion of shared environmental betterment programs.

Vessels

Oceangoing vessels are significant air polluters, but are among the least-regulated polluters. The power source of oceangoing vessels is residual oil (or bunker fuel) – a byproduct of the refinery process and thus the least refined of the petroleum fuels – and consequently is much dirtier than other petroleum products. It is used by oceangoing vessels because of its relatively low cost. The combustion engines of oceangoing vessels are the dirtiest such engines per ton of fuel consumed, producing 14 percent of the world's nitrogen emissions and 16 percent of all sulfur emissions from fossil fuels (Spice 1999). Bunker fuel used by some vessels has a sulfur content of 27,000 parts per million; by contrast, the sulfur content limit in gasoline used by U.S. automobiles is 15 parts per million.

Oceangoing vessels contribute 5 to 30 percent of the sulfur dioxide pollution found in coastal areas (Capaldo *et al.* 1999) and affecting the health of individuals that live in the coastal areas. While air pollution standards for motor vehicles have been established and tightened in many countries, the establishment of air pollution standards for oceangoing vessels is in its infancy. However, air pollution from oceangoing vessels is becoming more noticeable with the continuing growth in international trade. The IMO is currently conducting a study of air pollution standards for oceangoing vessels. However, IMO standards are not expected to be available until 2009 or 2010; their ratification and implementation by member countries may take several years. If these standards are too weak, individual states and provinces within countries may be encouraged to develop their own standards, e.g., such as those proposed by the state of California. Also, without international vessel air pollution standards, a variance in vessel air pollution standards among states and countries will likely occur. Proposals to reduce vessel air pollution in ports include cold ironing, speed reduction by vessels when approaching a port, and the burning of cleaner fuels by vessels.

Cold ironing occurs when vessels while in port receive energy from an external source, such as electricity from a shore-side electricity source – thereby enabling vessels to shut down their engines, i.e., to allow the vessels' iron engines to go cold and thus reduce the port's air pollution. The U.S. Navy has been using shore-side electricity for decades and cold ironing is a standard at U.S. Navy ports. The cruise line, Princess Cruises, utilized cold ironing in Juneau, Alaska in the summer of 2001 and at the Port of Seattle in the summer of 2005. Today, all Princess Cruises vessels that dock at the Port of Los Angeles utilize cold ironing.

In June 2004 at the Port of Los Angeles, the China Shipping Container Lines' vessel, *Xin Yan Zhou*, became the first containership in the world to turn off its engines while in port and use an onshore electrical power source, i.e., the first containership to cold iron. Furthermore, the Port of Los Angeles became the first container port in the world to have cold ironed a vessel. Containerships lend themselves to cold ironing, since their containers are loaded and unloaded by shore-side cranes. Tanker ships are less amenable to cold-ironing, since ship pumps are needed to unload cargo.

The expense of cold ironing a vessel, however, may limit its adoption. A shipping line may have to spend several million dollars to install electrical hookup capabilities in new vessels or retrofit older vessels. Ports and marine terminals may also have to spend several million dollars to install shore-side electrical facilities. The shipping line APL has experimented with an alternative cold ironing technology – a docked vessel's bow-thruster transformer is attached to a shore-side generator that runs on clean-burning liquefied natural gas. The cost per vessel for cold-ironing equipment with this technology is approximately $300,000 as compared to $1.5 million to retrofit a vessel to receive electricity from a shore-side electrical facility (Mongelluzzo 2007b). By utilizing clean-burning liquefied natural gas, there are significant reductions in harmful emissions such as nitrogen oxide, carbon monoxide, particulate matter, and carbon dioxide. In the UK wind turbines are being considered as an external electrical power source for vessels while in port.

UK ports and their shipping line customers have rallied against an IMO proposal to require ports to install cold-ironing systems. The concern is that UK ports and other ports of the world that adopt expensive cold-ironing systems will be at a competitive disadvantage (in terms of having to charge higher port prices) versus ports that do not adopt these systems. Also, some individuals argue that more energy may be consumed in powering a ship from the shore than with its own engine. However, a number of Asian shipping lines have ordered more than 100 vessels with the cold-ironing capability. Since these vessels are expected to at least initially operate in the transpacific trade, the Asian ports in this trade will have an incentive to equip their berths with shore-side electrical facilities.[1]

Speed reductions by vessels when approaching a port can result in significant reductions in nitrogen oxide emissions by these vessels. The Port of Long Beach in California, for example, has a voluntary program that includes discounted dockage fees for shipping lines that agree to reduce the speeds of their vessels to 12 knots within 20 miles of the port. The cost savings in dockage fees to shipping lines that have adopted this program now exceed more than $1 million. There is a 90 percent compliance rate among shipping lines that call the Port of Long Beach (Mongelluzzo 2007b).

Vessels emit the fine particulate matters, nitrogen oxides (NOx) and sulfur oxides (SOx), from their engines. Concern for these emissions prompted the European Commission to limit to 0.1 percent (as of January 2010) the fuel sulfur content for vessels operating in their ports. Traditional bunker fuel has a sulfur content of 2.7 percent.

The California Air Resources Board (CARB) established a vessel emission standard for the ports of Los Angeles, Long Beach, and Oakland as of January 1, 2007, by requiring vessels that call at the ports to use low-sulfur distillate fuel within 24 miles of the state's coast. The requirement was struck down by a federal court that determined that a state's jurisdiction extends only to three miles. The CARB filed an appeal and requested a stay pending the disposal of the appeal. The stay was granted by an appellate court on

October 23, 2007. Subsequently, the CARB announced that it would again start enforcing the vessel emission standard.

In March 2008 the Ports of Los Angeles and Long Beach announced a voluntary fuel subsidy program, whereby fuel subsidies would be provided to shipping lines whose vessels switch to low-sulfur fuel within 20 miles of the ports. The vessels must also run the low-sulfur fuel in their auxiliary engines while at berth and participate in the program that encourages vessels to reduce their speed to 12 knots or less as they near the ports. The one-year voluntary program was to begin July 1, 2008 and end June 30, 2009, at an estimated cost to the ports of $19 million – based upon the 5,700 vessel calls at the ports in 2007 (Joshi 2008).

Shipping lines may also voluntarily adopt vessel emission standards at ports. On May 26, 2006, Maersk Line announced that it would voluntarily phase in the use of ultra-low-sulfur diesel fuel (0.2 percent sulfur content) for its container vessels that call at the ports of Los Angeles and Oakland, reducing vessel SOx and NOx emissions by 92 percent and 10 percent, respectively (Mongelluzzo 2006). Although the ports of Los Angeles, Long Beach, and Oakland have no environmental regulatory authority, they may be able to establish vessel emission standards by requiring stricter emission-reduction standards from shipping lines as conditions for renewal of their terminal leases with the ports.

In 2007 there was a proposal to the IMO to require vessels to switch to distillate fuel for the purpose of reducing vessel air emissions. However, critics argue that such a switch would greatly increase vessel fuel costs, especially if the supply of distillate fuel does not keep up with industry demand, thereby possibly disrupting international trade. Other options available to shipping lines for reducing harmful vessel emissions include electronically controlled fuel injection, selective catalytic reduction, slide values on engines, the use of emulsified fuel and water in combustion, and the use of advanced lubricating oil. From the perspective of the shipping line, the preferred option will likely be the option that is the least costly to the line (Wang *et al*. 2007). However, this option may not be the one that would be chosen by the port authority or government.

Vehicles

In addition to vessels, port vehicles – trucks, cargo-handling equipment, and railroad locomotives – are also air polluters. Trucks, cargo-handling equipment, and railroad locomotives account for 40 percent, 23 percent, and 4 percent of the nitrogen oxide emissions at ports, respectively, in comparison to 32 percent for oceangoing vessels (Mongelluzzo 2007a).

The Ports of Los Angeles and Long Beach are leaders among U.S. ports in enacting measures for reducing port air pollution. The San Pedro Bay Ports Clean Air Action Plan that was announced by the two ports in April 2007 is a case in point. The plan requires that 16,000 old, polluting trucks calling at these ports be replaced with low-emission vehicles by 2012. Specifically, the plan calls for (1) replacing pre-1992 trucks with alternative fuel or cleaner diesel engines, (2) retrofitting 1993–2003 trucks with NOx and particulate reduction equipment, and (3) requiring all trucks by the end of 2011 to meet or exceed the EPA 2007 on-road particulate emissions standards and be the cleanest available at the time of replacement or retrofit with respect to NOx. All trucks that do not meet the EPA 2007 emissions standards by January 1, 2012 will be banned from the ports.

The expected cost to replace trucks under the plan is $2 billion. Owner-operator truck drivers who constitute the majority of the local harbor truck drivers are unlikely to have the financial resources to maintain and purchase new trucks (at a price exceeding $100,000 per truck).[2] In order to finance the purchase of new trucks, the Ports of Los Angeles and Long Beach have adopted a container tax of $35 per TEU. The tax is expected to raise $1.6 billion by 2012; the remaining $400 million (to finance the $2 billion) is expected to come from the state of California.[3] The plan has a provision to subsidize up to 80 percent of the cost of purchasing a new truck. For the Port of Long Beach, truck drivers would be eligible for up to $2 billion worth of loans for the purchase of new trucks with the port providing a subsidy of up to $1,000 per month toward a driver's loan payment.

The plan also includes a concession program in which the two ports would license harbor trucking companies. The Port of Los Angeles has a component in this program that states that only trucking firms (carriers) that hire drivers as direct employees would be eligible to be licensed, not owner-operator truck drivers. As a consequence, nearly 17,000 owner-operator truck drivers would be replaced with employee drivers from a small group of large truck carriers. The rationale for the employee-driver mandate is the stable workforce argument, i.e., a small group of truck carriers with employee drivers will provide a more stable truck driver workforce than a workforce of owner-operator truck drivers. If unionized, the employee drivers might also receive higher incomes than those received as owner-operator drivers. The Port of Long Beach, however, does not have such a component in its concession program, i.e., it is not in favor of the hiring of drivers as direct employees for eligibility for port licensing.

The hiring of direct-employee truck drivers, but not owner-operator truck drivers, for eligibility for port licensing is opposed by the American Trucking Associations and the owner-operator truck drivers, but supported by the Teamsters union. Further, a letter from the Federal Maritime Commission to both ports states that any attempt to restructure harbor trucking would invite legal challenges. In February 2008 the Port of Long Beach approved its concession program without requiring that port-licensed harbor trucking companies be employee truck drivers.

In March 2008 the Port of Los Angeles Harbor Commissioners approved the port's concession program, which included the component that harbor trucking companies are to hire employee drivers as a condition for receiving a license to dray containers to and from the port. This hiring is to be phased in over a five-year period; at the end of the five years, all harbor truck drivers at the Port of Los Angeles must be employee drivers. In addition, the commissioners passed an amendment that would allow port staff to audit trucking company applicants for financial soundness.

The San Pedro Bay Ports Clean Air Action Plan also calls for port cargo-handling equipment to meet EPA (Environmental Protection Agency) standards for new equipment. Older equipment will be retrofitted. If the equipment cannot meet the stricter standards, it will be taken out of service. The retrofitted equipment will use the cleanest available alternative fuel (most likely natural gas) engines. The EPA and the two ports are developing hybrid yard tractors – either using a hybrid electric system or a hybrid hydraulic system combined with the cleanest available diesel engines.

By 2008 all switch railroad locomotives utilized in the ports were replaced with Tier II engines that use emulsified fuels and are equipped with 15-minute idling devices. By 2011, all diesel-powered, line-haul locomotives entering the ports will have to use ultra-low-sulfur fuel and meet EPA Tier II rail standards.

The Port of Gothenburg in Sweden has estimated that approximately 70 percent of its carbon dioxide emissions are produced by its cargo-handling equipment. Consequently, it has adopted the program of "Working Eco Driving" to reduce these emissions. The program is a planned driving program that seeks to avoid stops and maintain a steady speed for its cargo-handling equipment for the reduction of fuel consumption and therefore carbon dioxide emissions. Fuel consumption is expected to decline by 30 percent and carbon dioxide emissions by 2,000 tons a year (Woodbridge 2007). The port has also adopted the policy that all newly acquired cargo handling equipment must be equipped with catalytic converters and particle filters. This policy is expected to reduce port air emissions by 90 percent (Woodbridge 2007). The port is also using wind power, a renewable energy source, to generate shore-side electricity for its cold-ironing program.

Hong Kong International Terminals (HIT) is the first terminal operator in Hong Kong to utilize electric rubber-tired gantry cranes (RTGs). By the year 2010, 70 percent of its RTGs will be electrically powered; the remaining 30 percent will be converted into hybrid RTGs. The Da Chan Bay Terminal 1 at the Port of Shenzhen was the first container terminal in the world to have an all-electric fleet of RTGs (Wallis 2008).

Noise and aesthetic pollution

Noise is unwanted sound. The magnitude of this unwanted sound is often measured on a scale of loudness expressed in decibels. Noise is unwanted by individuals, since it may interfere with their normal speech or other activities, cause them physical pain (e.g., if the sound pressure level of the human ear is 140 decibels or above), and create fear (e.g., fear that they may be harmed). At ports, noise is generated by ships, trucks, trains, ship-to-shore gantry cranes, yard equipment, and construction and maintenance activities. The noise levels of ship auxiliary engines while in port, for example, can reach 80–120 decibels; chainsaws by comparison average 110 decibels (Sharma 2006). Port noise may result in individuals suffering from hearing impairment and high blood pressure (hypertension).

Port noise can also affect wildlife. Low-frequency sounds emanating from ship engines can disorient marine animals that use sound for reproductive interactions and prey location (Bailey *et al.* 2004). At those ports that have adopted cold ironing, not only will there be a reduction in air emissions but also noise reductions from cold ironing.

Aesthetic pollution occurs when the appearance of the environment is made less beautiful. Examples of port aesthetic pollution include the colors of cranes and yard equipment that are quite different from those colors found in a port's surrounding environment (say the color pink as opposed to a light blue color that often appears on port equipment) and the flood lights and blinking vehicle lights in a night environment. Port lights at night can cause sleep deprivation, disrupt biological rhythms, and cause stress for individuals located in neighborhoods near ports. At the Port of Hong Kongs Modern Terminals, special devices have been installed on mast lighting to minimize glare.

Summary

Water and air pollution are major negative environmental impacts of ports. Port communities are placing greater pressure on ports to negate or lessen these environmental impacts. Port waters can be polluted from vessel ballast water, dredging, vessel waste disposal, vessel antifouling paints, and vessel oil spillage.

When ballast water is taken in by vessels, microscopic organisms and the larval stages of larger organisms indigenous to the region can also be taken. When ballast water is discharged in other regions, the discharged aquatic life may then thrive and disrupt the local ecological system. Dredging can be used to recover valuable materials or to create greater water depths. Environmental costs of dredging include turbidity plume and other harmful effects to the ecosystem. Vessel waste may include gray water (drainage from laundry, bath, shower, dishwasher, and washbasin drains), garbage (food waste and disposable items such as utensils, plastic cups, bottles, and tins), and sewage (water containing fecal matter and urine). Antifouling paints on vessel hulls can reduce the growth of biological material on the water-immersed surfaces of vessels, but are also harmful to the ecosystem. Vessels may spill oil from oil-cargo tanks as well as from fuel tanks.

Oceangoing vessels emit nitrogen oxides (NOx) and sulfur oxides (SOx) from their engines. Proposals to reduce vessel air pollution in ports include cold ironing, speed reduction by vessels when approaching a port, and the burning of cleaner fuels by vessels. Cold ironing occurs when vessels while in port receive electricity from shore-side electricity sources, thereby enabling them to shut down their engines. The fossil-fuel-burning engines of port trucks, cargo-handling equipment, and railroad locomotives also pollute the air of ports. Their emissions while in port may be reduced by using alternative fuels or cleaner burning engines.

Noise pollution is generated at ports by ships, trucks, trains, ship-to-shore gantry cranes, yard equipment, and construction and maintenance activities. Aesthetic pollution occurs at ports when colors of cranes and yard equipment are quite different from those colors found in the port's surrounding environment and by floodlights and blinking vehicle lights in a night environment.

Notes

1 In 2008 Canada invited its port authorities and terminal operators to apply for funds from its Marine Shore Power program ($6 million over four years). The funds are to be used by port authorities and terminal operators to purchase equipment such as transformers to power ships at docks, i.e., cold ironing.
2 In October 2007 the Virginia Port Authority announced its support for the U.S. Environmental Protection Agency's SmartWay Transport Partnership with the launch of a pilot program of offering low-interest loans to truckers for the purchase of new and more emission-efficient engines or to retrofit older trucks for such efficiency. Further, the truckers can join the SmartWay Transport Partnership Program, where they would be eligible to qualify for increased business from SmartWay Shippers that are committed to provide at least 50 percent of their cargo to SmartWay carriers.
3 Reductions in port truck air emissions are also expected to occur from limiting truck idling time while in port, e.g., requiring diesel engines to be shut off after five minutes of idling.

Bibliography

Bailey, D., Plenys, T., Solomon, G. M., Campbell, T. R., Feuer, G. R., Masters, J., and Tonkonogy, B. (2004) *Harboring Pollution: The Dirty Truth about U.S. Ports*, New York: Natural Resources Defense Council.

Bryant, D. (2005) "California: The Incredible Green Hulk", *Maritime Reporter and Engineering News*, November: 17–18.

Capaldo, K., Corbett, J., Kasibhatla, P., Fischbeck, P., and Pandis, S. (1999) "Effects of Ship Emissions on Sulphur Cycling and Radiative Climate Forcing Over the Ocean", *Nature*, 400: 743–746.

Corbett, J. J. and Farrell, A. (2002) "Mitigating Air Pollution Impacts of Passenger Ferries", *Transportation Research Part D*, 7: 197–211.

Demars, K. R., Richardson, G. N., Yong, R. N., and Chaney, R. C. (1995) *Dredging, Remediation and Containment of Contaminated Sediments*, Philadelphia, PA: ASTM International.

Dicks, B. (1998) "The Environmental Impact of Marine Oil Spills: Effects, Recovery and Compensation", a paper presented at the International Seminar on Tanker Safety, Pollution Prevention, Spill Response and Compensation, Rio de Janeiro, Brazil.

Evans, S. M., Leksono, T., and McKinnell, P. D. (1995) "Tributyltin Pollution: A Diminishing Problem Following Legislation Limiting the Use of TBT-Based Anti-Fouling Paints", *Marine Pollution Bulletin*, 30: 14–21.

Giuliano, G. and O'Brien, T. (2007) "Reducing Port-Related Truck Emissions: The Terminal Gate Appointment System in the Ports of Los Angeles and Long Beach", *Transportation Research Part D*, 12: 460–473.

Joshi, R. (2008) "Californian Ports to Bankroll Low-Sulphur Switch". Available online at http://www.lloydslist.com, March 26.

Keefe, J. (2007) "Ballast Water Management: Industry Leading the Way", *Maritime Executive*, September: 36–39.

Loy, J. M. (1999) "The Coast Guard and Ballast-Water Management", *Journal of Commerce*, October 27: 6.

Mongelluzzo, B. (2000) "California Law Targets Foreign Species", *Journal of Commerce*, January 4: 1.

—— (2001) "Clearing the Air", *JOC WEEK*, November 5–11: 31–32.

—— (2006) "Cleaning the Air", *Journal of Commerce*, June 12: 13–15.

—— (2007a) "Global Warming: Southern California's Environmental Initiative Begins to Take Root at Home and Abroad", *Journal of Commerce*, January 8: 42, 44–45.

—— (2007b) "Clean Machines: Carriers, Ports Want an International Standard on Air Pollution from Ships", *Journal of Commerce*, October 29: 11, 13–15.

O'Mahony, H. (2006) "Pouring over the Legislation Means Slow Progress on Ban on TBT Coatings", Available online at http://www.lloydslist.com, February 2.

Sharma, D. C. (2006) "Ports in a Storm", *Environmental Health Perspectives*, 114: 224–31.

Spice, B. (1999) "Ship Pollution Study: Emissions Cool Earth", *Journal of Commerce*, August 23: 2.

Staff (2004) "Little Harmony in Conducting European Waste Disposal Rules". Available online at http://www.lloydslist.com, May 3.

—— (2006) "New Ballast Water Management System from Greenship", *Maritime Reporter and Engineering News*, February: 27–29.

—— (2007) "Environmental Risks of Dredging", *World Dredging, Mining and Construction*, 43: 10–11, 20.

Talley, W. K. (2003) "Environmental Impacts of Shipping", in D. A. Hensher and K. J. Button (eds) *Handbook of Transport and the Environment*, Amsterdam: Elsevier, 279–291.

—— (2004) "Post OPA-90 Vessel Oil Spill Differentials: Transfers Versus Vessel Accidents", *Maritime Policy and Management*, 31: 225–240.

—— (2005) "Regulatory Issues: The Role of International Maritime Institutions", in D. A. Hensher and K. J. Button (eds) *Handbook of Transport Strategy: Policy and Institutions*, Amsterdam: Elsevier, 421–433.

—— (2005) "Post OPA-90 Vessel Oil Transfer Spill Prevention: The Effectiveness of Coast Guard Enforcement", *Environmental and Resource Economics*, 30: 93–114.

——, Jin, D., and Kite-Powell, H. (2001) "Vessel Accident Oil-Spillage: Post US OPA-90", *Transportation Research Part D*, 6: 405–415.

Tirschwell, P. (1999) "Terminating Aliens: EPA's Help is Sought by Environmentalists", *Journal of Commerce*, September 27: 9.

Vutukuru, S. and Dabdub, D. (2008) "Modeling the Effects of Ship Emissions on Coastal Air Quality: A Case Study of Southern California", *Atmospheric Environment*, 42: 3751–3764.

Wallis, K. (2008) "Hong Kong Cuts Sulphur Emissions: Terminal Operators Switch to Cleaner Power". Available online at http://www.lloydslist.com, June 10.

Wang, C., Corbett, J. J., and Winebrake, J. J. (2007) "Cost-Effectiveness of Reducing Sulfur Emissions from Ships", *Environmental Science and Technology*, 41: 8233–8239.

Woodbridge, C. (2007) "Clean Handling Ashore", *Containerisation International*, December: 78–79.

Yell, D. and Riddell, J. (1995) *Dredging*, London: T. Telford.

13 Port security and safety

Introduction

Maritime security incidents are intentional. They involve damage to property and/or injury to individuals for political reasons. They may occur on board ships and in ports and are undertaken by individuals (or terrorists). Maritime piracy incidents are also intentional but unlike maritime security incidents their purpose is theft. Maritime safety incidents, e.g., vessel accidents, are unintentional. However, maritime security, piracy, and safety incidents may have the same outcomes – property damage and injuries.

A port security incident cycle consists of four phases (Price 2004; Pinto and Talley 2006). The first phase (prevention) is to prevent security incidents from occurring by creating barriers that deny terrorists from planning and undertaking such incidents. The second phase (detection) is early apprehension of planned incidents. The third phase (response) is the mitigation of the impact of a security incident once it has occurred. In the fourth phase (recovery), the port seeks to return to normal operations following a security incident. The prevention and detection phases are *ex ante* security phases; the response and recovery phases are *ex post* security phases. The focus of port security planning has been *ex ante* as opposed to *ex post*. In the United States this is likely due to the fact that no major port security incident has occurred.

This chapter presents a discussion of port security. The chapter begins with a discussion of the economic effects of maritime security incidents, followed by a discussion of the International Ship and Port Facility Security (ISPS) Code. An in-depth discussion of U.S. port security follows – maritime cargo security initiatives; the SAFE Port Act; detection, response, and recovery; and security finance. Then, EU port security and a comparison with U.S. port security are discussed.

Maritime security incidents: economic effects

Maritime supply chains are susceptible to terrorism given that they are networks for the movement of international trade. Since ports are nodes in these networks, they are also susceptible to terrorism. Disruptions in maritime supply chains attributable to maritime security incidents can have significant negative effects on international trade, since the latter is highly reliant on safe waterways and ports. The impacts of terrorist attacks on maritime supply chains can include loss of lives, damage and destruction to property, and the decrease in economic activity.

A major security incident in a container port, e.g., a terrorist attack on and the sinking of a containership in the port's harbor, will not only result in the loss of the ship and its cargo, but also will disrupt vessel traffic to and from the port – thereby having a negative economic impact on the port, the port community, and international trade in general (e.g., from cargo arrival delays and increased transit times for ships using alternative routes). Although the 10-day closure of U.S. West Coast ports in 2002 was due to the lockout of dockworkers by the ports, this same closure could have been due to terrorist attacks. The closure resulted in (1) 200 ships being unable to berth and unload their cargo, (2) the delay of domestic export cargoes moving to U.S. ports, (3) mid-ocean diversions of ships to other ports, and (4) domestic businesses laying off workers and/or cutting back on production. The delay in the delivery of Asian cargo to the United States resulted in an estimated 0.4 percent decrease in the nominal GDP for several Asian countries; the decrease for Hong Kong, Malaysia, and Singapore was estimated to be 1.1 percent.

A maritime security incident may also result in higher marine insurance premiums. For example, insurance premiums tripled for ships calling at ports in Yemen after the terrorist attack on the oil tanker Limburg off the Yemeni Coast in 2002 (Richardson 2004). As a consequence, many ships canceled Yemen from their schedules or diverted to neighboring ports. The occurrence of a security incident may result in greater investments in maritime security prevention and detection technologies, thereby increasing the transportation cost of international trade.

The international ship and port security code

Following the terrorist aircraft attacks in New York City on September 11, 2001, the International Maritime Organization (IMO) sought to strengthen the security of the flow of maritime cargo around the world. A draft of the IMO maritime security regulation, the International Ship and Port Facility Security (ISPS) Code, appeared in December 2002. On July 1, 2004 the code was adopted by an IMO conference at which representatives of 108 member countries, observers from IMO associate members, and intergovernmental and nongovernmental international organizations were in attendance. This wide participation at the conference was an indication of the worldwide concern for maritime security.

The ISPS Code sought to enhance security on board ships and at ports. The primary focus of the ISPS Code is to address security of ships at sea and the security of the interface between ships and port facilities when ships are at berth. The code has requirements for governments, shipping lines, ships, and ports. Governments are required, for example, to (1) determine which port facilities are to designate port facility security officers (PFSOs); (2) ensure completion and approval of a port facility security assessment and the port facility security plan for each port facility that serves ships engaged in international voyages; (3) approve ship security plans (SSPs); and (4) issue international ship security certificates (SSCs) and enforce compliance measures.

Shipping lines are required, for example, to (1) designate a company security officer (CSO); (2) undertake a ship security assessment (SSAS) for each ship for which an SSC is to be issued; (3) develop an SSP for each ship that is issued an SSAS; (4) designate a ship security officer (SSO) for each ship; and (5) provide training for the CSO, the SSOs, and ship crews. Ships are required to have an automatic identification system, an identification number, and a security alert system. Ports are required to (1) carry out and have approved port facility security assessments; (2) develop port facility security plans; (3) designate a PFSO with skills and training roughly similar to the CSO; and (4) provide adequate training for the PFSO and other appropriate personnel.

The code established three maritime security (MARSEC) levels that indicate the severity of a security threat. MARSEC level 1 indicates that a threat is possible, but not likely;

MARSEC level 2 indicates that terrorists are likely active in an area; MARSEC level 3 indicates that there is the imminent threat of a security incident.

U.S. port security

Since September 11, 2001, the United States has established numerous programs to prevent and detect port security threats. On November 19, 2001, the U.S. Congress created the Transportation Security Administration (TSA) by passing the Aviation and Transportation Security Act. The TSA's initial focus was on aviation security, but today its mission is to ensure the security of the transportation of passengers and cargo. The Maritime Transportation Security Act (MTSA) that was signed into law on November 25, 2002 is designed to prevent security incidents in the maritime supply chain by focusing on the higher security-risk sectors of the maritime industry. The MTSA not only includes the requirements of the ISPS Code, but also imposes additional security requirements on certain U.S. flagged ships and port facilities.

The security defense for U.S. ports is layered, i.e., with respect to four zones: foreign port, offshore, coastal, and dockside zones (Emerson and Nadeau 2003). The foreign port zone (layer 1) is the far-out-to-sea-as-possible security defense for U.S. ports. For a vessel arriving at a U.S. port from a foreign port that has ineffective security measures, the Coast Guard may deny entry or prescribe conditions for entry. The offshore zone (layer 2) includes U.S. waters inside the 200-mile exclusive economic zone but beyond the 12-mile territorial sea. The coastal zone (layer 3) includes U.S. waters that extend inward from the 12-mile territorial sea to the docks and piers of a U.S. port. The dockside zone (layer 4) is the U.S. port.

The Coast Guard has established port security zones around ships and high-risk port facilities. Under the authority of the U.S. Ports and Waterways Safety Act, the Coast Guard may establish security subzones within the coastal zone to safeguard waterways, ports, vessels, and waterfront facilities from destruction, sabotage, or other subversive acts. To restrict vessels from nearing a particular facility, another vessel, or a specified geographic area, 115 security zones have been implemented at U.S. ports since September 11, 2001.

Port access-control measures include alarm systems, perimeter fencing, terminal lighting, closed-circuit television systems, port access/egress controls on trucks and rail cars (i.e., vehicle checks), employee background checks, and security patrols. Also, high-interest vessels may be escorted into and out of port with sea marshals (or armed Coast Guard personnel) on board.[1] The purpose of the High-Interest Vessel Boarding Program is to have sea marshals provide security to the pilot and crew during transit, thereby diminishing the potential for vessel hijacking.

Maritime cargo security initiatives

There are three major U.S. maritime cargo security initiatives – two voluntary security programs and the 24-Hour Advance Manifest Rule (24-hour rule). The voluntary security programs have been designed by the U.S. Bureau of Customs and Border Protection (CBP) to provide origin-to-final destination visibility and control over containerized freight movements. These programs include the Container Security Initiative (CSI) and the Customs–Trade Partnership Against Terrorism (C-TPAT) programs.

CSI was created to protect U.S. ports from terrorist attacks and to prevent the use of containers for the transportation of dangerous cargo. Specifically, foreign ports are asked to pre-screen containers (for dangerous cargo) before they are loaded onto U.S.-bound ships. Without CSI, containers arriving from foreign ports would likely have to be inspected at the importing U.S. ports. The CSI is a bilateral agreement between the U.S. and a foreign port (i.e., its government or port authority). The foreign port that handles substantial containerized cargo designated for the U.S. will identify high-risk containerized cargo and work with deployed CBP officers to target such cargo. As of the first quarter of 2007, 50 foreign ports, handling 85 percent of the container volume destined for the U.S., were designated as CSI ports. There are 23 CSI ports in Europe, e.g., Rotterdam, Hamburg, and Antwerp. The CSI benefits to CSI ports include reducing (1) the inspection times for their exports in U.S. ports, and (2) the delay in ocean transportation to the U.S., since the CBP will likely have more confidence in accepting cargo from CSI ports. The CBP also offers CSI reciprocity agreements, e.g., Canadian and Japanese customs personnel are deployed in some U.S. ports.

C-TPAT is a joint government–business initiative to build cooperative security relationships. These relationships, established under C-TPAT guidelines, are to reduce the vulnerability of the U.S. international supply chain to terrorism. Companies that choose to participate in C-TPAT are required to conduct a self-assessment of their security practices, submit a security profile of their international business practices to the CBP, develop a security plan that incorporates C-TPAT guidelines, and work toward the promotion of C-TPAT guidelines with other global firms (Thibault *et al.* 2006). The benefits of C-TPAT to participating companies include accelerated customs clearances at U.S. ports and, in the event of a terrorist incident, the companies will be allowed to clear customs faster than non-C-TPAT companies. C-TPAT membership was initially limited to shippers and manufacturers but now includes carriers, brokers, freight forwarders, terminal operators, and ports (Bichou 2004). By the end of 2004, C-TPAT members included 9,083 U.S. importing companies, 2,208 carriers, 1,412 brokers, 393 foreign manufacturers and vendors, and a small number of port authorities and marine terminal operators (Keane 2005). In June 2008, DP (Dubai Ports) World, the world's fourth largest global container port terminal operator (see Chapter 2), announced that it had been certified as a C-TPAT company.

In a 2007 CBP-commissioned survey of C-TPAT companies, 91.5 percent of the 1,756 responding companies noted that they had not considered leaving the program and more than one-half stated that the benefits of participating in C-TPAT were greater than or equal to the costs (Staff 2007). The vast majority of the companies stated that C-TPAT had provided predictability in the transportation of goods and greater work force security. Thirty-five percent noted that C-TPAT had eliminated 50 percent of the number of customs inspections that existed prior to C-TPAT.

The CBP is developing a "mutual recognition" C-TPAT status with other countries. That is to say, if a company receives C-TPAT status (or its equivalent) for exports to the United States (or a mutually recognized) country, it will receive C-TPAT status (or its equivalent) for exports to the mutually recognized country (or the United States). It is anticipated that New Zealand may be the first country with which the United States may reach a mutual recognition status. The CBP is also discussing the mutual recognition status with Jordan and Canada. Mutual recognition status with China is likely to be difficult, since China is opposed to United States validation of Chinese companies on the grounds of sovereignty. In November 2007 customs officials from the U.S. and the EU announced that they would begin extending reciprocal fast-lane customs clearances by 2009 for shippers that meet joint security standards. Mutual recognition status is a means by which the CBP is attempting to provide security to international supply chains.

The 24-Hour Advance Manifest Rule (24-hour rule) requires container shipping lines to provide information about container cargo on board ships calling at U.S. ports. Specifically, the carriers must submit this information electronically to the CBP at least 24 hours prior to the departure of ships from foreign ports. The submitted information allows for the pre-screening and targeting of suspected containers, which has been proven to be more cost effective and less time consuming than the traditional approach of random physical inspections (Bichou *et al*. 2007). Shippers and consignees, however, will have to adjust their inventory management processes to accommodate the 24-hour rule. If the electronic filings contain missing or inaccurate information, the container shipping lines, freight forwarders, and non-vessel operating common carriers (NVOCCs) that are convicted of doing so may face a violation fine from the CBP of up to $5,000.

A similar rule to the 24-hour rule on cargo also exists for ships. The 96-hour rule of the U.S. Department of Homeland Security (DHS) requires that all ships that are to call at U.S. ports are to provide the U.S. government with a 96-hour advance notice of arrival. The benefits of the rule include limiting the possibility of a terrorist sailing a ship into a U.S. port and providing the U.S. government with the ability to target particular ships for which it has security concerns.

The SAFE Port Act

On October 13, 2006, President Bush signed into law the Security and Accountability for Every (SAFE) Port Act. The Act seeks to strengthen port security by establishing technology initiatives and better data-collection programs. One of the Act's more important technology initiatives is the implementation of the transportation worker identification credential (TWIC) program that requires background security checks and biometric-based credentials for all those working in or around U.S. ports. Biometrics is the automated measurement of an individual's unique physical characteristics for the purpose of establishing identity. Measurements may include fingerprint pattern, hand geometry, blood vessel pattern, iris pattern, and face recognition. Biometric technology provides a higher level of assurance that a person is who they claim to be than conventional access control systems which typically rely on ID cards and/or a pin number.

A person's TWIC credential will ensure that this authorized person will have access to the port. Implementation phases of the program include (1) the TWIC applications, background checks, and issuance phase, and (2) the reassessing the TWIC card and reader technology, installation, and use issues phase. Pilot programs are to be conducted concurrently with the issuance of the TWIC credentials to test card and card reader interoperability. The cards will have an embedded computer chip that stores two fingerprint minutiae templates. The cost of the TWIC program is expected to be $3.2 billion. The standard user fee for a five-year TWIC card will be $132.25 and $105.25 for an applicant who has completed a prior comparable threat assessment. As of July 1, 2008 only 429,255 workers of an expected 1 million workers applied for TWIC cards (Shippers News Wire 2008). Further, the final compliance date for workers to have TWIC cards was moved from September 25, 2008 to April 15, 2009.

One of the biggest concerns about TWIC from the perspective of port workers is that a large number of them will likely lose their jobs from failing TWIC background security checks (because of criminal backgrounds and drug violations). Port operators are especially concerned for the loss in jobs for which there is a shortage of workers, e.g., harbor drayage truck drivers. The Ports of Los Angeles, Long Beach, and New York-New Jersey rely heavily on immigrant harbor drayage truck drivers. Twenty-two percent of the harbor drayage truck drivers at the Ports of Los Angeles and Long Beach, anticipating that they will fail background security checks, are not expected to apply for the TWIC card (Mongelluzzo 2008).

The SAFE Port Act also requires improvements in the U.S. automatic targeting system program that collects and analyzes container cargo data for the targeting of high-risk cargo.

Specifically, the data gathered on inbound containers to the U.S. from foreign ports will be encrypted and transmitted in near real time to the CBP's National Target Center. These data are to be combined with other data, such as manifest submissions, to improve the risk scoring for targeting high-risk containers. Participating governments will have immediate access to all data that is used to label a container as high-risk. The problem of a high-risk container will be resolved locally (i.e., by the foreign government or port), e.g., the foreign government may be asked to inspect the container's contents or shipping lines will be instructed not to load the container until the risk is fully resolved.

The Act instructed the CBP to obtain better data from U.S. importers for container security screening and targeting efforts. As a result, the CBP is seeking data for 10 additional variables on the containerized cargo of U.S. importers prior to the loading of this cargo on ships at foreign ports as well as information on ship stowage plans and container status messages from shipping lines (the "10 plus 2" Initiative for Containerized Cargo). International shippers are concerned about the cost of compliance, making changes in their information technology systems, and whether the initiative will improve port security. The SAFE Port Act also requires the development of a Post-Incident Trade Resumption and Supply Chain Security Strategic Plan and the promotion of International Container Security Standards.

The Act also instructed the DHS to establish at least three pilot overseas scanning programs to test the feasibility of 100 percent screening of containerized cargo and 100 percent scanning of high-risk containerized cargo destined for U.S. ports. The Act requires that the DHS increase the use of cargo inspection technologies in coordination with other federal agencies and foreign governments. The pilot programs have containers at participating foreign ports and destined for U.S. ports 100 percent scanned with both nonintrusive radiographic imaging and passive radiation detection equipment placed at the terminal arrival gates of these foreign ports.[2]

In 2007 the ports of Singapore, Puerto Cortes (Honduras), Southampton (UK), Salalah (Oman), Qasim (Pakistan), Busan (Korea), and Hong Kong agreed to participate in the DHS pilot overseas scanning program by conducting 100 percent scanning of shipping containers, bound for the United States, for nuclear or radiological materials. Also, data gathered from container scanning will be transmitted in near real time to the United States' National Targeting Center, where it will be analyzed to determine if the containers contain radioactive material. The results of the overseas scanning program will also be used to evaluate the effectiveness of the new radiation scanning technology that will be installed at U.S. ports for 100 percent scanning for radiation of all shipping containers that enter the United States by the end of 2008. Rather than waiting for the results of the DHS pilot overseas scanning program, the U.S. Congress in July 2007 passed the Implementing Recommendations of the 9/11 Commission Act that requires the scanning of all (i.e., 100 percent scanning of) U.S. inbound containers at foreign ports by the year 2012.

Detection

Inspection and tracking are procedures that may be used for detecting port security incidents in their early planning stages. Many U.S. ports inspect containers using radiation detectors. These detectors screen for nuclear devices, dirty bombs, natural sources, special nuclear materials, and isotopes commonly used in medicine and industry. The Ports of Los Angeles and Long Beach have radiation portal monitors (RPMs) that can screen all exiting container traffic and vehicles for radiation. The Port of Baltimore has a $6 million X-ray machine that can scan a 40-foot container in just 30 seconds.[3] In July 2006 the DHS awarded $1.16 billion worth of contracts to the three vendors, Raytheon, Thermo Electron, and Canberra, to develop a fixed radiation detection portal system that will become the standard port installation for screening cargo containers and truck traffic. In May 2007 the Port of Long Beach began using its new underwater security surveillance system – two portable underwater robots with high-frequency sonar imaging capabilities.

Containers can be tracked by using radio frequency identification (RFID) tags – devices on which data can be stored and remotely retrieved. Ultra-high frequency RFID tags are commonly used for container tracking and truck and trailer tracking in terminal yards. The tags are attached to containers, trucks, and trailers for their identification via radio waves. In a pilot project by Savi Networks, RFID-based e-seals have been placed on containers that broadcast signals at regular intervals to a Savi network, proving that no one has broken into the containers. Savi has agreements with port authorities and terminal operators in the U.S., Asia, and Europe. These agreements will allow Savi to eventually track containers in the transpacific, Far East–Europe, and transatlantic trades. Further, shippers can monitor the progress of their shipments via the internet, since shipment data will be linked to e-seal numbers. Effective December 1, 2007, the Ports of Los Angeles and Long Beach are requiring that trucks be equipped with RFID tags in order to gain access to these ports.

For tracking ships and obtaining ship cargo and crew information before ships reach U.S. ports, the Coast Guard is considering attaching transmitters to buoys of the National Oceanic and Atmospheric Administration (NOAA). The Coast Guard's current system allows it to collect such information only when the ship is within 25 miles of a port. NOAA uses the buoys to collect data on temperatures, winds, and waves.

In addition to detecting port security threats, port security initiatives may also negatively affect the performance of a port, e.g., the movement of cargo within the port and into and out of the port may be delayed due to port cargo and vehicle security inspections. Alternatively, port security initiatives may lead to an improvement in the port's quality of service. For example, security investments, and thus improvements, in a port's information technology (IT) and electronic data interchange (EDI) systems may lead to improvements in the reliability of port services, i.e., providing services on time, from improvements in the port's documentation and shipment tracing capability. IT systems may also be used to detect port cargo theft and unsafe port operations (Thai 2007).

Response and recovery

The Homeland Security Presidential Directive 13 (HSPD-13) of December 2004 states that "expediting recovery and response from attacks within the maritime domain" is one of six core elements of U.S. policy for enhancing the security of this domain. If a major security incident occurs at a port, the likely initial response is to shut down the port. If so, the economic loss to the port, its users, and the local community may be significant. Unlike the ISPS Code, which requires ports to develop security plans, the SAFE Port Act requires the DHS to develop protocols for resuming trade after a terrorist incident. Since no major security incident has occurred at a U.S. port, investigations into the response to and recovery from port security incidents must rely upon analyses of hypothetical port security incident scenarios.

For the marine terminal, Norfolk International Terminals in Norfolk, Virginia, U.S.A., the following security incident scenario was considered for which stakeholders noted their likely responses (Pinto and Talley 2006):

A slowly moving liquefied petroleum gas (LPG) tanker vessel in the port's harbor is approached by a small speeding boat with terrorists. The terrorists attach a bomb along the side of the vessel, which subsequently explodes, resulting in a gaping hole of about 30 feet long in the vessel's side; the loss of propulsion and electrical power and deaths and injuries to several crew members follow. The LPG vessel drifts toward Norfolk International Terminals (NIT). The vessel incurs a second explosion. It is damaged further. A containership berthed at NIT is also damaged; several of its containers fall into the water – some float and some sink. Several dockworkers that were working the berthed containership at the time of the second explosion are badly injured. The LPG vessel subsequently sinks, blocking the harbor channel. This channel is used by both commercial and U.S. Navy vessels. The Navy's marine terminal is adjacent to NIT.

The first responder to the security incident is the Coast Guard. Specifically, the Coast Guard's captain of the port, who is responsible for the security of the port, notifies its sector command and headquarters and the Federal Bureau of Investigation (FBI) of the security incident. Details of the security incident are reported. The Coast Guard implements security level MARSEC III, noting that a security threat is imminent. The Coast Guard ascertains the severity of the incident and whether secondary incident impacts (e.g., explosions) and further attacks are expected. The Virginia Marine Police is asked to establish police waterway security zones in order to mitigate any further attacks. The Coast Guard also asks for the assistance of the Virginia Port Authority's Maritime Incident Response Team in eliminating harbor fires and rescuing injured people from the water. Assistance from the local fire department is requested by this team.

NIT shuts down its inbound and outbound cargo movements and evacuates personnel. Other container terminals in the area do likewise. The sudden shutdown of the container terminals creates severe congestion at their gates and on adjacent roads – from trucks in route and the evacuation of terminal workers – restricting the arrival of emergency vehicles. The local police provide assistance in addressing the road congestion problem.

The FBI supports the Coast Guard in collecting intelligence with respect to the severity of the incident, the possibility of further attacks, and mitigating further attacks. The U.S. Navy secures its vessels and other assets. The CBP has little response except for checking suspicious cargo and accounting for personnel. The director of security and emergency management, Virginia Department of Transportation, notifies pertinent Virginia state agencies and the Governor's office of the occurrence of the security incident. The director also requests authorization from the Governor's office for additional state police as well as for troops from the state's National Guard to be sent (if needed) to the area.

Once the Coast Guard's captain of the port announces that the port is secure from terrorist attacks and secondary security incident impacts, the recovery phase for the security incident begins, i.e., the marine terminals that were shut down as a result of the terrorist attack are now open (even on a limited basis). The recovery phase ends when the terminals have resumed normal operations.

In the recovery phase of the security incident, the FBI is a major decision maker. It requests that the crime scene not be disturbed nor the channel be opened. It interviews eyewitnesses of the incident and gathers evidence from the crime scene, i.e., from the sunken LPG vessel and sunken and floating containers. However, the FBI is under major pressure to finish its investigation of the crime scene as quickly as possible so that the sunken ship and other debris can be removed from the channel so that it can be reopened. It is not only under pressure from the marine terminals and their users (shippers, truckers, railroads, and shipping lines), because of the economic losses that they are occurring, but also from the Virginia Governor's office because of the economic losses to the local and state economies.

Once the FBI has given its permission for the sunken ship and other debris to be removed from the channel, the National Oceanic and Atmospheric Administration (NOAA) is asked to survey the harbor waterways for debris. The sunken ship's owner and the owners of sunken and floating containers are responsible for their removal from the channel. If the channel's depth and turn basin area have been altered, the U.S. Army Corps of Engineers will be asked to dredge the channel to the specifications that existed prior to the security incident. The Coast Guard will decide whether the MARSEC level should be reduced and if so, to what level. The channel is officially opened when so designated by the Coast Guard's captain of the port.

In May 2007 the Port of New York-New Jersey also considered a hypothetical port security scenario at a stakeholders' meeting for the purpose of developing a port plan for resuming operations after a terrorist incident (Edmonson 2007b). The scenario involved an assumed terrorist attack that left a containership and a tanker disabled in the Kill Van Kull channel, a channel between Staten Island and Bayonne (New Jersey), where ships transit to reach New Jersey's container terminals. The plan called for ship traffic to be managed on a first-in, first-out basis. The stakeholders discovered that the first-in, first-out plan had to be tempered by the region's immediate needs.

Port security finance and cost

In fiscal year 2007 the U.S. Congress appropriated $202.2 million to the DHS to assist port authorities in paying for port security improvements. The Port of Los Angeles received $6.5 million from this appropriation for improvements to the port's waterside surveillance systems, command and control center, and other communication systems. The Port of Long Beach received $4.6 million to improve its underwater surveillance and to integrate its security systems. On the East Coast, the South Carolina State Ports Authority received $3.7 million for security improvements. The DHS port security grants are for the purchase of equipment to ward off terrorist attacks, but not for funding security operating costs, e.g., the costs of maintaining and operating security. Hence, a number of U.S. ports are charging security fees to defray these costs.

In the U.S. the security fees for container terminals are between $2 and $5 per container as opposed to between $9 and $11 per container at mainland European terminals (Woodbridge 2007). Ports that are members of the Florida Ports Conference, for example, charge a wharfage security fee based upon the type of cargo that is handled, i.e., $0.10/short ton for breakbulk; $0.02/short ton for bulk; $0.02/short ton for liquid bulk; $2 per container box; and $1 per embarking multiday passenger. In addition, a security fee of 5 percent of the ship's dockage fee is charged. These charges are minimum fees. If justified, member ports may charge higher fees.

Ports that are members of the Gulf Seaports Marine Terminal Conference charge security fees similar to those of the Florida Ports Conference. The Virginia Port Authority assesses security charges based on the cargo moving through its marine terminals. The charges include a $2 fee per container (regardless of size, loaded or empty) and $0.10/short ton for breakbulk cargo. The charges are billed to shipping lines.

Security fees that are not uniform across competing ports may affect the competitive position of ports. Costs of U.S. port security programs that are not borne by government and port users will be borne by port operators. If the costs for the latter are relatively high, then smaller as opposed to larger ports may find it difficult to finance these costs. If so, the competitive position of smaller ports versus larger ports will deteriorate.[4] The Port of Long Beach has received $51 million in federal grants since 2001, but has spent or plans to spend an additional $20 million of port funds on security projects. The Virginia Port Authority, a port authority for a much smaller port, has received $11 million in federal grants since 2002, but has spent an additional $11 million of its cargo-generated revenue on security projects (Woodbridge 2007).

EU port security

In non-U.S. countries, port security initiatives have generally been based upon the IMO ISPS Code and those of the United States. Among countries, the United States has been the leader in developing port security initiatives.

The EU's Regulation 725/2004 sought to transpose the provisions of the ISPS Code into a binding EU law. Its focus is the security of the ship/port interface. Regulation 725/2004 requires that ports have security plans, identify and monitor restricted areas, and prevent dangerous materials from being taken onto ships or into port facilities. In addition to ships involved in international voyages and their ports (as for the ISPS Code), Regulation 725/2004 also covers ship voyages within the EU and their ports. The Regulation created a security inspection program that is to be managed and monitored by the EU Commission. Member states retain the right to develop security initiatives for their ports beyond those of the ISPS Code, e.g., in ports that only occasionally serve international voyages.

By January 1, 2004, 70 percent of EU port facilities (primarily marine terminals) were in compliance with Regulation 725/2004. The average investment compliance cost per port facility was 464,000 euros with an average operating compliance cost per port facility of 234,000 euros. Landside compliance accounted for 44 percent of investment compliance cost, followed by 34 percent for electronic systems and 14 percent for seaside access (Dekker and Stevens 2007).

Regulation 648/2005 is similar to the U.S. C-TPAT and 24-hour rule programs. The Regulation has risk-based controls, i.e., pre-arrival and pre-departure information requirements for cargo coming into and going out of the EU. Further, the authorized economic operator (AEO) was established. When a company is awarded the AEO status, it is eligible to receive a reduction in custom inspections (similar to the C-TPAT program). The criteria for granting AEO status include (1) a compliance record with customs requirements, (2) a satisfactory system for managing commercial records, (3) financial solvency, and (4) appropriate security and safety standards. As of January 2008, 266 companies had applied to become AEOs in the EU (Stares 2008a).

Whereas Regulation 725/2004 addressed security of the ship/port interface, Directive 65/2005 seeks to secure the remainder of the port, thereby supplementing Regulation 725/2004 (Pallis and Vaggelas 2007). Port boundaries are to be designated by the member states. If a port is subject to Regulation 725/2004, it is also subject to Directive 65/2005. Ports must develop a port security plan that contains actions and necessary procedures to be undertaken in the event of a security incident. A state's monitoring and dissemination of information are the responsibility of the state's port security authority (to be established by the state).

In 2006 the EU proposed a regulation to protect the security of the remaining parts of the supply chain. Four supply chain activities were recognized: (1) preparing goods for shipment from production sites, (2) transporting goods, (3) forwarding goods, and (4) warehousing, storage, and inland terminal operations. A secure operator (SO) status for supply chain operators that meet certain security requirements would be established. As in the case of AEOs, SOs would benefit from lesser security control. However, due to strong opposition from transport operators (based upon the expected high costs in implementing the proposed regulation), the EU postponed discussions, with a reevaluation of the proposed regulation undertaken in 2008.

The U.S. CBP is pursuing a "mutual recognition" security status with the EU. The AEO and C-TPAT standards are being compared. The next steps are to compare the validation approaches of the two programs and investigate how each party can grant reciprocal agreements to companies that meet the AEO or C-TPAT standards, thereby providing exporting companies the benefit of fast-track clearance through customs.

In February 2007 the International Organization for Standardization (IOS) stated that it would formally adopt a standard for establishing and verifying international supply-chain security, i.e., the IOS 28001 (Edmonson 2007a). The World Customs Organization has also advocated the establishment of international supply-chain security. Companies seeking to become IOS 28001 companies must establish and document a minimum level of security within their supply chains. The secured international trade network will consist of AEOs that have been certified to have established sufficient security in the network.

Port safety

Given the difficulty of directly observing safety in the operation of a port, proxies for reductions in port safety have been used, i.e., reductions in port ship and worker accidents. These accidents are unintentional and may involve damage to property and/or injury to individuals.

Port accidents

A discussion of fatal and nonfatal injuries from vessel accidents at the Port of Hong Kong over the time period 1992–2004 appears in a study by Yip (2008). Among the vessel accidents 5 and 20 percent resulted in fatal and nonfatal injuries, respectively; 47, 19, and 10 percent of the accidents involved cargo ships, barges, and passenger vessels, respectively; 54 percent of the vessel accidents were collision accidents; and 12 percent of the accidents occurred when vessels were in anchorage.

In an investigation of the determinants of the number of nonfatal injuries in vessel accidents at the Port of Hong Kong, Yip (2008) found that this number is (1) greater for cargo ships and passenger vessels, (2) greater for fire/explosion, capsizing/listing, and vessel structural failure accidents, and (3) less if the vessel's registry is the Hong Kong Registry. The number of fatal injuries in vessel accidents at the Port of Hong Kong is greater for fishing vessels.

Information on worker accidents at ports is sparse. However, a survey of 1985–1986 longshoremen accidents by the U.S. Bureau of Labor Statistics (1987) found that (1) 15 and 9 percent of the accidents involved forklift/tractor and clerk/checker longshoremen, respectively; (2) the nature of the accident was bruise/contusion and hernia for 61 and 9 percent of the accidents, respectively; and (3) the part of the body affected for 19 and 16 percent of the accidents was the head/neck and upper extremities, respectively (U.S. Bureau of Labor Statistics 1987).

Port state control

Enforcement of ship safety (construction and operation) rules worked well under flag states until the adoption of flags of convenience (FOCs), the registration of ships in countries other than those of its citizen owners. By 1996 over one half of the world's shipping fleet was under FOCs. At the same time, there was rising concern for enforcement of international safety rules – given that some FOCs have no interest in adopting or enforcing ship safety rules and confine their interests to collecting registration dues. The ineffective enforcement of international safety rules by FOCs was addressed by some countries with the establishment of port state control (PSC) systems. In 1982 twelve European countries signed the Paris PSC Memorandum of Understanding, arranging to inspect safety and other certificates carried by ships of all flags (including each other's) visiting their ports, and to insist, by detention if necessary, on deficiencies being rectified.

Although PSC systems are often found in developed countries, e.g., in Australia, Canada, the United States, and EU countries, much of the world remains unaffected by PSC. In 2007 Australia averaged 57 PSC inspections of ships and three ships detained per week. Bulk ships accounted for almost 60 percent of all inspections. The number of ships detained in 2007 was 159, half of which were attributed to structural and equipment deficiencies (Staff 2008).

An investigation of the effectiveness of PSC inspections of ships is found in a study by Cariou *et al.* (2008a). The effectiveness of PSC inspections for ships is defined as the likelihood that ships will register a lower number of deficiencies from PSC inspection at a future time period as opposed to a previous time period. The study is based upon PSC inspections of ships carried out by the Swedish Maritime Administration from January 1, 1996, to December 31, 2001. The study found that 27.1 percent of the inspected ships had no deficiencies over the time period (never deficient), 58.6 percent exhibited no or some deficiencies over the time period (sometimes deficient), and 14.3 percent consistently had at least one deficiency over the time period (always deficient). More than 63 percent of the ships exhibited a reduction in the total number of deficiencies from earlier to subsequent inspections, thereby providing evidence of the positive effectiveness of PSC ship inspections.

Port safe working conditions

Safe working conditions for port workers have been promoted by unions, port operators, and government (Russell 2008). The International Labour Organization (ILO) of the UN supports decent working conditions for workers around the world. The ILO's Occupational Safety and Health Convention details port safe operating procedures for handling (stacking and storage) various types of cargoes and operations along berths and throughout marine terminals. The International Dockworkers Council (IDC) promotes port safe working conditions for its dockworker members by being proactive in decreasing port accidents and worker health problems.

Port operator safety plans are often developed subsequent to worker accidents on port property. At the Port of Hong Kong, for example, worker accidents have occurred from workers falling from high-stacked containers and being involved in object collisions. Hong Kong International Terminals created its safety and health policy to address worker high-risk operations (such as working on high-stacked containers), fire safety, and procedures for handling, storage, and transportation of dangerous cargoes. A decrease in port accidents leads to fewer workplace disruptions and ultimately improves the production efficiency of ports.

In the United States, the Occupational Safety and Health Act of 1970 created national workplace safety standards for millions of U.S. workers. Specifically, the Act put in place (1) workplace safety and health standards, (2) a reporting system for on-the-job accidents and injuries, and (3) inspectors to enforce workplace safety and health guidelines. The Act also created the Occupational Safety and Health Administration (OSHA) to administer the Act's guidelines. OSHA's Office of Maritime Standards and Guidance is responsible for identifying hazardous situations at ports. Also, its maritime terminal guidelines address

(1) proper handling of hazardous cargo, manning of lines, and use of conveyors and winches, (2) accessing barges and handling of hatches and crane operations, and (3) certification for workers in the manning of equipment.

Summary

Port security incidents are intentional and undertaken to damage property and/or to injure individuals for political reasons. Port security incidents can disrupt maritime supply chains and thus have significant negative effects on international trade. The IMO's ISPS Code was adopted to address the security of ships at sea and the security of the interface between berthed ships and port facilities.

Following the September 11, 2001, terrorist attacks in New York City, the United States adopted numerous security programs to prevent and detect port security incidents. Three major maritime cargo security initiatives – two voluntary security programs (CSI and C-TPAT) and the 24-hour rule – were adopted. The CSI requires foreign ports to prescreen containers (for dangerous cargo) before they are loaded onto U.S.-bound ships. C-TPAT is a joint government–business initiative to build cooperative security relationships. C-TPAT companies benefit from accelerated customs clearances at U.S. ports. The 24-hour rule requires container shipping lines to submit information electronically to the CBP about their container cargo at least 24 hours prior to the departure of ships from foreign ports.

The U.S. SAFE Port Act seeks to strengthen port security by establishing technology initiatives and better data-collection programs. The TWIC program requires background security checks and biometric-based credentials for all those working in or around U.S. ports. The Act instructed the DHS to establish pilot programs to test the feasibility of 100 percent screening of containerized cargo. Also, the Act requires improvements in the U.S. automatic targeting system program that collects and analyzes container cargo data for the targeting of high-risk cargo.

Inspection and tracking are procedures that may be used for detecting planned port security incidents. Containers can be tracked by the placement of RFID tags on containers. Since no major security incident has occurred at a U.S. port, U.S. investigations into the response to and recovery from port security incidents must rely upon analyses of hypothetical port security incident scenarios. Port security costs have been financed by government funding, user fees, and by port operators themselves.

EU port security programs are adaptations (in many cases) of the ISPS Code and U.S. port security programs. Port security regulations require EU ports to have security plans, identify and monitor restricted areas, and prevent dangerous materials from being taken onto ships or into port facilities. Pre-arrival and pre-departure information is required for goods coming into and going out of the EU. Ports must develop a port security plan that contains actions and necessary procedures to be undertaken in the event of a security incident.

Given the difficulty of directly observing safety in the operation of a port, proxies for reductions in port safety have been used, i.e., reductions in port ship and worker accidents. PSC inspections inspect ships while in port for safety, and insist that safety deficiencies be rectified, by detention if necessary. Safe working conditions for port workers have been promoted by unions, port operators, and governments.

Notes

1 On March 1, 2003, the Coast Guard became a component of the newly formed Department of Homeland Security (DHS).

2 NYK Line has criticized the U.S. overseas 100% scanning program. The criticisms include (1) who is to perform the container scanning at the foreign port is not specified by the program, and (2) who is to purchase, operate, and maintain the scanning equipment is not specified by the program.

3 The effectiveness of detectors in detecting biological, chemical, nuclear, and explosive terrorist devices may be investigated via mock threat training exercises.

4 "Small port entities are particularly sensitive and most likely targets to be used by terrorist – not as the attack aims, but as the entry points allowing people and explosive devices to be transported unnoticed into and out of that country" (Szulc 2007: 29).

Bibliography

Allen, N. H. (2006) "The Container Security Initiative Costs, Implications and Relevance to Developing Countries", *Public Administration and Development*, 26: 439–447.

Barnes, P. and Oloruntoba, R. (2005) "Assurance of Security in Maritime Supply Chains: Conceptual Issues of Vulnerability and Crisis Management", *Journal of International Management*, 11: 519–540.

Bichou, K. (2004) "The ISPS Code and the Cost of Port Compliance: An Initial Logistics and Supply Chain Framework for Port Security Assessment and Management", *Maritime Economics and Logistics*, 6: 322–348.

——, Lai, K.-H., Lun, Y. H. V., and Cheng, T. C. E. (2007) "A Quality Management Framework for Liner Shipping Companies to Implement the 24-Hour Advance Vessel Manifest Rule", *Transportation Journal*, 46: 5–21.

Blumel, E., Boeve, W., Recagno, V., and Schilk, G. (2008) "Ship, Port and Supply Chain Security Concepts Interlinking Maritime with Hinterland Transport Chains", *WMU Journal of Maritime Affairs*, 7: 205–225.

Brooks, M. R. and Pelot, R. (2008) "Port Security: A Risk Based Perspective", in W. K. Talley (ed.) *Maritime Safety, Security and Piracy*, London: Informa, 195–216.

Cariou, P., Mejia, Jr., M. Q., and Wolff, F.-C. (2008a) "On the Effectiveness of Port State Control Inspections", *Transportation Research Part E*, 44: 491–503.

—— (2008b) "Port State Control Inspection and Vessel Detention", in W. K. Talley (ed.) *Maritime Safety, Security and Piracy*, London: Informa, 153–168.

Cooperman, S. (2004) "Tracking Cargo", *Security*, 41: 20–22.

Dekker, S. and Stevens, H. (2007) "Maritime Security in the European Union – Empirical Findings on Financial Implications for Port Facilties", *Maritime Policy and Management*, 34: 485–499.

Edmonson, R. G. (2007a) "ISO Security Standard on Track", *Journal of Commerce*, 8, February 5: 32, 34.

—— (2007b) "Recovery Plan: Industry Group Works on Ways to Restore Maritime Commerce After a Terrorist Attack", *Journal of Commerce*, 8, May 14: 22–23.

Emerson, S. D. and Nadeau, J. (2003) "A Coastal Perspective on Security", *Journal of Hazardous Materials*, 104: 1–13.

Fortner, B. (2002) "Electronic Seals Track Containers to Improve Port Security", *Civil Engineering*, 72: 37.

General Accounting Office (2004) *Port Security: Better Planning Needed to Develop and Operate Maritime Worker Identification Card Program,* Washington, DC: U.S. Government Printing Office.

Goulielmos, A. M. and Anastasakos, A. A. (2005) "Worldwide Security Measures for Shipping, Seafarers and Ports: An Impact Assessment of ISPS Code", *Disaster Prevention and Management*, 14: 462–478.

Harrald, J. R., Stephens, H. W., and van Dorp, J. R. (2004) "A Framework for Sustainable Port Security", *Journal of Homeland Security and Emergency Management*, 1: 1–21.

Haveman, J. D., Shatz, H. J., and Vilchis, E. A. (2005) "U.S. Port Security Policy after 9/11: Overview and Evaluation", *Journal of Homeland Security and Emergency Management*, 2: 1–24.

—— Jennings, E. M., Shatz, H. J., and Wright, G. C. (2007) "The Container Security Initiative and Ocean Container Threats", *Journal of Homeland Security and Emergency Management*, 4: 1–19.

Heaney, S. (2008) "100% Scan=100% Headaches", *American Shipper*, July, 50: 21–24.

Keane, A. G. (2005) "Applauding C-TPAT's Reach", *Traffic World*, April 25: 9–10.

Knapp, S. and Franses, P. H. (2007) "Econometric Analysis on the Effect of Port State Control Inspections on the Probability of Casualty: Can Targeting of Substandard Ships for Inspections be Improved?", *Marine Policy*, 31: 550–563.

Koch, C. L. (2007) "Review of U.S. Maritime Security Issues", *Propeller Club Quarterly*, Spring: 4–10.

Lewis, B. M., Erera, A. L., and White, III, C. C. (2006) "Impact of Temporary Seaport Closures on Freight Supply Chain Costs", *Transportation Research Record: Journal of the Transportation Research Board*, No. 1963: 64–70.

Li, K. X. and Zheng, H. (2008) "Enforcement of Law by the Port State Control (PSC)", *Maritime Policy and Management*, 35: 61–71.

McDonald, L. and O'Sullivan, R. (2004) "Integrated Harbor Security System Enhances Port Protection", *Sea Technology*, 45: 27–30.

Mongelluzzo, B. (2008) "Clean-Air Proposals, TWIC Product Uncertainty for Port Trucking Industry", *Journal of Commerce*, 9, January 7: 23–24.

Natter, A. (2007) "Reading the Cards", *Traffic World*, July 23: 15.

Ng, K. Y. A. and Gujar, G. C. (2008) "Port Security in Asia", in W. K. Talley (ed.) *Maritime Safety, Security and Piracy*, London: Informa, 257–278.

Pallis, A. A. and Vaggelas, G. K. (2007) "Port and Maritime Security: A Critical Analysis of Contemporary EU Policies", *Proceedings of the International Symposium on Maritime Safety, Security and Environmental Protection*, Athens, Greece.

—— (2008) "EU Port and Shipping Security", in W. K. Talley (ed.) *Maritime Safety, Security and Piracy*, London: Informa, 235–255.

Pinto, A. and Talley, W. K. (2006) "The Security Incident Cycle of Ports", *Maritime Economics and Logistics*, 8: 267–286.

—— , Rabadi, G., and Talley, W. K. (2008) "U.S. Port Security", in W. K. Talley (ed.) *Maritime Safety, Security and Piracy*, London: Informa, 217–233.

Price, W. (2004) "Reducing the Risk of Terror Events at Seaports", *Review of Policy Research*, 21: 329–349.

Pruitt, T. (2004) "Maritime Homeland Security for Ports and Commercial Operations", *Sea Technology*, 45: 20–24.

Richardson, M. (2004) "Growing Vulnerability of Seaports from Terror Attacks, to Protect Ports while Allowing Global Flow of Trade is a New Challenge", Hong Kong: Institute of South East Asian Studies.

Russell, S. (2008) "Port Safety and Workers", in W. K. Talley (ed.) *Maritime Safety, Security and Piracy*, London: Informa, 123–152.

Shippers' NewsWire (2008) "TWIC Card Delivery Lagging Behind Applications". Available online at http://www.shippers.com (accessed 4 March 2009).

Staff (2007) "Industry Backs C-TPAT, Study Shows", *Journal of Commerce*, 8, September 17: 11.

—— (2008) "AMSA Gets Tough on High Risk Vessels at Australian Ports", *Lloyd's List*. Available online at http://www.lloydslist.com, April 25.

Stares, J. (2008a) "EU Inundated by Early Rush for AEO Status", *Lloyd's List*. Available online at http://www.lloydslist.com, February 19.

—— (2008b) "Rotterdam May Scan all Export Boxes", *Lloyd's List*. Available online at http://www.lloydslist.com, May 30.

Stevens, T. (2007) "The SAFE Port Act: Using the Latest Technology to Secure Our Ports", *Sea Technology*, 48: 13.

Szulc, D. (2007) "Small Ports: Are they Prepared to Face Threats", *Maritime Reporter and Engineering News*, November: 26–27, 29.

Talley, W. K. (2002) "Maritime Safety and Accident Analysis", in C. T. Grammenos (ed.) *The Handbook of Maritime Economics and Business*, London: Informa, 426–442.

—— (2005) "Regulatory Issues: The Role of International Maritime Institutions", in D. A. Hensher and K. J. Button (eds) *Handbook of Transport Strategy: Policy and Institutions*, Amsterdam: Elsevier, 421–433.

Thai, V. V. (2007) "Impacts of Security Improvements on Service Quality in Maritime Transport: An Empirical Study of Vietnam", *Maritime Economics and Logistics*, 9: 335–356.

—— and Grewal, D. (2007) "The Maritime Security Management System: Perceptions of the International Shipping Community", *Maritime Economics and Logistics*, 9: 119–137.

Thibault, M., Brooks, M., and Button, K. (2006) "The Response of the U.S. Maritime Industry to the New Container Initiatives", *Transportation Journal*, 45: 5–15.

U.S. Bureau of Labor Statistics (1987) *A Comprehensive Report, Injuries Involving Longshore Operations*, Bulletin 2326, Washington, DC: Government Printing Office.

Wengelin, M. (2006) "The Swedish Port Security Network – An Illusion or a Fact", *Journal of Homeland Security and Emergency Management*, 3: 1–12.

Woodbridge, G. (2007) "Rising to the Terminal Security Challenge", *Containerisation International*, October: 72–74.

Yip, T. L. (2008) "Port Traffic Risks – A Study of Accidents in Hong Kong Waters", *Transportation Research Part E*, 44: 921–931.

14 Ports in the future

Introduction

Traditionally, ports are sea/land interfaces for the provision of services to their users – carriers, shippers, and passengers. Ports are also an integral part of the world's transportation system. Further, ports are engaged in nontraditional port activities such as property development and financial, management, and logistics activities.

Ports in the future are expected to become more involved in vertical and horizontal integration (Bichou and Gray 2005). Vertical integration occurs when the port owner/operator and the port user enter into an arrangement where the port owner/operator or the port user controls the activities of the other through ownership or leasing. For example, carriers and shippers may own ports or terminals. Horizontal integration occurs when port owners and operators cooperate among themselves through mergers (e.g., Copenhagen and Malmo Ports) or agreements (e.g., the Port of Singapore Authority Corporation owning and managing ports and terminals in other countries as a global container port terminal operator). Ports and terminals may also be owned and managed by institutions other than port service suppliers and users (e.g., insurance companies).

Container ports are expected to have sufficient infrastructure in the short term to handle the growing number of containers worldwide, but may not in the long term. The planning and construction cycles for new container ports and terminals may last 10 to 12 years from initial planning stage until they open for business. Pressure to increase port infrastructure (or terminal capacity) and especially hinterland infrastructure (or landside connections) are expected to become more intense over the long term.

This chapter discusses ports in the future. Specifically, ports in the future are discussed from the perspective of port challenges (port congestion, size of containerships, and size of containers), the Panama Canal and vessel port calls (Panama Canal expansion and competitors), port information and communication technologies, port pollution, port logistics activities, port security, port cooperation, and LNG marine terminals.

Container port challenges

Container ports in the future will face challenges that include increases in (1) port congestion, (2) size of containerships, and (3) size of containers.

Port congestion

Port congestion arises when port users interfere with one another while in port, thereby increasing their time (delays) and associated costs in port. Port congestion has been a problem at major container ports worldwide. However, under the current global financial crisis, this congestion has diminished at a number of these ports. Prior to this crisis, the growth in global container traffic (measured in revenue FEU-kilometers) was forecasted to be 8 percent for 2008–2009 and 6 percent per year for the 10-year period starting 2010 (Staff 2008a), thereby outpacing the worldwide growth in container port capacity. A revenue FEU-kilometer is a revenue-generating 40-foot equivalent unit (FEU) transported 1 kilometer.

The top-three ranked container trades in 2007 (excluding Intra-Asia) are Asia/Europe, Asia/North America (transpacific), and North America/Europe (transatlantic) with 173.6, 140, and 20 billion revenue FEU-kilometers, respectively (see Table 14.1). Prior to the current global financial crisis, the Asia/Europe trade was forecasted to grow by 9 percent over the 2007–2012 timeframe (Staff 2008a).

A congestion delay by a ship at one port may lead to a delay in the ship's arrival at the next port of call. During the first quarter of 2007, 73 percent of containerships arrived late at EU ports because of docking delays at their previous ports of call as opposed to 45 percent of containerships during the first quarter of 2006 (Drewry Shipping Consultants 2007). In 2007 the Ports of Hamburg and Rotterdam turned away ships because of the lack of docking space at the ports, attributable to the ships not adhering to docking schedules at their previous ports of call.

Size of containerships

Since 1996 the largest containership in service has more than doubled in size. In 1996 the *Regina Maersk's* carrying capacity was 6,000 TEUs; in 2005, the Hapag-Lloyd *Colombo Express's* carrying capacity was 8,750 TEUs; and in early 2007, the *Emma Maersk* was placed in service with a carrying capacity of 13,000 TEUs. The *Emma Maersk* is 1,302 feet long and 184 feet wide, with a draft of over 50 feet. By comparison, the U.S. Navy's largest aircraft carrier is 1,220 feet long and 132 feet wide, with a draft of 39 feet. The largest new containerships (with carrying capacities of 8,000 TEUs and above) are placed in service in primary east–west trades; the existing 5,000 to 6,000 TEU ships in these trades are placed in secondary east–west trades. This displacement process of ships into smaller trades continues until 2,500 TEU ships are moved into north–south trades and 1,700 TEU or smaller ships are placed in new trades (Berrill 2006).

The average size of containerships in service is increasing annually, while increases in port capacity are lagging behind. Container ports are under increasing pressure to provide capacity for larger containerships, e.g., dredging channels and berths to deeper water depths,

Table 14.1 Containerized ocean freight flows (2007) (billions of revenue FEU-kilometers)

Trades	Revenue FEU-kilometers
Asia/Europe	173.6
Asia/North America	140.0
Intra-Asia	97.3
North America/Europe	20.0
Central–South America/Europe	19.5
Central–South America/North America	17.9
Africa/Europe	14.8
Middle East/Europe	14.1
Total	497.2

Source: Staff (2008a) "Value Creation in Container Shipping", *American Shipper*, 50: 69.

providing wider ship turning basins and utilizing larger dock cranes. Container ports that are unable to accommodate the larger containerships will likely experience a decline in their container throughput over time.

In the United States, the Ports of Los Angeles and Long Beach have channel depths of 60 and 63 feet, respectively; hence, their channel depths are deep enough to handle the world's largest containerships, even the *Emma Maersk*. However, many U.S. ports are dredging their channels to deeper depths to attract larger containerships. For example, the Port of New York-New Jersey is dredging the depth of its channel to 50 feet and the Port of Savannah is dredging its channels from 42 to 48 feet. The Port of Virginia has dredged channels of 50 feet, the deepest channels of any U.S. East Coast container port. Also, U.S. container ports are installing larger dock cranes to service the larger containerships. The Port of Seattle, for example, has installed three dock cranes at a cost of $7.8 million each that can work containerships that are 23 containers wide.

With the rising trend in the delivery of containerships with capacities ranging between 7,500 and 15,500 TEUs, containership overcapacity in trades may occur. If so, container shipping lines will attempt to solve this problem by: (1) increasing the number of ships assigned to trades, thereby increasing the frequency of port calls in these trades, (2) reducing the speed of ships, thereby requiring a greater number of ships in a given service string in order to maintain ship carrying capacity in the string, and (3) taking ships out of service, i.e., laying up ships.

Size of containers

The size of containers has gradually increased over time, i.e., from the 40-foot container to 45- and 48-foot containers. The shipping line APL introduced the 45-foot container to the shipping industry in 1980, the 48-foot container in 1986, and the domestic 53-foot container in 1989. In November 2007, APL introduced the Ocean53 – the first 53-foot ocean-capable container. Unlike the domestic 53-foot container, Ocean53 is built to handle the stresses of ocean voyages and repeated lifts.

The U.S. domestic 53-foot container has been used for a number of years by the U.S. trucking and railroad industries. The domestic 53-foot and smaller international containers have been involved in transloading, i.e., the transfer of cargo to and from each other. For example, the cargo in a smaller international import container is unloaded and then reloaded into a domestic 53-foot container and conversely for an international export container.

The 53-foot container appeals to the shipper, because its capacity is 60 percent greater than that of the 40-foot container, thereby allowing the shipper to consolidate more cargo into fewer containers. Two 53-foot containers can hold the contents of three 40-foot containers. Hence, by using 53-foot containers, the shipper will incur lower handling (given that there are fewer container lifts) costs and lower transportation (given that there are fewer containers being transported) costs. By using an Ocean53 container in the transportation of international cargo from one country to another, the need to transload international cargo in 20- and 40-foot containers to and from domestic 53-foot containers will be avoided.

If Ocean53 containers are accepted by the shipping industry, container ports in the future will have to adapt to handling these larger containers. However, the adaption may not be to the extent experienced by container ports in adapting to servicing larger containerships. Current port equipment should be able to handle the slightly heavier 53-foot container. However, adjustments to container stacking will be required (given that 53-foot containers take up more space), i.e., 53-foot containers will need to be mixed with 20-foot and 40-foot containers so that the stability of the stacks is maintained.[1]

Panama Canal and vessel port calls

The Panama Canal will affect vessel port calls in the future directly by its expansion and indirectly by the activities of its competitors.

Panama Canal expansion

The Panama Canal began operating in 1914. Today, 14,000 vessels pass through the canal annually, carrying 5 percent of the world's ocean cargo tonnage (Panama Canal Authority 2008). The canal's locks, however, are not large enough to allow post-Panamax container-ships, i.e., containerships that exceed 5,000 TEUs in size, to pass through the canal. Alternatively, Panamax containerships (not exceeding 5,000 TEUs in size) are able to pass through the canal. Given the increasing number of post-Panamax containerships in service worldwide, the Panama Canal Authority realized that it had to expand the canal to handle large containerships or risk losing calls by containerships traveling from northeast Asia to the U.S. East Coast.

In 2006, the voters of Panama approved a U.S.$5.25 billion plan to expand and modernize the Panama Canal (to be completed in 2014). Two new lock facilities will be constructed, one on the Atlantic Ocean side and the other on the Pacific Ocean side of the canal. Also, the Gatun Lake's navigational channels will be widened and deepened – widened to no less than 280 meters in their straight sections and 366 meters in their turns, permitting post-Panamax ship encounters (where the ships are moving in opposite directions) in the channels. The deepening of the channels will accommodate ship drafts of up to 50 feet. The expansion will allow post-Panamax containerships up to 12,000 TEUs in size to pass through the canal and will be self-financed by canal tolls that will be increased annually over time.

The Panama Canal expansion will benefit U.S. East Coast ports to the detriment of U.S. West Coast ports. Forecasts indicate that the percentage of containerized cargo from northeast Asia passing through the canal destined to U.S. East Coast ports will increase with (decrease without) the expansion from 38 percent in 2005 to 44 (36), 46 (29), and 49 (23) percent in 2015, 2020, and 2025, respectively (Panama Canal Authority 2006). Post-Panamax containerships that previously called at West Coast ports (since they were too large to transit the Panama Canal prior to its expansion) will be able to transit the expanded Panama Canal for calls at East Coast ports. The Panama Canal expansion will also likely lead to an increase in trade between northeast Asia and countries on the Atlantic side of South America, e.g., Brazil, therefore benefitting the ports of these countries.

Panama Canal competitors

Railroads

North American railroads that provide intermodal rail service (e.g., double-stack train service) to and from North American ports are competitors of the Panama Canal. However, these railroads have been increasing their intermodal rates in recent years when contracts with shipping lines are renewed. The significant increases in intermodal rail rates (in some cases double-digit increases) to and from U.S. West and East Coast ports have forced container shipping lines (especially those calling at West Coast ports) to reevaluate their services. Some have increased their all-water service through the Panama Canal.

Some container shipping lines have also reduced their U.S. door-to-door services, thereby placing the burden on shippers to obtain and pay directly for inland transportation services to and from U.S. ports. For example, Maersk Line, facing significant increases in intermodal rail rates and deteriorating profits from inland transportation services, has eliminated a number of U.S. inland locations that it has served on through bills of lading (i.e., under door-to-door rates). A decrease from 250,000 to 50,000 through bills of lading to U.S. destinations is planned by the shipping line (Mongelluzzo 2007). Roughly two-thirds of the cost incurred by Maersk Line in moving a container from China to Chicago is attributable to inland costs (Dupin 2007). At the APM terminal at the Port of Los Angeles, Maersk has discontinued four weekly double-stack trains carrying 1,000 containers; on-dock rail container lifts at this terminal were 40 percent fewer in 2007 than in 2006 (Mongelluzzo 2008a).

Suez Canal

Another competitor of the Panama Canal is the Suez Canal. The Suez Canal is 118 miles long and 984 feet wide at its narrowest point. Vessels with drafts of up to 53 feet are allowed passage. The Suez Canal Authority has plans to increase this draft to 72 feet by 2010, which would allow for passage by supertankers. The canal has no periodic tidal surges, nor locks (as in the case of the Panama Canal) to negotiate. However, the canal has only one shipping canal with several passing areas. Vessels transit the canal in tug-escorted convoys of 15 or 20 vessels. Vessel passages take between 11 and 16 hours and a pilot on each vessel is required for passage. The Suez Canal Authority is a part of the Egyptian government.

The demand for U.S. East Coast all-water Suez-Canal container service has increased significantly. Factors contributing to this increase include (1) the increasing demand for all-water services in general, (2) the deeper drafts at East Coast ports that can accommodate post-Panamax ships, (3) the rising U.S. intermodal rail rates, and (4) the rising Panama Canal tolls and surcharges. The Suez Canal containership route to the U.S. East Coast from North Asia takes a week longer than the Panama Canal containership route. Consequently, shipping lines are having to utilize post-Panamax ships of at least 5,500 to 6,500 TEU capacity to make the Suez route TEU rates competitive with those of the Panama route TEU rates, i.e., to incur TEU cost savings from the economies of ship size at sea from using post-Panamax ships (Mongelluzzo 2006a). The main disadvantage of the Suez route to the U.S. East Coast from Asia for container shipping lines is the deployment of a greater number of ships for maintaining weekly service through the Suez Canal, i.e., ten containerships are needed for a weekly service from Asia through the Suez Canal as compared with eight ships through the Panama Canal (Leach 2006a).

Increases in all-water services through the Panama and Suez Canals have benefitted U.S. East Coast ports. From January 2006 to mid-2007, the TEU capacity of containerships sailing from Asia to the U.S. East Coast increased 22 percent, while the capacity from Asia to the U.S. West Coast decreased by 3 percent (Kulisch 2007). In the first quarter of 2008 the share of U.S. container imports from northeast Asia that were destined for U.S. West Coast ports declined from the same quarter in 2007, i.e., 72.4 percent for the first quarter of 2008 versus 74.9 percent for the first quarter of 2007; by comparison, the percentages for U.S. East Coast ports increased from 23.4 percent for the first quarter of 2007 to 25.7 percent for the first quarter of 2008 (Mongelluzzo 2008b).

Arctic sea route

A potential competitor of the Panama Canal is the Arctic sea route, the Northwest Passage. The Northwest Passage across northern Canada is currently used during a short period of time in summer; otherwise ice conditions prevent its use. However, recent milder ice conditions in the region and forecasts of global warming have led to the speculation that the Northwest Passage is likely to become a viable alternative in the future to the sea routes associated with the Panama Canal – especially since east–west shipping routes through the polar latitudes are shorter in distance than the southern alternative routes associated with the Panama Canal.

The United States and the EU regard the Northwest Passage as an international strait to be used for international navigation under Part III of the Law of the Sea Convention. States bordering international straits such as Canada for the Northwest Passage may not impede, e.g., by imposing tolls on transiting vessels, the right of transit passage through such straits. Canada claims the waters of the Northwest Passage as internal waters, i.e., in Canada's territorial sea, for which it has complete sovereign control. However, the Law of the Sea Convention ensures that Canada may not unilaterally control passage of international commercial shipping.

In a study by Somanathan *et al.* (2007), the Canadian Northwest Passage route versus the Panama Canal sea route between eastern North America and Japan was evaluated. Specifically, costs of moving containers over sea routes from New York and St. John, Newfoundland in North America to Yokohama, Japan, were compared. A capital cost premium of 30 percent for a Canadian Arctic class ship (a commercial ship for ice service) and a 50 percent premium for insurance were assumed for the Northwest Passage route. The results indicate that a 10 percent cost savings would occur for transporting containers from St. John's to Yokohama over the Northwest Passage route (a shorter route) versus transporting the same containers from St. John through the Panama Canal and then to Yokohama (a longer route). Alternatively, cost savings would occur if the containers are transported from New York through the Panama Canal (a shorter distance) versus transporting the containers from New York to St. John to Yokohama over the Northwest Passage route (a longer route).[2]

Port information and communication technologies

"It is no longer enough to just handle cargo in the most efficient manner; the market increasingly expects ports to be sophisticated at handling data" (Marianos *et al.* 2007: 8). "Most ports will have to expand their capacity through operational and information technology improvements" (Mongelluzzo 2006b: 20). By allowing port stakeholders to communicate transparently and efficiently, port communication systems promote competitive ports as well as competitive global product markets. Ports in the future are expected to seek (1) the elimination of paper documentation from their operations, (2) the use of standardized information and communication technologies, (3) greater integration of these technologies in daily port operations, and (4) greater use of wireless communication technologies.

Ports have introduced a number of new information and communication technologies into their operations since the introduction of electronic data interchange (EDI) systems in the mid-1980s. The internet has been an enabling technology, allowing ports, shipping lines, and shippers to submit data electronically without the need for expensive information technology (IT) systems. Various web-based technologies that are currently used by ports and their stakeholders (Marianos *et al.* 2007) include Web Services, eXtendible Markup Language (XML), and Resource Description Framework (RDF).

Although the radio frequency identification (RFID) communication technology has been in existence for a number of years, only in recent years has it been adopted by ports. In 2006 the Ports of Los Angeles and Long Beach issued 10,000 RFID tags to its harbor truck truckers as a part of the Pier Pass program. RFID is an automatic identification (auto ID) technology. Other auto-ID technologies include bar-code, optical character reader, and biometric (e.g., retinal scanning) technologies. However, unlike RFID, information has to be manually scanned in the above auto-ID technologies. RFID revolutionized auto-ID technologies by being wireless. That is to say, RFID identifies an object by wireless transmission using radio waves. RFID tags have been attached to port cargo and mobile equipment in order to, for example, identify the location and condition of port cargo and mobile equipment, alert port management of unauthorized container breaches, reduce cargo inspection time by customs, and reduce the waiting times of vehicles and their cargo at terminal gates. Also, data can be stored on RFID tags.

The three types of RFID tags are passive, active, and semi-active tags. Passive tags have no power source; power from readers is used to scan tags to retrieve stored information. Active tags have a power source for both internal circuits and data transmission. Semi-active tags have a battery power source that powers only the circuits. RFID readers of RFID tags, e.g., to obtain information from tags, can be handheld or mounted units on port mobile equipment and fixed structures. In the future, greater use of solar-powered RFID readers is expected, especially at ports where power supplies are inadequate.

A problem with the use of RFID tags in ports is that tags and their radio frequencies may differ from one port to another. Thus, information stored in a tag attached to a container in one port may not be readable when this container is transported to another port. Also, RFID tags may utilize different computer languages. Another problem is that radio waves can be jammed; this is problematic for port security. For more effective use of RFID tags in global trade in the future, standards will need to be established, e.g., regarding the frequencies and amount of power to be used by tags and the standard computer language.

Port pollution

Ports in the future will be under increasing pressure to reduce pollution (i.e., to become greener), in particular to reduce air pollution. The number of ports worldwide requiring port vessels to either cold iron or burn cleaner fuels while in port is expected to increase. A similar increase is also expected for port vehicles and mobile equipment – to either burn cleaner fuels or not power vehicles and equipment with fossil fuels but rather by electricity. At the C40 World Ports Climate Conference held in Rotterdam in July 2008, an environmental charter was signed by port authorities worldwide to promote a sustainable reduction of greenhouse gas emissions through cooperation, exchange of information, and best practice (Hailey 2008). California will continue to be the leader among U.S. states in addressing the reduction of port air pollution.

Rising prices for vessel bunker fuel worldwide will have short-term and long-term indirect effects on port air pollution.[3] In the short term, rising bunker prices have led to a number of container shipping lines reducing the transit speeds of their vessels. By doing so, a significant reduction in vessel fuel consumption occurs; in fact, the percentage reduction in vessel fuel consumption (or the increase in fuel savings) is greater than the percentage reduction in vessel speed, i.e., the relationship of vessel fuel consumption reduction to vessel speed reduction is elastic. However, in order to maintain the same level of vessel TEU carrying capacity (see Chapter 2) for a given service string, a shipping line will need to add another vessel or vessels to the string, all else held constant.[4] With an increase in the number of vessels utilized in the string, there will be an increase in the number of vessel port calls and therefore an increase in vessel air pollution at the string's ports.

As opposed to increasing port air pollution in the short term, rising bunker prices may lead to a decrease in port air pollution in the long term. Two possibilities come to mind. First, bunker prices may reach such high levels that it becomes economically feasible for container shipping lines to switch from bunker containerships to nuclear containerships. A scenario where such a conversion becomes feasible is as follows (Gillis 2008):

> Three 9,000-plus-TEU nuclear-powered containerships provide non-stop transpacific container service between the Port of Hong Kong and the Ports of Los Angeles/Long Beach. The ships travel at a sustained 35 knots between the Port of Hong Kong and the Ports of Los Angeles/Long Beach. The three nuclear containerships replace four bunker-fueled containerships in the service string traveling at 25 knots. The FEU rates for the nuclear-powered containership service are $600 above the current FEU rates. A 9,000-TEU nuclear-powered containership costs upwards of $835 million to build compared to the construction cost of $150 million for a bunker-fueled containership of the same size. Every five years, a nuclear-powered containership requires refueling at a cost of $113 million. The price of bunker fuel is $455 per metric ton. The ports' load/unload rate is 300 container moves per hour.

Since nuclear containerships would not emit greenhouse gases, their replacement of bunker containerships in the above service string would reduce vessel air pollution at the ports of Hong Kong, Los Angeles, and Long Beach.

Second, steeply rising bunker prices, followed by steeply rising container rates, may in the long term realign world trade (Changqing 2008) – by threatening the low-wage comparative advantage of many countries in Asia, in particular China, i.e., rising ocean container transportation costs may offset the lower labor manufacturing costs of China. Some Chinese manufacturers, for example, may relocate their manufacturing sites closer to major consumer markets, say in the United States. If so, fewer post-Panamax containerships would be traveling from Asia to the U.S., resulting in a decrease in vessel air pollution at U.S. ports from the decrease in the number of vessel port calls.

Port logistics activities

Ports in the future will not only provide traditional services to port users, but are expected to increase their provision of profitable nontraditional port activities such as tourist, recreational, and logistics activities. Many ports have created logistics parks in their immediate and distant vicinities. Types of port-based logistics parks include the following (Theys *et al.* 2008):

1 Container Oriented Logistics Park – large warehouses located close to container terminals and intermodal terminal facilities.
2 Specialized Port-Based Logistics Park – warehouses and offices of companies specializing in different logistics activities, e.g., third-party logistics firms, logistics software firms, and financial service providers to maritime companies, located in the immediate vicinity of the port.
3 Peripheral Port-Based Logistics Park – offices of companies that supply the port with materials and resources located in the immediate vicinity of the port.
4 Virtual Port-Based Logistics Park – distribution centers for port cargo located in the distant vicinity (e.g., up to 100 kilometers or more) of the port.

The Virtual Port-Based Logistics Park also has been described as an inland (land-locked) terminal of the port. The U.S. Port of Virginia has an inland (land-locked) terminal, named the Inland Port of the Port of Virginia, at Front Royal, Virginia, that is approximately

210 miles northwest of the port's marine terminals in Hampton Roads, Virginia. Specifically, the Inland Port is an intermodal container transfer facility that serves as an interface between rail and truck for the transportation of containers to and from the marine terminals of the Port of Virginia. Containers are transported by double-stack trains to and from the Inland Port and the port's marine terminals, thereby reducing port congestion at the latter. At the Inland Port, truckers retrieve import containers (that were delivered to the Inland Port on double-stack trains from the port's marine terminals) for delivery to their final destinations or deposit export containers (that will be delivered on double-stack trains from the Inland Port to the port's marine terminals) for loading on departing ships. Consequently, with the existence of the Inland Port, the economic impact of the Port of Virginia is spread over a wide geographical area. Inland ports are also found in other areas of North America (e.g., Dallas) as well as Europe and in the Yangtze basin of China.

Ports have developed logistics activities by handling transshipment cargo as opposed to just handling import/export cargo and by profiling themselves as logistics center ports. Ports (e.g., Singapore) located near major shipping lanes are more likely to become transshipment hub. Ports with major consumer markets in their hinterlands are more likely to develop into logistics center ports. An example of a logistics center port is a port that has a free trade zone that adds value to import cargo. The added value may range between 50 and 80 percent of the value of the import cargo (Frankel 1987).

Port security

Ports in the future are expected to devote more resources to security, especially since the passage of the U.S. Implementing Recommendations of the 9/11 Commission Act of 2007 that requires the scanning of all (i.e., 100 percent scanning of) U.S. inbound containers at foreign ports by the year 2012 (see Chapter 13). The 100 percent scanning provision was passed by the U.S. Congress "as a political reaction to public perception that limited physical inspections by border security authorities left the nation vulnerable to a smuggled weapon of mass destruction or other dangers" (Kulisch 2008: 58). A major fear among U.S. maritime stakeholders is that the U.S. government would effectively shut down maritime trade to and from the U.S. following a domestic maritime terrorist incident in order to investigate the source of the security breach and the possibility of other security breaches.

The EU has criticized the U.S. 100 percent scanning provision as being "unnecessary, costly and counter-productive in that it ignores other types of trade, such as bulk shipping or even cruise ships, which could be used to carry weapons of mass destruction" (Stares 2008). Others have argued that a sampling, risk-based approach to container inspection would be preferable (to 100 percent container scanning) in terms of being less costly and less counter-productive. The cost of the 100 percent scanning of U.S. inbound containers at foreign ports will initially be borne by foreign port operators, but then transferred to port users, shipping lines, and shippers. A "100 percent scanning would cause an immediate slowdown in world trade and snarl port operations in the short term" (Heaney 2008: 21). "On the plus side, the scanning law will renew confidence in containerized transportation and result in extra productivity in the medium term due to port reorganization" (Heaney 2008: 22).

Port cooperation

Cooperation among ports is expected to increase in the future. In the United States the ports of Charleston and Savannah have formed a joint chassis pool. Shipping lines that are unwilling to place their chassis in the pool will not be able to keep them at the ports' container terminals.

Truckers hauling containers to and from port terminals can use a chassis of any member of the pool to haul a member's container. Fourteen container shipping lines (to increase to 18 lines) are members of the South Atlantic Consolidated Chassis Pool. The benefits of the pool include (1) freeing up space in container yards that otherwise would be occupied by chassis,[5] (2) reducing the time incurred by truckers in searching for a chassis owned (or leased) by the same carrier that owns (or leases) the container to be transported, (3) increasing the speed flow of containers moving into and out of port terminals, and (4) reducing the total number of chassis needed by the pool's members (Leach 2006b).

Also in the United States, virtual container yards have been organized by the Ports of Los Angeles and Long Beach on the West Coast and the Port of New York-New Jersey on the East Coast. Virtual container yards provide for a more efficient exchange of empty containers among truckers at ports by reducing the time in acquiring empty containers. A description of empty containers held by truckers, the shipping lines that own or lease them, and their location would be posted by the truckers on a website. Truckers that are members of the virtual container yard program would then have access to the site and thus empty containers. The benefits of the program include (1) increasing the availability of empty containers to truckers in port areas without increasing the container yard capacity at ports for the storage of empty containers, and (2) reducing port air pollution by truckers exchanging empty containers at locations away from ports. It has been estimated that if 4 percent of the empty containers at Southern California ports are exchanged by truckers on the street, i.e., are street turns, thousands of unnecessary truck trips to these ports for empty containers could be saved annually (Mongelluzzo 2006b).

LNG marine terminals

Liquefied natural gas (LNG) is natural gas that is stored and transported in liquid form at a temperature of minus 260 degrees Fahrenheit. By converting the gas into a liquid form, its volume is significantly reduced for transport by LNG tanker ships and for handling by LNG marine terminals. An LNG marine terminal may be a liquefaction (for exporting natural gas) or a regasification (for importing natural gas) terminal. Indonesia is the largest LNG exporter in the world, but with only two liquefaction marine terminals, and Japan is the world's largest LNG importer with 23 regasification marine terminals.

LNG is poised to occupy a greater role in the future in meeting the world's energy needs. However, the environmental, safety, and negative economic concerns of LNG marine terminals in populated areas may result in a lower rate of growth in the construction of LNG terminals in these areas in the future. Citing environmental, safety, and economic concerns, the U.S. state of New York, for example, rejected a 2008 proposal (by Shell U.S. Gas and Power and TransCanada Pipelines) to construct a floating LNG marine terminal on Long Island Sound (Aichele 2008). Specifically, the state noted that the terminal would be a potential terrorist target and the requirement of a 2,040-acre moving security zone for an LNG tanker vessel from which most other vessels would be excluded would disrupt commercial and recreational fishing and other waterway activities in the area.

Summary

Port congestion is a problem at major container ports worldwide and is expected to increase in the foreseeable future, since the growth in global container traffic is expected to outpace the global growth in container port capacity. The average size of containerships in service is increasing annually, while increases in port capacity are lagging behind. If Ocean53 containers are accepted by the shipping industry, container ports in the future will have to adapt to handling these larger containers.

The Panama Canal expansion will benefit U.S. East Coast ports to the detriment of U.S. West Coast ports. The increase in intermodal rail rates by U.S. railroads that provide intermodal rail service to and from U.S. West Coast ports and the U.S. East Coast have led to some container shipping lines switching to all-water service through the Panama Canal. Increases in all-water services through the Panama and Suez Canals will generally benefit U.S. East Coast but not West Coast ports. A potential competitor of the Panama Canal is an Arctic sea route.

Although radio frequency identification (RFID) communication technology has been in existence for a number of years, only in recent years has it been adopted by ports. For more effective use of RFID tags in global trade in the future, standards will need to be established.

Ports in the future will be under increasing pressure to reduce pollution, in particular air pollution. Rising prices for vessel bunker fuel worldwide will increase port air pollution in the short term – i.e., from shipping lines reducing the transit speed of vessels, thereby requiring additional vessels on a service string to maintain the vessel carrying capacity on the string and leading to more vessel port calls on the string. If nuclear-powered vessels replace bunker-fueled vessels in the long term, port air pollution from vessels will decrease.

Ports in the future will not only provide traditional services to port users, but are expected to increase their provision of profitable nontraditional port activities such as tourist, recreational, and logistics activities. Ports in the future are also expected to devote more resources to security, especially since the passage of the U.S. 100 percent scanning requirement of U.S. inbound containers at foreign ports by the year 2012. Also, cooperation among closely located ports is expected. The environmental, safety, and negative economic concerns of LNG marine terminals in populated areas may result in a lower rate of growth in the construction of such terminals in these areas in the future.

Notes

1 With the decline in the value of the U.S. dollar, there has been an increase in the demand for U.S. exports, but U.S. imports still exceed U.S. exports – thereby resulting in thousands of empty containers located across the United States. Prior to the export demand increase, container-leasing companies would often pay container shipping lines to transport empty containers back to Asia. Now, with the export demand increase, the leasing companies are willing to lease their containers to U.S. exporters for free, rather than paying container shipping lines to reposition empty containers to Asia. The leasing company may also be willing to pay a part of the cost of draying the empty container to the exporter's facility.

2 It is interesting to note that on the Russian side of the Arctic, Russia's northern sea route is used for commercial shipping. Also, within the last 40 years, the efficiency of icebreaking vessels in polar Arctic waters has improved 30 to 40 percent – attributable to improvements in vessel designs, superior surface coatings, and other refinements in all phases of icebreaking (Gray 2008).

3 At the beginning of 2007, the bunker price per ton was U.S.$296; at the beginning of 2008, the price was U.S.$500 and by mid-July 2008 the price was U.S.$767 (Staff 2008b).

4 A service string is defined as a service offered by a shipping line that involves several of its (or alliance) vessels performing outward and return voyages among ports in two distinct geographical areas, say in the transatlantic trade between North America and Europe.

5 At the U.S. Port of Virginia, space needed for chassis in container yards has been reduced by stacking chassis vertically.

Bibliography

Aichele, R. O. (2008) "New York Rejects Proposal for Floating LNG Terminal on Long Island Sound", *Professional Mariner*, August, 116: 16–17.

Airriess, C. A. (2001) "Regional Production, Information-Communication Technology, and the Developmental State: The Rise of Singapore as a Global Container Hub", *Geoforum*, 32: 235–254.

Berrill, P. (2006) "Matrix of Liner Links", *TradeWinds*, August 25: 12–13.

Bichou, K. and Gray, R. (2005) "A Critical Review of Conventional Terminology for Classifying Seaports", *Transportation Research Part A*, 39: 75–92.

Carluer, F. (2008) *Global Logistics Chain Security: Economic Impacts of the U.S. 100% Container Scanning Law*, Brussels, Belgium: World Customs Organization.

Changqing, L. (2008) "A Sharp Intake of Breath", *Containerization International*, August: 41.

Drewry Shipping Consultants (2007) *Annual Container Market Review and Forecast 2007*, London: Drewry Shipping Consultants.

Dupin, C. (2007) "Maersk Restructuring Inland Services", *American Shipper*, March, 49: 60–63.

Frankel, E. G. (1987) *Port Planning and Development*, New York: John Wiley & Sons.

Gillis, C. (2008) "Nuclear Shipping", *American Shipper*, July, 50: 86–88.

Gray, B. (2008) "Arctic Has Its Place in the Sun", *Lloyd's List*. Available online at http://www.lloydslist.com, June 6.

Hailey, R. (2008) "World Ports Unite on Climate Declaration: Ecological Framework Based on Data Sharing", *Lloyd's List*. Available online at http://www.lloydslist.com, July 21.

Heaney, S. (2008) "100% Scan=100% Headaches", *American Shipper*, July, 50, 21–24.

Kulisch, E. (2007) "Imports Tilt East for NS", *American Shipper*, December, 49: 71–72.

—— (2008) "Off Target: Flynn Faults U.S. Maritime Security Policy as Inconsistent, Non-Inclusive", *American Shipper*, February, 50: 58–60.

Leach, P. T. (2006a) "Split Decision: The Suez Canal is an Increasingly Attractive Alternative for Trans-Pacific Shippers", *Journal of Commerce*, June 19, 7: 12–14, 16, 18.

—— (2006b) "Ocean Carriers Pressed to Join Chassis Pool", *Journal of Commerce*, November 27, 7: 32.

Marianos, N. N., Lambrou, M. A., and Nikitakos, N. V. (2007) "Emergent Port Services in the Context of Information and Communication Technologies", a paper presented at the Annual Conference of the International Association of Maritime Economists, Athens, Greece.

Mongelluzzo, B. (2006a) "East and Gulf Coast Ports Race the Clock as All-Water Services Escalate", *Journal of Commerce*, June 19, 7: 20, 22, 24–25.

—— (2006b) "Virtual Container Yard: New System for Off-Port Swapping of Empty Boxes Debuts in Southern California, New York", *Journal of Commerce*, October 2, 7: 18–19.

—— (2007) "Move It Yourself: Maersk Plans to Sharply Reduce Points Served Through Inland Bills of Lading", *Journal of Commerce*, February 5, 8: 38.

—— (2008a) "Changing Times for Intermodal", *Journal of Commerce*, February 25, 9: 18–19.

—— (2008b) "Head East", *Journal of Commerce*, June 9, 9: 12–14.

Notteboom, T. and Vernimmen, B. (2008) "The Impact of Fuel Costs on Liner Service Design in Container Shipping", a paper presented at the Annual Conference of the International Association of Maritime Economists, Dalian, China.

Olivier, D. and Parola, F. (2007) "The Success of Asian Container Port Operators: The Role of Information Technology", in J. Wang, D. Olivier, T. Notteboom, and B. Slack (eds) *Ports, Cities and Global Supply Chains*, Aldershot, UK: Ashgate, 205–220.

Panama Canal Authority (2006) "Master Plan for the Panama Canal". Available online at http://www.pancanal.com/esp/plan/documentos/plan/acp-plan-maestro.pdf and http://www.pancanal.com/eng (accessed 23 March 2008).

—— (2008). Available online at http://www.pancanal.com/eng (accessed 23 March 2008).

Pinder, D. and Slack, B. (2004) *Shipping and Ports in the Twenty-First Century*, London: Routledge.

Somanathan, S., Flynn, P. C., and Szymanski, J. K. (2007) "Feasibility of a Sea Route Through the Canadian Arctic", *Maritime Economics and Logistics*, 9: 324–334.

Staff (2008a) "Value Creation in Container Shipping", *American Shipper*, 50: 69–70, 72, 74, 76, 78–85.

—— (2008b) "Trans-Pacific Fuel Surcharge Headed for Record Level", *Journal of Commerce Online*. Available online at http://www.joc.com, August 25.

Stares, J. (2008) "Rotterdam May Scan all Export Boxes". *Lloyd's List*. Available online at http://www.lloydslist.com, May 30.

Talley, W. K. (2008) *Maritime Safety, Security and Piracy*, London: Informa.

Theys, C., Ryoo, D. K., and Notteboom, T. (2008) "Developing Logistics in Ports: Creating a Global Framework", a paper presented at the Annual Conference of the International Association of Maritime Economists, Dalian, China.

Tsilingiris, P. S., Psaraftis, H. N., and Lyridis, D. V. (2007) "Radio Frequency Identification (RFID) Technology in Ocean Container Transport", a paper presented at the Annual Conference of the International Association of Maritime Economists, Athens, Greece.

Index